☑ Other

☑ Other

√ Other
Copyright © 2014 by Cindy Campopiano.

All rights reserved, including the right to reproduce this book or portions thereof in any form whatsoever, except for brief quotations in printed reviews with the prior permission of the author and publisher.

Published by Sothic Rising
Berkeley, California

ISBN 978-0-9915188-0-7
Library of Congress Control Number 2014902205

Book cover design by Cindy Campopiano. Cover photo by Vincent Xarya. Back cover photo by Cindy Campopiano.

Author's Note

This is a work of nonfiction. Some names and minor characteristics of people and places have been changed to protect identity.

☑ Other

Acknowledgements

Huge thanks to the people who have encouraged me in writing this memoir. To my editors, Kristy Biluni, Marcia Trahan, Margaret Diehl, and Ed Robertson: I appreciate your challenges as well as your favorable and detailed assessments. Ongoing thanks to Vincent Xarya for his enthusiastic and loving support. Much gratitude to Sal Sanflippo for the parting gift. Reverent thanks to Dr. Clarissa Pinkola Estes for being a light in the dark for so many years. Thanks to Judy Wyatt for wading through an entire second-draft manuscript, and for her immense, caring assistance. A much-deserved hat tip to Cecilia Phillips: you might consider going professional with your feedback skills. (And here's to *Suppah Cluuuub*!) Heartfelt appreciation to Josephine Davenport for her permission to reprint a portion of the letter she wrote to my grandfather. And many thanks to everyone I've met who didn't hesitate to tell me they wanted to read this book.

☑ Other

"Who has ever ascended from the underworld, has ascended unscathed from the underworld?"

-The gala-tura and the kur-gara (emissaries of the Sumerian sky god Enki).

☑ Other

Contents

Prologue	1
1. Passage	3
2. Fortitude	12
3. Knowledge of Good and Evil	28
4. The Wandering	55
5. Perseverance	104
6. Acceptance	129
7. The Question	163
8. Satori	207
9. The Return	241

☑ Other

Prologue

I want to ride the two-headed cow," I whispered to my aunt Nell at a summer carnival. I was four. I loved getting away from home for a day to the transformed fairgrounds, loved the vivid fleeting world of traveling carnies.

The shade from a sycamore almost reached the picnic table where we ate with Nell's friends and my one-year-older brother, Chris. Now and then a faint breeze lifted the edges of the white paper holding our cold cuts and cheese.

"What?" Nell asked, leaning down to listen. She had soft, fine brown hair and slender hands. Again I whispered my secret longing.

"The two-headed cow. I wanna ride it." Here and there among the spinning chair-o-planes, ponies, kiddie carousel and booth games we had spotted white signs promising a double-headed cow, represented by two cartoon smiles and four enthusiastic eyes. The signs looked left over from previous years, with dust edging the paint along the wood grain.

Aunt Nell gave me an *Awww, that's so cute* look.

"Hey, guess what Cindy just said? She thinks the two-headed cow is a ride." Cringing while everyone laughed, I didn't even protest that I knew the cow was real. If I could sit nimbly atop the bare back of the exotic beast as it raced away, over a long-grassed field in bloom, everything would be better. After lunch we followed the signs to the correct tent.

Besides having two heads, it was a normal cow that stood in the dusty light of its stall and stared from four half-lidded eyes. Just seeing it, I felt content. I hadn't expected the weird creature to be beautiful.

☑ Other

Some believe that the ordinary and common — regular cows, square lawns, motes of dust — contain something extraordinary, which might be obvious only to babies and cats, who are agog at light and color. Common enough throughout history stand the extraordinary works of art and architecture fashioned by people who wanted to carve out a measure of greatness against the trampling of time. Growing up, I thought the greatest feat would be to venture all the way around the world. I imagined riding not only mythical creatures but flying carpets and wooden boats to far-flung lands. Nights warm enough to be sleeveless outside, the humid air tinged with barbecue smoke, were the best time to sense the possibilities.

Eventually, in adulthood, I would go the whole way around. After a year in Japan I would take the global trip. I would float in warm clear waters off the coast of Thailand, ride a dappled gray horse over Sahara sands to the Great Pyramids, and meander with locals along a rocky Mediterranean shoreline in Cinque Terre, Italy. Things would finally go well, and I would leave a long, dark road behind. On the journey around the world, each new experience would hint that destiny was aligning.

Enthusiasm, like any strong emotion experienced in full for the first time, can form a mask blocking a full range of vision. Once back from the journey, I would soon see only that my fate looked no more extraordinary than that of an animal trapped in a pen, from which I would have to escape.

☑ Other

1.

Passage

In Japan I fell in love with the land and its people. From there, I frolicked westward through ten countries only to slam into the brick wall of America — a country I'd had a tough time growing up in. Moving to San Francisco, I warded off a deep dread by subletting a room with a fireplace and high ceilings. The antique breakfast table and throne-like wicker chair near one window made it look like a comforting place where I might be able to prolong my journey.

On my travels, people had welcomed and befriended me. San Franciscans, though, excelled at standoffishness. Worse, job prospects were slim. Those two factors knocked my optimism off its elephant and drove me to walk. Up and down hills I paced, out to the strip of sand by the bay, through Strybing Arboretum in Golden Gate Park with its groves of prehistoric trees. Floundering on the last day of the sublet, I did nothing but watch movies and have food delivered. *What next?* got shoved to a back burner.

For the first time that month, the silence of the building broke. The insistence of a vacuum motor intruded — fainter then louder, farther then closer. Roll of toilet paper in hand, about to head to the shared bathroom down the hall, I opened the door. There stood a tired middle-aged Japanese woman whose vacuum powered down beside her.

"Can I show you some other room we have available?" she asked, her worn face set. The young Japanese woman who had sublet the room to me hadn't introduced me to Miyako, the landlady. I stared a moment before answering.

"Give me a minute." I walked past her. Having recently lived in this woman's home country, I was taken aback. The Japanese were known

☑ Other

for cushioning big questions within polite phrases, and only after asking about the listener's well-being.

The bathroom had just been cleaned. When I came out, the landlady led me halfway down the hall to a room with a brown faux-leather couch and nothing else. A mausoleum-level stillness silenced us both.

"Come upstair," she said. I followed her up, along the corridor and around a corner to a door with its own little hallway, which lead to a window and a fire escape. "This one is my favorite," she said, unlocking the door.

The corner room, spacious and carpeted, had three bay windows on one wall and two flat windows on another. Late afternoon sun glimmered through drawn shades of tiny bamboo rods. Not bad, except for the faint smell of dog urine.

"No pet," she said.

"How much?" I asked.

"Five hundred. A money saver," she added.

"I'll take it if I can cook in here," I said. She beamed.

"For you. What do you eat? Chicken? Keep the window open, you know, these other people, they use microwave. But for you, sure. What color curtain you want?"

"Red would be good," I blurted, regretting not having said "no thank you." My guard rose around this woman, but I needed a cheap place to live.

Miyako and I met again the following afternoon to seal the deal. All my belongings, a few bags and boxes, rested on the floor in the hallway.

"So. Five hundred?" I asked to confirm.

"Five fifty," she said with a nervous laugh.

"Five fifty." I stared at her.

"A money saver," she repeated. I hesitated a moment.

"OK," I finally said. Once she'd gone I whispered to the emptiness, "Sheisty," and left to buy a powdered enzyme designed to eat nasty smells. With some of my savings I outfitted the room with a bed, a

☑ Other

small table and a convection oven, cozying things up with a few houseplants and accessories.

At an English Language school where I found a temporary teaching position, a student named Raita introduced himself, as students often did. We discovered that we shared a couple interests: reggae music and its longtime accompaniment, ganja.

Sitting at my little table, Raita and I smoked and listened to music, drinking beer out of bowls because I hadn't yet bought glasses. The fire escape became a balcony, the sounds of traffic floating through the dusk while fluorescents from a gas station on the opposite corner illuminated a green sign, UNION STREET. As evening fell, candlelight flickered on walls and windows.

"Heyyyy, Cindy," Raita said, grinning. "I like your room is how my mind when smoking."

"Ah. Thank you very much," I answered. "It's probably the lighting." I pointed to a string of mini lanterns that cast a red glow on the diamond-shaped leaves of a fichus and on a poster for Miyazaki's *Howl's Moving Castle*. Glancing around, I saw a slip of paper on the floor near the door. Picking it up I noticed the name at the bottom — Riley. Miyako's son.

"Hmm. My neighbor is inviting me over."

"A writing?" Raita scoffed. "Why he doesn't just ask you or text?" He looked askance at the note.

"Maybe shy," I said.

"This is like childhood. How old? Come on, how old this guy?"

"I don't know yet. More beer?"

When Raita left California a few days later I sharply noticed my lack of new friends. The teaching job raced to the end of its six weeks. I shuffled through days, going to bed early and dreading the next morning. I had reached my 30s, and it seemed I had scaled a steep mountain — only to realize I had climbed the wrong one. Pointing out that I had given up a contented and financially stable situation in Japan to struggle back in America, my closest friend, Mike, offered me a

☑ Other

couple of mind-clearing months in the spare Paris flat he and his wife paid every month to keep. Refusing would have been folly even had my return to America gone as planned.

I took the retreat, paying Miyako in advance for the two months I'd be gone. Anxiety over whether I could pull off my return to the States made me ping-pong back out of the country.

"I'm going to do this right," I told my new room the night before I took off from San Francisco International Airport. "As soon as I get back."

In Paris I roamed through museums, gardens, and cathedrals, enthralled suddenly to be alive. I deeply inhaled the aroma of the fresh baguettes I carried back to the French apartment. I went dancing at my favorite Montmartre bar. I photographed the city. On my last night, my vacation-boyfriend, Karim, and I lounged against each other on his couch. Our brief romance would end when I left The City of Love, no need to worry about pesky relationship issues.

We sipped wine and kissed occasionally. I nestled against his bicep, refusing to think about leaving Paris until the next morning when I had to catch my flight. Karim surfed channels and settled on a Swedish drama, subtitled in French. The lead actor threw a television out a window during an argument with his girlfriend. Karim laughed while I thought how it is from French we get the term *defenestrate*, to throw something out a window.

The next afternoon I made a second hopeful attempt at returning to the States. After twenty-two hours in transit I arrived at the tiny pub next door to my rented room. Standing on the splotched sidewalk and still wearing my backpack, I squinted through pale winter sunlight at the memento-strewn walls and draft taps. The bartender beckoned.

A drink to welcome myself back, I thought, although I felt no American solidarity — despite the accomplishments of Martin Luther King, Jr. and the First Amendment. I slipped onto a barstool as an onlooker among a gathering of customers shoulder-to-shoulder in the

☑ Other

holiday atmosphere. James, the bartender and owner, had gray at his temples and a lean frame. His smile revealed amusement and compassion, but his eyes betrayed a life that had turned out sadder than he had perhaps expected.

"Guess what happened the other day?" he called out, and paused for attention. "Our little friend upstairs threw a TV out the window."

Odd.

"Smashed right there on the street," he said, pointing with his thumb. "And guess who came running out to clean it up?" He waited again, eyebrows raised. Everyone had stopped talking. *"The mother."* He shook his head and laughed.

I resumed sipping, and through the steamed-up window saw the guy James was talking about: Riley. The street darkened as dusk fell around him. He wore a black vest, a purple shirt and an '80s-looking black-brimmed hat. A cartoonish smile floated beneath the hat. He appeared to look skyward. I may have heard a whoop.

"Speaking *of.* He's not allowed in here," James said, aiming a distasteful glance outside.

"Why?" I asked.

"He's had a restraining order against him. He has *guns.* He knows he can't come in here." The pub sat between the building I lived in and Miyako's house, where Riley occupied the top floor.

Outside looked cold and windy. With a sigh, I returned to my beer. Every last drop of Paris-inspired enthusiasm had evaporated. My savings plummeted by Christmas. For the holiday I took a train sixty miles south to Cupertino where my brother Chris, a programmer in Silicon Valley, lived with his wife and two kids.

After the culture of major international cities, San Jose's suburbs confronted me with newness, all shiny and watered down. As Chris drove away from the station, I noticed few people on foot and nothing much to stroll by — only strip malls, car sales lots and the same giant chains that had spawned across the country. Just how crucial was one more Panda Express?

☑ Other

"What do you think about Bush getting reelected?" Chris asked as he steered. Growing up, people often said that he and I looked alike. One kid in junior high went so far as to say I was my brother with boobs.

"I saw the news in Japan," I said. "And could not believe people voted for him again. I got mad and then didn't look at a newspaper or online news the whole time I was traveling."

"Mm-hmm." he replied. A world journey didn't appeal to him. "Isn't seeing famous places and monuments just as good in videos?" he asked. "Going all the way there — is it really that much better?" He approached his driveway.

"Way better," I answered.

"And you weren't scared in any of those big cities by yourself?"

"No," I said. "Other things scare me." *Dying alone, giant fish, angry drunks.* I wouldn't have to worry about any of those on Christmas. Playing video games with my young niece and nephew and competing at board games with Chris and his friends made for a comforting holiday.

The next day, post-travel blues echoed in the cracked sidewalks of a ghetto-like area of San Francisco known as the Tenderloin, through which I walked en route to my nicer neighborhood. In no overseas city from Shanghai to Amsterdam had I seen as many dispossessed people as on the streets of major American cities.

The Tenderloin drew vagrants dressed in oily tatters, limping and crying out. Some shuffled like zombies that announced twenty details per minute. A man wearing one torn shoe had only a stump at the end of his other leg. Leaning on a cane and looking anguished at the sky, he kept shouting.

"I'm *so sick* of this! I'm *so sick* of this!"

Although blessed with my own room and no missing limbs, a depression like a sinkhole whirled around in my mind. I missed having enough money. I missed traveling. I missed Karim. After dating him I

☑ Other

decided to seek out non-American men for romance, figuring there would be less chance of arguing in the absence of common languages.

My imaginary ideal boyfriend was a U.S.-born Japanese man who abided by some ancient code of valor but spoke fluent English. He would be *genki* — hearty — and use polite respect, as well as have experience with American subculture. He would not be mainstream, no way, but not criminal either. He would know how to dance, make a mean pork cutlet donburi and pronounce rice wine "sah-kay," which we would pour for each other.

So specific was my longing that I had put Riley, Miyako's son, in this category before even meeting him. TV out the window? Guns? Hearsay. When it came to romance, I had long wandered the Land of Nod, guided by fantasies.

I did not need a ladder this time. I had locked myself out, but told Miyako otherwise so she wouldn't think I was an idiot.

"Please tell him to bring the ladder up when you see him," I said into my phone as I paced the hall. The drab walls sapped my energy. From behind one of the nearby doors came the muffled sounds of a football game.

"OK, I will," Miyako replied.

I climbed out a window onto a fire escape and up a thin metal ladder to the top of the building. Rooftops usually provided mood-lifting views. In the mid-distance to the west, a windblown San Francisco Bay and dark orange Golden Gate Bridge, cloaked in fog, heralded a dull blue January ocean. Ancient was the low sky and silence that seemed to ask, *Why are you even here?*

Returning to America now looked like backing into a corner. Trudging to the edge of the roof, I peered down onto Miyako's deck where Riley stood, his luscious black hair curling across his forehead. I hurried back inside, thinking he was getting ready to come over with the ladder that I didn't actually need. I would admit I'd locked myself out and ask for a key.

From the stairwell at the far end of the hall I saw him one floor down, inside the building. He looked twenty-five, maybe thirty. Instead of a ladder he held onto a staircase post, leaning back as if contemplating something he had unlimited time to think about. He wore shorts and a light T-shirt even in the cold of January.

"Hey," I said.

"Hi," he returned, looking up and smiling. He had perfect teeth.

"Did your mom tell you I called?" I asked.

"No," he answered, shaking his head.

"Could you let me into my room?"

"Awww. How long have you been waiting? You shouldn't have to stand around like that. I'll find the key. Hold up." He pushed open the door that led to their patio. "Be right back."

I waited on the fire escape, staring into the fog while periodically checking the hall in front of my door. After a few minutes a man dressed in white pants and a long-sleeved white shirt rounded the corner, his dark hair slicked back. He held an open box of See's chocolates. I wondered if someone in the building had a Mexican husband. Realizing it was Riley I climbed back in, lowering the slatted blind.

Not only did he look different than he had a moment before — and the time I had seen him from the pub — but he also looked different than the last time I'd seen him, the day he had actually brought a ladder so I could post prints high on my wall. That afternoon he had been wearing bike clothes, all spandex in various hues. He had walked up the stairs ahead of me, his muscular legs flexing as he bragged in a California accent that he had "a *recording* studio" next door.

Now he stood in his white outfit, a blank canvas. His ochre eyes appeared to wear a touch of eyeliner though he had no makeup on. He kept returning my gaze, but I couldn't read his expression. With silken motions he leaned forward and handed me the room key. I took it, and a chocolate from the box he tilted in my direction.

"Thanks . . ." I said. "I'm gonna order pizza. Would you like some?"

"Mmmm," he murmured. "The timing is bad."

"Another day then," I said.

Riley nodded with assurance before breaking our locked stare.

☑ Other

2.

Fortitude

The only way for me to answer *What am I doing here?* was to go back before the beginning. Every tough question pointed to the past. For some reason I had always felt uncomfortable in my skin, and not only because the Irish kind burns even on cloudy days. I sometimes wondered if I was supposed to be human, or whether some mistake had been made.

Whoever came up with "We all come into this world alone" must have been grown in a test tube. Emerging from a living body ranks high on the scale of the least solitary moments of life. Maybe the "alone" part refers to pre-conception. A cultural teacher once told me that we choose our parents, which he said he had learned while living on a Navajo reservation.

"We choose the circumstances, people, and the location," he said. Making my own birth plans without a brain sounded improbable. "Some people who had terrible childhoods get angry," he told me. "They don't believe they would pick that. But we have good reasons. We not only choose whom and where, but three things to work on: one main mission and two side tasks. Then it's up to us to remember."

Even if that were true, as far as I could tell, entering the world proved too big a distraction. My mom, Betty, has said she doesn't know whether my hip got dislocated before or during birth, but whichever, I arrived with my butt at a sassy angle and my face crumpled in distress.

"The first brace didn't fit right or the material was too soft or something," her story goes. "We had to take you back to the hospital after two days because you wouldn't stop crying." It helps to think my parents waited the two days with some purpose in mind, like early Native Americans who threw their babies into snow for a moment to encourage tolerance to pain.

☑ Other

On the muggy August afternoon in Denville, New Jersey when I struggled into the world, North Vietnam celebrated an "international day of solidarity with the black people of the United States" in response to a visit from a delegation of Black Panthers. Maybe that's why an old African-American man's voice has rumbled up in my mind at key times.

Who dat? he might say. Or, *This is some kind a* bull*shit right here.* Then he retreats to the back porch of my mind.

The doctor refitted me with a metal brace I wore for my first six months. In one family photo I'm lounging, with an extreme case of bed head, in a baby swing while a rod capped with stirrups props my legs open. Chris is standing next to the swing with his hand to his chest as if to say, "Oh, *my*."

"You were *very* loved as a baby," my mom assured me once when telling stories of the past. At the time, I wouldn't have been surprised if she'd added, "but not as a child or adult."

"But you were real clingy," she assessed. I learned to crawl while wearing the brace. Could that have been part of my plan before birth?

I've heard the first memory is crucial, a key that unlocks the adult persona. Some claim to recall the comfort of the womb while others say they remember nothing before the age of ten. My first is of lying in a crib, aware of light and voices from downstairs where my parents had company. The murmurs of toddler Chris and a family friend's son, Andre, approached.

"Let's take off her little sockie," Andre whispered. I felt the thin cotton sock slip past my left ankle, over my toes and disappear. One *whoosh* defined the world as unreliable. The spaces between early memories are black, not gray or purple or white, embossed in swirling pinpoints forming two oaks that arch serpentine into each other, wrapping back on themselves and into the ground that bore them. They guard some entrance, and one bright day, a voice could have said, *you will walk between them.*

I was a Jersey kid, born to a land where people spoke loudly and confidently about whatever they were thinking. I had a good chance of pushing past the birth-injury challenge, but my dad made that

☑ Other

impossible by ruining every day. He drank so much that by dinnertime he was both beat down and worked up. In Joe Campo we had two fathers. Daytime Dad worked in one of the three hair salons he owned, an easygoing boss who focused on his craft and had loyal customers. In the morning he would practice karate in the cellar or skim the pool for fallen leaves. Every evening he turned into the drunken father we dreaded. Sober Dad would ask,

"You want me to make lasagna for dinner? We still got those sausages." Minutes later Buzzed Dad would snarl, "You don't know what the fuck you're talking about," to whatever our mom had just said. Head and torso unsteady, he scowled like a crazy bearded stranger and referred to his family as "you assholes," including our beagle Jones. I would get lightheaded when I heard sick anger creep into his voice, and my heart would start hammering when his growling turned into ferocious shouting. As if on a never-ending run of scheduled performances, each evening's verbal rampage stole center stage from tender London broils, broccoli spears and any attempted table talk. Often I couldn't eat for nervousness. In the days before going stormily silent during his ranting, Mom would interject, rolling her eyes at his domineering tone as if he were an uninvited guest at a barbecue — and not her husband, the man we feared.

Bottle after bottle bore the blame. Betty and her sister Nell, a second mother to me, often talked about how much better things would be "if he would just stop drinking." The sisters, united in worry over Joe's booze consumption, didn't know how to lessen it. Nothing in their upbringing had prepared them — Mom, Nell, and their brothers had grown up during the '50s and '60s in a Beaver Cleaver home devoid of addiction. Mom, the first girl after four boys, got pampered. The transition to life with Joe must have been jarring.

Sometimes repeats of *Leave it to Beaver* would be on when I stayed home sick from school. Mom would set me up in front of the TV with a bowl of soup and go about her day of housecleaning.

"Hey, Beave," the father would say with no pall of sorrow cast over his eyes. Seeing sitcom families giving each other supportive smiles and kind advice cheered me way up. I could forget where I was, pulling my

☑ Other

Winnie the Pooh blanket tight around me while basking in temporary safety. All too soon, Dad's evening spiel would crack that illusion.

"There iszh no right and there iszh no wrong," he would slur. "No good and no evil, no puniszhment and no rewardhh. No God and no Devil. In other wordzh," he lifted a wavering finger, "I am." Following a moment of silence to allow emphasis he would continue. "I, am. No — you don't unnerstan. I ... am. Lissin," he yelled. "You aren't *lissining*."

Not listening didn't keep the words out, and I had nothing to measure them against but his craziness. Some parents tell stories to their children. Raging is like storytelling with destruction added, which can trip *fright* or flight, and there wasn't anywhere to go.

I learned to tune out the chaos. When the kitchen turned into a war zone I might notice a blue label bearing a piece of fried chicken on a Crisco can that contained, when investigated, no chicken. I looked at the white gel that had been plowed into and felt sad. Far from flinching when my dad threw a tray of ice across the room, I just wondered where the chicken was supposed to be.

When he made crass gestures like sidling up to my mom and requesting an early evening lay, I'd wander into our entrance hall and stare at the pretty, gradated blue of the slate flagstones. I could still hear his thick insistent voice and would glance into the living room where he stood, swaying next to my mom, breathing into her ear. They looked like flustered giants. In jeans and a form-fitting shirt, Mom was slim yet curvaceous, her pale blue eyes downcast as she turned partway away from my sweaty dad.

Anywhere had to be better than inside the walls of our house. Nature drew my eyes to the windows. Warm evenings brought fireflies swerving like fairy lights over our yard. Storm-wild branches threw bright green wet maple leaves flat against the sliding glass back door. In winter, snow whirled and banked up higher than the roofs of cars. Even when angry, nature was gorgeous and didn't scare me, except for thunder.

As a child, I never asked where I had come from. Uncle John didn't call me an old soul as he had Chris, who at three years old told our mom he wanted to go back home to God. We didn't even go to church.

☑ Other

We did go to Dad's salon, "the shop." In the early years, he held to a practice of not drinking before closing time, and he looked sane. I loved getting my hair washed by any of the friendly girls who worked for him. Ensconced in a chair tilted back to a giant sink, I savored the warm water pooling in a cupped hand against my scalp while spray from the nozzle sent shivers down my neck. The sharp scents of perm chemicals and hair spray were more comforting than those of coffee and bacon. The salon, with its lively buzz of conversation and warm, beige-gold wallpaper reflected in the mirrors, was a welcome change from home. Instead of acting insecure and then terrifying, Dad stayed confident and upbeat as he cut, styled and applied dye to hair. I believed that the girls and the customers saw our family as normal, and I thought with relief that all our darkness stayed hidden.

"He was real nice to me," Mom has said when asked why she started dating Dad. A young man of twenty, he courted her, a girl of sixteen. Thin but muscled, he had a chip-on-the-shoulder, James-Dean look and a trace of vulnerability in his dark brown eyes. She lived in Montclair, a more affluent city than its working-class neighbor Bloomfield, where my dad came from.

Like the frog in the slowly heated water, she had begun at "cool and calm." She dated him all through high school and for two more years before he proposed. In their first married months she greeted him with shrimp cocktails and sparkling wine in their new house when he got home from work. With business steady at the shops — his brother and his closest friend ran his other two — and their new lives ready to begin, he grew sullen. He had nothing to shadow box now that he had proven himself marriage-worthy to her parents, who had never fully approved of him.

By the time Chris and I arrived, he was in a rage stage. A barely contained wrath awoke in him when he poured alcohol on it, and up raced the flames. His shoulders would droop, but his eyes would get fierce and challenging. When we were still too young to realize we could hide in our rooms, we cowered in silence, not looking at him as he thundered. *Make it stop. Make it stop. Make it stop,* I would think. Sometimes Mom attempted to dissuade him.

☑ Other

"C'mon, Joe," she would say, looking harassed. "Can't you see we're trying to relax and watch TV?" Undeterred, he would just laser-hone the yelling in her direction. Her whole body would go rigid and her eyes unfocus. When he finally ran out of steam, when every cubic inch of air in the room had been poisoned with his mocking, enraged voice, he would pass out. Chris and I tiptoed around him like novice ninjas, making absolutely sure he did not reawaken.

My defenses only rested around him when we played chess, which he taught me early, or when his eyes flashed hesitation. Every night he resorted to his Black Russians or wine, strutting room to room like he'd just vanquished the enemy. Now and then he pulled out a stack of bills, holding them up and saying,

"Here, you assholes like money," as he let fifties and twenties rain onto the carpet. "Take it." Though in debt, he always brought us out for lobster, steak, expensive Italian food.

Every fourth or fifth house in our middle-class neighborhood had the same design, sometimes flipped. Ours rested in a four-block enclave bordered by spruce and maples. People entertained themselves by fixing up their homes and yards. Despite the ho-hum community, the state of New Jersey held the prestige of being an original colony. English forces had attacked and won New Jersey from the Dutch in 1664. Some kids in our neighborhood said "melk" instead of "milk," keeping Dutch alive in a way I couldn't seem to appreciate.

Every few weekends throughout our early childhood Chris and I went to a sitter, a widow named Mrs. Collins who lived a few miles away in White Meadow Lake. Mr. Collins, her ailing husband, was still alive the first time we went to her house. He sat motionless in a simple chair. The oldest person I'd ever seen, his skin appeared to drip from his body. He passed away a few weeks later. Mrs. Collins never let her grief affect the children in her home. As well as having her own three kids, she had long been a foster mother. She offered support and fairness, and best of all, responsiveness. She never allowed any child to try for her attention in vain — and then with urgency — only to snap, "What?"

☑ Other

She required the use of *please* and *thank you*. She didn't tolerate belittling others. A compliment from her felt earned, and she never reached boiling-point anger. She also made the best oatmeal I've ever eaten and have failed to replicate. Ladled into bowls from a huge pot that bubbled half the morning, shimmering with sugary rivulets and ribbons of milk, every spoonful assured me that good existed. Sometimes we entered the kitchens of the housewives in our own neighborhood as part of a local group of kids. Mothers would pour us hot chocolate in winter after we skated on the lake or went sledding, and in summer lemonade or Coke after we swam.

I loved activities that brought me out of the mundane. Biking no-hands down an incline called Third Block Hill was a rite of skill blissful to earn. I enjoyed riding upside down in our dad's boat-sized Buick, feet on the headrest and head below the dash. I didn't have to worry about seatbelt laws for children, restrictive car seats or lethal airbags.

Have you ever noticed how the roads on a map of the U.S. loosen up as they roll westward? When settlers first built them, they laid winding paths that meandered with shortsighted purpose. Then as if everyone from Fargo to Kansas City to San Antonio decided to open up at once, there is one edge along which the old-style roads give way. The frenzied knot work relaxes, and from there remains loose all the way to the West Coast. I would come to travel those roads, back and forth across the country as if pacing, trying to wake up and remember.

By kindergarten Dad's no-such-thing-as-good-or-evil routine caused me trouble. It didn't matter if I acted good or bad, whether Santa was coming or not. I decided that bedroom furniture was an acceptable surface for writing practice. I got the idea on Halloween morning when I noticed words on the sidewalk in front of our house.

The night before Halloween was known as Mischief Night. Houses would get splattered with raw eggs or draped in toilet paper. Rude messages appeared, written with soap on car and garage windows. I bent down to read what had been scrawled on the sidewalk in front of our lawn and saw *fuck you* underneath an arrow pointing at our house. Up in my room, black pen in hand, I carefully copied the letters and the

☑ Other

arrow onto the white cloth atop my dresser. The sloppily written message pointed out the window. Mom came in and stared aghast.

"You know better than that," she said. I looked away from her disappointed face, feeling betrayed. I had thought she would praise my writing skill. It seemed that Betty felt more comfortable raising a son, and Chris in turn delighted the family from the start. Relatives praised him as smart, mature and mannerly. Mom had taught him to read when he was four.

She likewise sat me down at four, opening a children's book and pointing to each word, asking me to sound it out. I got the word "he" right. She pointed to "was."

"Wuh. Wuh," I remember saying, enjoying how round the *w* felt in my mouth. Connecting the visual to the voice struck me as fun and funny, and I started giggling.

"Well, I guess you aren't taking this seriously," Mom said, closing the book without asking what was funny. I slid awkwardly off her lap.

I just couldn't measure up to my brother, but I knew he wasn't perfect. That year we both had to get glasses for nearsightedness. Reasonable as always, he accepted them without complaint. I hated wearing mine. Leaving the house in the morning, I would put on the brown-and-yellow-tortoiseshell frames, only to pocket them on the walk to school. I feared my classmates would tease and dislike me for having "four eyes." They were kids who always spoke up. Sure-footed and bounding with life, they were like golden retrievers, huskies and chocolate Labs, while I slunk around like a mangy mongrel. I didn't arrive at this conclusion by any kind of reasoning, but I was convinced that wearing glasses would push me over an edge I couldn't come back from. One wintry trek to class, I ditched the glasses in a snow bank, greatly relieved afterward. The replacement pair came with a lecture on expense. It seemed I often did things wrong.

"Wiggly Wanda," Mom would sigh. "You have no patience. Just sit still." She wanted me to stay motionless next to her on the couch while I wanted to build a fort with cushions and blankets. Watching movies curbed my motoring. I enjoyed my share of Disney and other cartoons, but since almost no censoring happened in our house, I saw two horror

☑ Other

movies by summertime. Years later when I asked Mom why she let me watch them, she said nonchalantly that scary films were "just entertainment."

"There's a good movie on tonight," she had announced that warm evening as we finished dinner. After filling and starting the dishwasher while Dad sat (quietly for once) getting loaded at the kitchen table, Mom led Chris and me down to the TV room. When *The Exorcist* began, everything seemed normal but gloomy, and I couldn't understand what anyone was talking about. I froze when the girl in the bed had heart palpitations. That night I did not want to get into bed. What if my heart started beating five million times a second? That's what could happen when girls got in beds.

Insofar as stories from childhood helping to form character, I learned how to be a misunderstood outsider from *Carrie*. Chris sat this one out while Mom and I made ourselves comfy on the couch. In the beginning, a pale girl showered at school. As she stepped out, the girls in her gym class taunted her.

"Why are they throwing towels at her?" I asked.

"Those aren't towels," Mom answered, staring straight ahead.

Carrie looked nervous and unhappy. Nobody liked her. This made her extra angry, especially when they played a trick on her involving pig's blood. She ended up burning most of her classmates and school faculty by starting a fire with her mind and then went home, using her telekinesis to murder her shrill and somehow less sane mother. My mom had fallen asleep halfway through, and I sat riveted until the gruesome end.

TV room light on, TV off. Kitchen light on, TV room light off. Stairway light on, kitchen off. I ran up but stopped short at my dark doorway. I feared the evil girls appearing out of nowhere. If they entered my dreams I don't remember, but one night I dreamt my mother and I rode a roller coaster alone. We whizzed around corners and climbed white wooden-framework hills. The air closed in, hot and a little dry. During a long swerve downward I could see past an approaching turn to where the clattery tracks fell away. Could it be true?

☑ Other

Yes. We lurched up, up, and the guide rails disappeared. Arcing high, still sitting in the coaster car, my mother and I sailed toward the ocean. What waited in the water scared me more. Rushing toward us as we lost momentum, a shark opened its mouth, staring from eyes as big as airplane jets. I woke overcome by uncertainty about whether my mom liked me or not, her Wiggly Wanda.

Chris and I walked into the kitchen on a midsummer morning to find Mom sitting on a chair placed in the middle of the room. We leaned against her legs and looked up at her tear-streaked face.

"Why are you crying? What's the matter?" we asked.

"The way we're living," she said. She drew a trembling breath and got up to walk us to the table, placing paper and pens before us.

"Write down how you feel when Dad drinks," she instructed. When she read mine she frowned.

"Oh, *Cindy*," she sighed. In uneven lines I had scrawled *When dad drinks he hurts us, he kills us.*

He didn't hesitate to drive me to ballet lessons drunk, to continue raging or to try his hand in Vegas when Mom had gallstone surgery instead of holding her hand in the hospital room.

Dad's mom, our grandmother Zita, prayed for him often. Once in a while, starting when we were five and six, she brought Chris and me to Catholic Mass. I liked the spicy smell inside the stone church, but the mumbling at the faraway pulpit went on too long. I loved gazing at the giant stained-glass windows that showed how brilliantly sunlight could prism. Walking back to the car one Sunday, holding our grandma's hand, Chris asked where our last name came from.

"Your great-grandparents had the name Campopiano," she explained, pronouncing it Kom*pop*iano. "But when they got here from Italy, they changed it to Campo."

"Why?" I asked, thinking the longer name prettier.

"The piano was just too heavy to carry around," she said, chuckling. After a lunch of MacDonald's Happy Meals, she dropped us off at home.

A shattering smash and a thunderous thud yanked me from sleep one night. I woke to indifferent light in squares on my bedroom walls.

☑ Other

The cacophony came from downstairs. Dad was shouting and throwing every breakable in his reach. From my doorway I peered down and saw a plate, distorted and oblong, soaring out of sight where it crashed. Something heavy broke the glass front of the armoire in the dining room. Shards rained and Dad became hoarse. He stumbled up to the landing, dragged Mom from their bedroom to halfway down the stairs and pinned her against the wall. He held up an orange and purple box printed Dunkin' Donuts Munchkins and demanded,

"What doesziszsay?" She looked down and started crying. Because she didn't answer he knocked her head against the wall, which started my tears. He let go of her and looked up, hair wild.

"Fuck you, Cindy," he yelled, as Mom ran back into their bedroom and slammed the door. I turned toward my dresser, now blurred, my throat surging as if it would leap out. An hour of stunned silence went by before I dared believe he had passed out. My nerves resisted sleep. Late the next morning, when my friend Maureen knocked on our door, I opened it an inch and told her I couldn't come out.

"Why are you still in your pajamas?" she asked and I shrugged, closing the door. I trudged up to my room and curled on my side on the unmade bed. Downstairs, Mom put the house back in order, bit by broken bit, while Dad slept off his drunk.

No hand smoothed my hair as I stared at the pink wall. No arms held me, or helped my bruised spirit up from where it had sunk in a heap. In the absence of comfort, I put on *Free to Be ... You and Me*, an album of stories and songs that described a land where children were well cared for. I liked that the girls in the stories were as smart and as fast as the boys. It was all right to feel things, one song said, though the feelings might be strange.

What I was sensing right then was that, as I embarked on life in this world, neither of my parents would be making the way easier. Strange, indeed. I *would* have to be a smart girl, and probably a fast runner too, relying on my own wits — especially if I ever found myself alone.

Chris seemed unaffected by our home, except for picking up our dad's habit of cursing every sentence or two.

"Shit," he would say in his little-kid voice. "My shoelace broke." Or, "Fuck the playground. Let's go get candy." We'd stop by and pick up Maureen. She and her sisters lived in a house with the same shape and dimensions as ours, but rather than feeling like a psych ward, it held the welcoming charm of a bed and breakfast. With every visit to Maureen's, I was ensconced in an unfamiliar but welcome sheath of protection. I could relax over a board game without pausing, arm frozen in mid-reach like the foreleg of a hunted deer testing the silence for danger. As at Mrs. Collins's house, sheltered in the knowledge that no one would roar obscenities or treat me any differently than Chris, I floated through Maureen's in delicious security.

No amount of "normal" things at home, from baking cookies to swimming at pool parties in our backyard, could provide the missing stability. Though I hung out with the kids in the neighborhood, it seemed REJECT had been stamped on my forehead. Sitting one warm afternoon with a group on Maureen's lawn, my eyes locked onto two tough older boys jumping off their bikes and striding toward us. One picked up an old dried piece of cat feces. While I stared, he placed it on my head. The boys spouted harsh laughter and hopped back onto their bikes. The turd fell off my head when I hung it in embarrassment.

Animals turned out easier to bond with than most people. I spent quality hours with Jones the dog and the litter of Calico kittens born to Aunt Nell's cat, which she brought to our house because her tiny apartment couldn't accommodate an entire feline family.

"You're good with the kittens," Nell observed. I glanced up with appreciation and noticed her eyes appeared blue-gray that day; often they looked hazel like Chris's. I decided on the spot I would become a veterinarian.

☑ Other

On St. Patrick's Day in second grade I walked the halls of Stony Brook and noticed one of the teachers striding in the opposite direction. She wore a "Kiss me I'm Irish" button like mine. My Irish came from a maternal grandfather and a paternal grandmother. This lady proved the world's family of Irish was more encompassing than I'd thought. She had kinky black hair and dark, chocolaty skin.

"Hey," I said up at her. "We have the same pin." She smiled and replied,

"Why, baby, yes we do." She leaned down, laughing. Her lips, full to begin with, grew larger as they closed in and warmly covered my cheek. I wanted to follow her down the hall, climb in her lap and stay encircled in her warmth and safety. In the schoolyard I picked a bunch of wildflowers to bring home.

Spring leading to summer marked the mildest time of year. Warm but not yet intolerable, the days lengthened and the woods near our house lit up in green majesty. Once sweltering summer struck, alleviation began with the sharp smell of garden-hose water hitting hot concrete. The water warmed as it flowed around our feet. There would be no pool party for my eighth birthday, no splashing with cousins or eating barbecued hamburgers, only sitting next to Chris in the backseat of the Buick on the road west.

Within ten years of his wedding day, Dad had amassed so much debt, and a couple of driving-under-the-influence tickets, he decided we would all flee New Jersey for the Golden State of California. I worried that the people there would speak a different language. As it turned out, they would. In Southern California, a ball became a "bahhl" instead of a "baul." Pencils were, nauseatingly, "pincils."

No, they weren't. And how would you know if you were hearing about a Dawn or a Don? All those flat words sounded worse than any uttering of "melk." Still, I'm glad we got out of Jersey before I started

☑ Other

saying things like *Order me some disco fries, would yuzz? I gotta go spray my hair.*

Dad decided to fly out ahead and work on opening a new salon near Los Angeles while the rest of us, including Aunt Nell, chugged out in the Buick. In Pennsylvania, one state westward, our muffler fell off. We tied it to the car. Mom and Nell cheered themselves up with a new CB radio that they planned to find the best truck stop restaurants with.

At every convenience store I saw evidence of Indians. Among Doritos, sodas and shot glasses hung mini drums on sticks, suede-clad squaw dolls and feathered earrings, but I saw no actual Indians. I had to imagine them, which I did enviously, picturing a group of Native American siblings on a couch in a tepee, laughing in their secure camaraderie.

We rolled dusty and sweaty into the has-been town of Bellflower, California, where the sister of one of Dad's shampoo girls lived. She had gone on vacation so we had her dismal house to ourselves. Dad joined us, and we spent our first week in California surrounded by thin walls, drab carpeting and closed drapes. Mom wanted to use the oven and noticed the pilot light out. She opened the broiler door and leaned forward, holding a lit match to the gas port.

Vvvhhhooooomf! She backed away from the oven with the front of her hair singed into an afro. California did not know how to treat people. I hated it already and wondered what other bad things this outpost of hell would hold.

Dad chose a new place quickly. We moved into a small rental house, shingled in redwood, in the nicer town of Torrance. The shop he opened looked great. All the hairdresser's stations were well equipped and the new mirrors perfect. We had no idea the location was bad. Not to be defeated, he came up with another idea to make money. He collected gnarled pieces of driftwood at the beach and built lamps. The two he completed tottered on mismatched end tables in our living room. Forgoing the Kahlua portion of his nightly cocktails, he now drank cheap vodka straight.

"'Lazereth isn't dead,' Jesus said, and people thought it was a god damn miracle," he might inform us again. Sometimes Mom and Chris would huddle together glaring from the couch. I felt like prey out in the open.

"Cind, go ahead and cry. Ain't nothin' wrong with that," Dad reasoned.

Sitting clenched, Mom still tolerated his ranting, but her patience threatened to blow out. She threw off the housewife mantle and took a part-time clerical position. When she got home from work she would prepare an easy dinner for everyone and retreat to her room. I hardly saw her.

Now sharing a bedroom, Chris and I would sometimes turn in early too, avoiding Dad's incoherent rambling we could still vaguely hear through the wall. One night when he was snoring on the living room floor, having passed out solid by 7:00, Mom poked her head into our room.

"We need to talk. Let's go." She drove us to Denny's. She needed to vent.

"I think we should kill him," she said, turning to me. "Chris agrees. What do you think?" Not sure if she were joking or not, I imagined all three of us stalking him with a knife, pushing his body into a trash can after the unthinkable act. *Bad idea*, I thought. Not wanting to look mutinous I shrugged, which drew scorn. Mom's eyes narrowed.

"What do you mean you don't know?" she asked.

"I don't know why we even ask what she thinks," Chris said. I pretended not to hear that.

I meant to ask Aunt Nell, who had been staying with us, if she thought Mom had been joking. A few weeks later, when Nell moved out, I had already buried the Denny's night in my graveyard of unwanted information and forgot to ask. I felt privileged to inherit Nell's bedroom and the waterbed in it, which I got to enjoy twice.

Another night of Dad's ranting erupted.

"Nobody gezzit," he said. "What people think is their presshusz reality is illusion."

Mom brought us to her coworker Wayne's till morning. We returned to find a note staked to the front door with a knife. *Go fuck yourselves.* Inside, Dad had demolished every room except Chris's. My father probably still thought of the room with the bunk beds as both of ours, and my new room as Aunt Nell's, which explained why the waterbed's mattress had been slashed and the wooden frame hacked into. Huge puddles had formed on the carpet.

Dad had flown back to New Jersey, it turned out, where he entered a rehab clinic. Mom sent Chris and me back East also, to Grandma and Grandpa Quinn's to finish out the school year and spend the summer. I didn't mind. I loved Grandma Quinn.

When she smiled, a huge warm grin that several of her children and grandchildren had inherited, I realized how seldom I'd seen it on our mother. Able to spruce up the ordinary, Grandma could make going for a walk to search for pinecones sound exciting. When she looked at me, I felt something close to pretty.

☑ Other

3.

Knowledge of Good and Evil

Chris and I joined a public swimming pool for the summer. Hordes of kids swam there, leaving little room to play. The best thing about the pool was getting evacuated when branch lightning spread beautifully down the heavy summer sky. On a sunnier day, I lounged on a towel with my neighbor, a skinny girl who lived next-door to my grandparents. We spoke a made-up language we thought fooled everyone around us. My neighbor stood up.

"Let's get hot dogs," she suggested.

"Where?" I asked.

"The truck across the street."

"OK," I agreed. Even though I didn't like hot dogs, I happened to be hungry.

The truck stood out as the only vehicle on the two-lane road that ran past the pool grounds. Behind it sat a hill where groups of kids hung out. As usual I wasn't wearing my glasses, and saw only a long stretch of road in either direction. I stepped into the street. Just as I noticed my neighbor wasn't beside me, I saw a blurry car approaching from the distance. I picked up my pace, certain I would make it to the other side.

I don't know where on my body the Ford station wagon struck, but after soaring through the air I saw the pavement rushing toward me. As my face hit the road, my leg got tangled under me. I heard someone from the hillside say, "She was hit!" and then the sound of mass people running. As a crowd formed I heard a voice.

"I'm a nurse." A woman in a blue bikini rolled me over and laid my head on the curb. She looked down with concern, her blond hair curling around her face. "Where do you hurt?" she asked.

☑ Other

"My foot," I said, dazed. I saw Chris pushing his way to the front of the crowd. Someone said,

"You can ride with your sister in the ambulance."

I lay on a gurney rolling into a hospital. The hallways and rooms glared white under strong lights, the waxed floors extra shiny. The air smelled like Band-Aids. My foot throbbed and there was pressure in my bladder, yet I felt a little important. At the hospital I would be treated officially for a severely sprained ankle. Men and women in loose, pale green clothing x-rayed my limbs and released me on crutches. Had they x-rayed my neck, though, they would have discovered that I had also injured my spine. That oversight would come back to haunt me several years later.

Couldn't evolution have integrated useful traits from earlier life forms? Vertebrae could have unhook and re-hook ability, like the jaws of a snake, used only in emergencies. But, no. Over time, teams of muscles would pull on my injured spine in a useless effort to realign it, causing those muscles to malfunction like soldiers applying the same command to any situation.

For a week after the accident, I got to stay in bed, happy to enjoy meals and watch TV all day while leaning against pillows. I found that I liked using crutches. I could lift myself up and take long, ground-covering strides.

By the end of the summer, my ankle had mended and I could walk unaided off the plane we took back to L.A. I almost didn't recognize our smiling mom hurrying toward us in a slender white skirt. Back from a supposed rehabilitation, Dad waited in a new apartment in Redondo Beach. Within a month Mom found Popov and Smirnoff bottles lining one of the kitchen cabinets. Grandma Quinn came to visit.

"Oh, Betty," she sighed. "He's zonked." She had run out of suggestions and did not even urge our leaving. After a couple months of good behavior, Dad began the rants again, weekly but with just as much malice. We closed our doors against him.

I noticed that I couldn't run as fast as before. The previous year on Field Day at school, I had beaten the fastest boy in my class at the 50-yard dash. Now, excited to race the same distance on Presidential

☑ Other

Fitness Award Day, I lost to an overweight girl. I blamed the car accident. Sulking on the walk home, I targeted ants along the sidewalk, killing one after another by aiming and bouncing a soccer ball I was carrying.

Books, I discovered, held the power to displace reality. Absorbed in a good story, I heard and saw nothing around me. Whatever room I sat in magically disappeared, and I became whichever protagonist I was reading about. Most of the books I chose in fourth grade involved sassy young girls facing the challenges of how to fit in at school or deal with an older sister's teasing. My favorite novel, *Island of the Blue Dolphins*, had more impact. It was based on the true story of a Native American woman left behind on an island alone. Before getting rescued she survived eighteen years through ingenuity and strength of spirit, staving off the dangers of the wild. I yearned for an adventure, preferably far off in a beautiful landscape.

Later that year, when Nell relocated to Campbell, a suburb of San Jose (about 300 miles north of us), Mom took me up there. She and Dad were ten months into their failed retry. Though she had told him she was fed up with his drinking and his behavior, she granted him a last summer with just him and Chris, which they spent together back East. In the meantime, Nell helped Mom find a new apartment in Campbell. My family's musical chairs didn't even strike me as abnormal anymore.

When Chris returned to California, Mom didn't expect Dad to return with him — or that he would spend the night outside our apartment, sleeping in his car. Out of pity, she told him in the morning he could come in and take a shower. He mistook that as an invitation to stay, and for some reason he was irremovable, like advanced rust.

Our apartment on Echo Avenue in Campbell crowded in on us. It was a distant cry from the New Jersey house. There was no upstairs, no pool, no back yard. The second-hand furniture we'd bought looked as if it had been made for some very poor dolls and enlarged to human size by mistake. Mom tried to combat increasing clutter and an infestation of fleas from our cats.

☑ Other

Chris and I enrolled in our fourth primary school. Once more, we learned the layout of a different suburb, street by street. Dad worked all day painting houses (his latest career move). Mom, moving up the ranks of an accounting department at a retail company, came home exhausted every night and fell asleep by 8:00 on the couch in front of the TV. Her face began to look haggard, and I felt a pang of sympathy for her. I knew it pained her to be married to Dad, to work so many hours.

"No waaaay," I replied to her offhand suggestion that we all move back to New Jersey. I loathed switching schools. We had just come back from grocery shopping, which Mom said was getting too expensive for all four of us.

"Well," she reconsidered, handing me a long package of chicken drumsticks to put away. "We won't move again till you graduate high school. How about that? I promise." She halfway smiled, eyes locked on the grocery bag.

"OK," I said. "Good."

One of my fifth-grade classmates, Sandra, was assigned as my partner for a field trip to Point Lobos, a National Park along the coast. As we walked the trails, the scant breeze lifted her thin blond hair off her shoulders. She mentioned a place she knew to ride horses.

"Wanna go?" she asked.

"Um, sure," I replied. Sandra was a bit of a loner, and I thought she might be weird.

Mom nodded with approval when she heard I had plans with a schoolmate, and gave me the ten dollars I needed for a one-hour ride. Sandra's dad dropped us off at a mountain ranch. The horses looked gigantic, but our guide easily hoisted us up. We headed out along a narrow inclining trail, leaning forward to help the horses gain traction. I felt tall and wonderful, swaying in the crisp autumn air.

"Watch," Sandra said as she urged her horse to a gallop. She pulled back on the reins when I caught up, and cantered next to me. "Know how to sing?" she asked.

"Why?"

☑ Other

"Let's make up lyrics," she said. I looked skeptically at her, and she suggested we practice what we knew first. Taking a deep breath, she sang the opening lines to a song by her favorite band, Cheap Trick. I gave her a sidelong stare as the horses slowed to a walk. Sandra had a lovely voice.

"I've never really tried," I admitted. "Maybe we can after I practice."

"It's easy," she said as we galloped once more to reach the guide. The hour flew by and left us wanting more time on horseback. Using Christmas money from my grandparents, I went riding with Sandra three more times that year. Neither of us needed a guide by summer. The ranch owners trusted us to bring the horses back on time and in good shape. I adored the exhilaration of racing over long-grassed slopes and climbing trails to breezy lookouts, giving the horses a cool-down on the meander back to the ranch.

At home in my room I tried singing into my cupped hand so I could hear my voice, which sounded off key and flat. I gave up and decided to write in my diary. I had been working on a story about a girl finding a portal to another world. Through it she escaped to a forest where she lived in a mahogany treehouse and could talk to all animals. She grew strong on hearty broth and barley. She made friends with forest-dwelling minstrels and good witches. Whenever I sat down to write I felt powerful, which made me feel joyful and let me take command of my world.

I couldn't find the journal. Thinking it might be in the hallway closet, I sat on the floor rummaging through crumpled blankets and junk.

"Cindy," came my mother's brisk voice from above. I looked up, ready to explain why I was on the floor with my head in the closet. Businesslike waves of brown hair framed her no-nonsense expression. "Don't you think it's time you got a bra?"

"I don't know," I replied in a meek voice.

"Well haven't you looked in the mirror lately?" she asked, sounding a little irritated. *She doesn't think I look at my own body in the mirror?*

Like any girl, I looked all the time. Concerning development, I hadn't liked what I'd seen. Changing one day I stopped short at my reflection, because while my left new breast barely budded out, the right looked round already. The nipple on the left had shrunk to a pinpoint — perhaps due to the cool air in the room — while the right nipple remained soft, like an inflated bull's-eye. My chest appeared to have a pair of lopsided eyes.

Really? Was that how it could happen, that one might grow faster than the other? Life suddenly seemed more complicated, and merciless.

Mothers could reassure their growing daughters, easing the awkwardness of puberty. My mom asking if I hadn't looked in the mirror surprised me, even though by that time I had gotten used to the joyless air between us. When I didn't answer, she turned and walked to the kitchen. I got up to call Aunt Nell.

"Did Betty talk to you about getting a bra?" Nell asked.

"Kind of," I said in a low voice, having brought the receiver into my room and shut the door. "She seems annoyed." "Well," Nell said. "It was no fun when our mother bought us our first bras either."

"Hmm," I said, not convinced that excused the uncomfortable dialog we'd just had in the hallway.

"Oh, it was terrible. Our mother dragged us into a department store and demanded the sales girl find bras for us. We had to try them on in front of her."

"Ready?" Mom called. "Let's go." I got off the phone, and we went to a girls' clothing store where I picked out a few bras that she allowed me to try on alone. I rushed through it, wishing I were shopping for jeans and sweaters. I couldn't hook a bra behind my back and had to scoot the clasp around to the front. I'd have to do this every day from now on? Growing up was not going to be fun.

When we got home I decided, while standing shirtless in front of the bathroom mirror, that the new bra actually looked nice. On the next horse ride I appreciated it even more, as well as the measure of independence provided by the hour on the mountain trails.

As a present for Chris's thirteenth birthday, Mom gave him the "master" bedroom of the apartment, which had its own bathroom. The

☑ Other

switch wouldn't affect her — the couch was her bedroom. Dad could have Chris's old room.

"That's not fair," I said. "Why does he get that room? What about when I turn thirteen next year?" She and I were sitting in the living room after Saturday breakfast.

"He needs that room, to study," she answered. Someone had given Chris a huge wooden desk, which Mom said would only fit in the largest bedroom.

I study, too.

"I know what you'll get," Mom said with amusement. "Before he ever does."

I knew, too. Anytime I heard that word, *period*, coldness trickled down my organs. When the first dark blood did come a few months later, I didn't tell my mom that I had "gotten it," but told the concerned eyes reflected in my mirror,

"I don't want this. I don't want this."

Coincidently, I had stayed home from school that day. Unable to find any clean jeans, I yelled to my dad that I couldn't go to school. Between painting gigs he had become house-husbandly, sending us off with lunches he had prepared. He frowned over my wanting to skip school but let me stay home. Using the bathroom less than an hour later, I found a spot of blood on my underwear. I borrowed from my mom's supplies and kept the unwanted discovery to myself.

Oh, to become tiny and hollow, plucked by a bird and dropped in a brook that joins a creek and hurries toward a river flowing into the ocean, where I might have turned into a powerful creature and gone free.

I could visit my classmates, but not invite them over. What could I say? *Oh, who is that yelling drunk man? Well, he's my uncle whose family left him. We're just letting him stay with us for a while.*

"It's not true, is it?" a friend from school, Amy, asked one day after class. She stared hard at me. "Kristen thinks you might have an alcoholic dad."

"No," I whispered. Amy and Kristen lived the modern version of Cleaverworld, in houses that were not only neat and clean, but that teemed with inviolable safety. When visiting, I stood out as a ragged weed among lilies and sweet pea blossoms. The parents still included me in their relentless kindness. A warm hug hello and goodbye, a luxuriant hair brushing before sleep. I could hardly believe my schoolmates got this royal treatment on a regular basis.

One of our upstairs neighbors, a quiet man, lived with his girlfriend, who hopped around on one leg and had a stutter. Next door in the back lived an older couple. The husband rarely spoke, but his wife, Anna, shrieked to the sky that our cat Lady was possessed by demons, when in fact the feline was pregnant. For weeks, Anna stalked Lady in our little front yard. When she finally lunged and grabbed Lady, I could only stare with outrage from the living room window as she paced the sidewalk, muttering while holding Lady by the neck.

Dad flung our front door open, launched across the yard and punched Anna in the temple. Her grip loosened and Lady fell. For once I felt proud of him.

The cat lay on the sidewalk, staring blankly and breathing shallowly. The police arrived, and I watched them ease the dispassionate Anna into the back seat. Two of the kittens were born with deformed legs, yet we found takers for them all.

Late one night as Chris and I watched *Saturday Night Live*, we heard Dad get up, go to the kitchen, open and close the fridge. He came in sober and yawning as he cracked open a Coke.

"Hey. Can I have one of those pieces of pizza?" he asked. From his expression he could have been one of our classmates. The following Saturday evening, in the bathroom in front of the mirror, he leaned back as he did when cutting hair. He concentrated on his own brown mop, combing and spraying. His face hung in red saggy pockets with deep lines around his mouth and on his forehead. The flames behind his eyes had grown faint.

For parent-teacher night Dad had dressed in his only suit, which was thick and brown. The bottoms of the pants stopped just above the ankles. He wore a creased yellow shirt and a mustard paisley tie. He was steaming drunk. Just before seven o'clock Chris told Mom,

"I don't want him to come."

☑ Other

None of us had ever stood against him and when Mom told him that he wasn't welcome, he did not become furious as we expected. Instead he looked as if he would cry. Although girls are usually the balm of wounded families, I said nothing and left with Chris and Mom.

What did I see on the faces around me? Undertones of boredom and nothing to be proud of. Daily I cruised those school halls, unnoticed in a hoodie and jeans.

My thirteenth birthday found me on our scrap of lawn in the August heat, petting one of the cats.

"What are you doing?" a young neighbor girl asked.

"It's my birthday," I told her.

"That's sad," she noted. "You're just playing with a cat."

"For *now*," I said, and went inside to the cool shade to microwave some nachos. Later Mom came home with a gardenia that she set in a bowl of water on the coffee table. Without a word she walked into the kitchen to make a birthday dinner. I stared surprised at the floating flower that gave off a scent far better than the best perfume. I wondered where my mom had first seen gardenias, wondered if she missed her parents or her brothers and their families. She rarely talked about her personal life. I meandered into the kitchen to see what she was cooking.

I started paying more attention to the world beyond our front door. It glittered with the spazztastic flash of the mid-'80s. For me, its best and brightest left one impression: ugly. Subcategory: fake. A prime example: shoulder pads. Instead of having gotten closer to remembering what I had chosen to work on in my lifetime, if that had

☑ Other

actually happened, I only knew that the world did not look good. Except for punk, break dancing and graffiti, '80s art and fashion seemed infected with cheesiness. As if they got dressed in the dark, people left home wearing neon green stirrup pants with orange trim, skewed wide shirts with tubular cuffs, huge scrunchy socks and asymmetrical belts. Women's pants pinched their waists, sectioning their bodies like insects. Pastels blared from every store and billboard. Style sickness spread like a massive Zima spill, spawning flammable fright-wig hairstyles and black rubber bracelets crammed twenty at a time onto wrists to cover, perhaps, the self-cutting on the rise. The general public had dumbed down enough to buy T-shirts printed with ungrammatical slogans like FRANKIE SAY RELAX and baseball caps that read CAP across the front.

The dominant music of the era leaned heavily on thin plastic keyboards. Worse, at home, my parents almost never listened to any music, although Neil Diamond's lounge-y voice sometimes filtered through while a Johnny Cash hit may have also shouldered its way in. On bended knee, Johnny listened to the voice of Galilee — the heavy clang-and-stomp of fallen times.

For those in the margins, alternative artists staved off mainstream madness and provided flip-side fashion. Like a dark mirror glancing off Madonna's bolero jackets, white lace, purple ribbons and drag-you-to-the-floor religious pendants of conflicting faiths, Siouxsie Sioux wore blood-red ostrich feathers, fishnet stockings on her arms, cupless bustiers and Cleopatra makeup. Somehow she seemed more real.

It would take a few years for me to understand that '80s culture displayed resurfaced '40s-and-'50s goofiness, warped after being held under for a few decades. Though tracers still rippled before the eyes of the many on acid, few traces of real social upheaval remained from the '60s and '70s. Americans could have found plenty to protest. When Reagan said that government was not the solution to the problem; government *was* the problem, he didn't mean that he ran an objectionable administration. Instead he implied, "Sink or swim, everybody." If you fell between the cracks, too bad. Meanwhile his wife launched the laughable *Just Say No* drug "awareness" campaign. Nancy

☑ Other

Reagan practically issued blindfolds as anti-drug gear. Her "do not think" message aligned with the political tone of the decade — which I didn't know much about, though at least I understood that a blanket *No!* spelled anti-freedom.

The town of Campbell languished as the dirt under the fingernail of San Jose. A few weeks before high school started, the suburb's turf became the entry point to a deeper level of hell — because of an unfortunate incident I tried desperately to forget. Like the fog of a coma, thick was the rug under which I stockpiled anything painful. Fear reigned over my emotions by the time I stepped onto the school bus on the first day of ninth grade. Spirit-crushing dread lurked beneath my surface, though I didn't reflect on its cause right away.

I'd managed to find a few new companions: Savannah, a smart, self-assured girl I'd met during junior high, and Janet, a new girl in the neighborhood. Mostly, though, I escaped into novels, music and schoolwork. A hope that growing up might mean inclusion in long-awaited knowledge had faded. Life started looking like an endlessly whirling spiral of school, meals, time to kill, and sleep. I kept wondering which could change — fate or destiny.

When Aunt Nell became a reborn Christian, she focused on converting anyone who hadn't. She took Chris and me aside and lay hands on our shoulders, praying for God to guide. Sometimes we went with her to church, a new building that looked nothing like the gorgeous cathedral our grandma had brought us to. No stained glass or fragrant incense, just bright modern walls and parishioners jumping up, fluttering their hands and thanking Jesus.

I thought it would be great if there were a God or gods — anything beyond this world that could help it. But when Nell's church friends tried to get Chris and me to go down to the preacher's podium during the part of the service when newbies were sworn in, neither of us were feeling it.

"Something happens spiritually when people have sex that we don't understand," Nell took a moment to point out one afternoon. I had reached prime sex-talk age. "Only after they fell, Adam and Eve did it. Nothing but marriage, in God's eyes, makes sex all right."

☑ Other

Not what I wanted to hear. Rather than scoffing at Nell, though, I jolted, seeing the memory I had been pushing away.

Back in August, a few nights after my fourteenth birthday, I had waited nervously on the edge of a children's slide at John D. Morgan Park, yards from where I'd played field hockey and soccer during junior high. I'd agreed to meet up with Rodney, a schoolmate I had a crush on. He was your stereotypically popular, good-looking boy. Sandra knew Rodney, and had given him my number. Acquainted with only the mildest social interactions (sleepovers and pizza outings), I figured this hangout would be just as casual.

"Be there at eleven," Rodney had said on the phone. I didn't know what to expect. I just felt lucky that he wanted to meet up with me, a nobody.

By 10:45 that Thursday night, Mom and Dad had fallen asleep. Chris's door was shut. I put down the book I was reading. Dressed in jeans, a boat-necked knit shirt and running shoes, I quietly slipped out of the apartment and walked the five minutes to the park.

From the darkness at the edge of the playground, Rodney strode toward me, his T-shirt stretched tightly over his chest muscles. He looked intently off to his right until he reached me. He didn't smile and neither did I. Nonchalantly we told each other hi. In his right hand he held a plastic Sprite bottle filled with a flat clear liquid.

"I've been drinking already," he said. "So you need to drink this."

"What is it?"

"Seagram's Seven."

At our mom's suggestion when we were four and five, Chris and I poured out all the booze we could find in the house. Standing on chairs, emptying each bottle into the kitchen sink, we thought we were ridding our lives of the scourge. Yet when offered straight whiskey that summer night, I drank it like I'd been waiting for it. The Seagram's tasted like fiery cough medicine.

As we walked toward a little grove of pine trees, I took one big swig after another, just glad to be next to Rodney, who smiled down at me now and then. I began to feel light as air. A breeze floated by, grassy and fresh. We sat down on a little hill that overlooked the site of our eighth-

☑ Other

grade graduation. Nearby crickets went silent. I remembered the congratulatory hugs with classmates, and especially how Rodney's embrace had dazzled me with sweetness and warmth.

"This stuff is affecting me," I said as the stars above dipped and swayed. My eyelids got a little heavy. My head wanted to nod forward. I sat up straight and tried to come up with something to say. Realizing that I didn't know this boy at all, and probably had nothing in common with him, I wondered why I had a crush on him. His deep blue eyes? Broad shoulders? An airplane passed overhead, the sound of its engines ripping the sky in two. I didn't understand why it was *that* loud, or why Rodney wasn't making conversation.

"Have you ever been kissed?" he finally asked, taking my never-held-by-a-boy hand.

"No."

I could feel the heat off his skin. He leaned forward and delicately touched my lips with his, parting them and edging his tongue in. So new, warmth sliding against warmth, it felt like the first notes of a song you knew you were going to love. This was why people adored kissing. *It's beautiful.* The night air mixed with Rodney's soapy scent, the sultriness of the kiss lingering. But something in me lurched. *This is all wrong.* My head felt thick and I had no control of my limbs. He maneuvered me easily onto my back.

"I want to fuck you," he said in the same soft tone he'd been using, now edged with menace. *This isn't supposed to happen.*

"No," I said and tried to sit up, only to find that my body wouldn't obey, as if I were in a terrible dream. While I gaped in panic at the spinning, glittering sky, he pushed up my shirt. I shivered. He undid my jeans. "Stop," I said. He pulled off each of my shoes, followed by the jeans. Then my underwear. Blades of grass poked against my skin. I just wanted to rewind to the kiss. My mouth had gone numb, but I held onto the warm sweet feeling of five minutes before.

"Kissz me instead," I slurred. That's all I desired. The moment of my first kiss, even better than I had imagined, like a gift I thought I barely deserved, had morphed into this grotesque procedure. I felt horribly disoriented. Here I'd thought Rodney was this cool guy who liked me enough to hold my hand and give me romantic kisses. Now he pinned my wrists to the ground and thrust his hips toward me. I yelled, "Owwwwww!" as pain tore through the growing numbness. I pushed uselessly against his grip. He shifted his weight off me for a minute and switched tactics. While I tried not to vomit, he positioned himself over my face and cautioned,

"Don't bite."

I was suffocating, my mouth crammed full. Just before blacking out, I wished I wasn't me. When I came to, Rodney was carrying me uphill to the same spot we just were. He set me back down on the grass. Confused and tired, I reached for my underwear, noting the bloodstains on my thigh.

"I gotta go," Rodney said as he slithered away. I slowly put my clothes back on. In order to balance standing I had to lean forward with my hands on my knees. Eventually I stumbled out of the park.

One old Irish blessing starts *May the road rise to meet you*. That night it proved true. The road home rose to meet me again and again. Every time I fell during that long walk home, it was harder to get back up. I hated being drunk. I had no idea why people enjoyed it.

That was the adult world of sex? Blue with bruises under my clothes the next day, I didn't tell anyone what had happened. I considered myself an even more pathetic person in an even uglier world. I didn't trust my parents and feared my mom's scornful disapproval. She would think I was an idiot, and I believed she would be right. Embarrassed about my incredible naiveté and getting played like a fool, I didn't think I had anything to say that my family would have respected me after.

See, this kid who must have gotten held back 'cause he's sixteen had gym class with me last year, and I noticed him when we collided during a soccer game. I love soccer because it makes me feel strong and fast, and I liked Rodney because I liked his looks — a simple mistake.

I had been used like a toy, had gotten stripped of an already fleeting sense of identity, and was now more "what" than "who" — a *thing* to be acted upon, not someone who carried out her will. I sensed the same sick feeling as when I'd first heard of serial killers, and about what mindset it took to consider another person yours to do with whatever

☑ Other

you wanted. And to *have been* a living doll, powerless and helpless, nauseated me.

Hatefully angry at Rodney, I felt astounded a week after ninth grade started when a girl at school mentioned that he wanted to know if I still liked him. *Liked* him, as if he thought what he did was anywhere near normal or right.

Maybe something had indeed happened spiritually that I didn't understand. *If ye partake in the Sprite bottle full of Seagram's*, I thought, *ye shall surely be filled with pain, and plummet into thine own vomit for eternity.* It made sense that humanity lay face down in the dust. Eve had been naïve, and God had lied, saying whoever ate of the tree of knowledge of good and evil would die. That would have been easier, considering how broken I felt. How wrong our dad had been, trying to convince us those opposites didn't exist.

Definitely bad: Not being able to choose your first.

Good: Not getting pregnant by the boy who stole your adolescence.

Also good: That it wasn't a gang of boys.

Evil: That this destructive act, whether of a few minutes or hours, happens every day all over the world and usually affects the victim for life. Rape rams messages in: *You don't decide what is done with you. My pleasure is what you are here for. You're damaged goods now.*

I had been interested in another boy — my brother's friend Chris Robinson. We called him by his last name instead of "the other Chris" or some nickname. Robinson had dropped out of tenth grade to play piano all day. His forearms and hands were the most beautiful I'd ever seen. His laugh burst like tiny fireworks. He had no idea how much I liked him. The night before the Rodney debacle, Robinson had come over to play video games. After my brother had fallen asleep, Robinson and I sat, controllers in hand, swilling pitchers of iced tea till the early hours. I had decided he would become my first kiss. One day later, I understood that liking someone led to getting duped, and kisses to violation. First love had bypassed me, and I no longer cared if I saw Chris Robinson or not.

Until that night, I had enjoyed making sketches in ink or pencil. That hobby no longer held interest, and my music tastes turned to

☑ Other

macabre, dark sagas of pain. I took to reclining on our smaller couch with my eyes half closed, staring at the sparkly white paint of the living room ceiling and working on a poem about having fallen like a burned-out star. To assist the cocooning process, LSD leapt out and shouted,

"Need a distraction? Fret not, young lady." On the bus home one afternoon, one of my two new friends, Janet, tore a tiny piece off of a sheet of paper and drew a dot on it. One of Janet's best features, her celebrity smile, did not appear as she held the torn corner of paper in her palm for me to see.

"This is what acid looks like," she said.

"What do you mean?" I asked.

"You eat the paper, then go into the B world."

I considered Janet of sound mind and optimistic spirit. So instead of saying, *That's like, totally lame, burnout. We're in ninth grade*, I asked her what happened next.

"Well, there's the P world and the B world," she began, like a beer aficionado winding up for a long uninvited explanation. *Ya gotcher lagers and ya gotcher ales.* She bent over her notebook and drew. It looked like this:

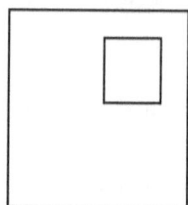

She labeled the smaller box P and the larger one B.

"The P world is the regular world we're in now — the people world. The B world is when you're on acid. My friend can grab some anytime 'cause her mom and dad make it at home. We call it 'bears' so nobody knows what we're talking about. One time, she was on it at school and this guy tapped his pen on his desk, but it sounded like 'doi-oi-oi-oiiing, doi-oi-oi-oiiiing.' And one time when *I* was, this kid gave me chocolate and it tasted like toothpaste."

Well. Hmmm. Clearly this reality bender called for investigation. With Janet and Savannah I ate bits of paper with dark dots on them — reminiscent of candy dots — in the morning before classes. The taste revived memories of sticking my tongue on the contact point of a nine-volt battery. By second class I could barely recognize my schoolmates. Anyone with a slightly big face now resembled a Disneyland character staggering under the weight of a giant head covered with actual skin.

Testing flavors was out of the question. My stomach bobbed like a weightless glass ball. My palms got sweaty, and I felt both hot and cold, and neither hot nor cold. When I did try to eat (popcorn), it wasn't clear where in my throat I should be swallowing. Worse, my jaw and neck hurt — not as if they'd been injured recently, but a deep ache that I hadn't noticed before.

I had French class for fourth period. The teacher asked us to come to the board one by one, but I could have sworn he gave the instructions in a language other than French. Swishy non-words landed ashamed on the vibrating linoleum. When my turn came I went up, took the chalk in hand, and listened. He said something I couldn't quite make out but started writing an answer to, then turned to where he "sat" at the back of the class.

"*Non*," he boomed, granny glasses pinching the end of his beak. "*Pas correct*." I faced the board again. This was *pas bon*. I considered myself a good French student. I looked at the chalkboard eraser, which surprised me by leaping to its death, fluffy gray and innocent. It hit the floor without making any sound, and I started laughing. When I finally turned around to go back to my seat, the muscles around my ribs aching, the entire class had become one undulating fabric of guffawing faces. I pronounced acid weird and ugly, feeling so myself by association.

At P.E., which I had with Savannah and Janet, we tried to play tennis. Savannah stepped onto the court, her head whipping right then left, her tall thin body edging sideways, cat-like. Janet held her racket in the ready pose, her forehead and eyes enlarged by an invisible fish-eye lens. It seemed that several balls rocketed by so they were impossible to hit. After school we recapped the strangeness.

"I saw Skeletor."

"This girl was in a bubble —"

"I looked in the mirror and I had a guy's face."

"Didn't know walls could breathe like that."

Instead of running from the twisted funhouse of acid, homemade or otherwise, I just never did it at school again. As distorted as it could get, the B world was definitely bigger than the P world. After a few more trips with Savannah, an old man's voice now familiar piped up: *You need you something new and different, girl.* A senior who sat in front of me in French class dealt cocaine. He had the greasy hair, blemished skin and name "Tony" appropriate to such an occupation.

"I wanna try it," Savannah told me. Although she rolled her eyes at how her palm-reading, astrology-charting hippie parents got weird using drugs, this would be different. Tony and I executed the deal in class. Later, having snorted two huge lines apiece, Savannah and I scaled one of the three dome movie theaters in San Jose. My heart pounded as we gained the top rungs of the curved ladder that hugged the entire height of the dome. Above the tree line, away from people, our mundane city looked pretty.

Oh, fast speech and slow mind, filthy-fingered twitching, place of gnashing teeth. Even so, I could swear I'd seen shades of beautiful colors that hadn't existed before, running through the dull streets. We lifted up our eyes and in a torment of come-down hunger saw dinner in the distance. At our parting corner I told Savannah,

"See ya when I see ya." She replied,

"Not if I see you first."

Sometimes I'd watch Savannah draw as she tilted her head for perspective, long blond bangs hanging over the page. During endless classes she would sketch everyone as 90-year-olds bent over their desks, about to die of boredom. She had bright blue-green eyes, a nicely angled jaw line and a slender body, but she considered herself ugly. She must, I thought, be identifying with her mother, who looked like she'd

☑ Other

been plucked from a wax museum of Quakers. Savannah's dad, Marv, who was twenty years older than her mom, seemed to be hurtling toward an even older age prematurely. He was an intelligent, artistic collection of twitches. His wiry eyebrows jerked independently, like the legs of a jazz drummer.

Marv offered to take Savannah and me out for driving practice. At school our driving instructor, Mr. Carr, had pointed out how nervous Savannah, Janet and I seemed. I tried slowing my movements and acting calm, though my stomach still felt jumpy, and Mr. Carr bought it. I put on the same nonchalant demeanor when Savannah's father took us out, and kept an eye on the speedometer, maintaining twenty-five. The old man kept a jittery hand on the dash and made no attempt to hide the terror in his eyes. Exasperated, I pulled into a parking lot to switch places with Savannah.

"Why is he all freaked out?" I whispered, and she whispered back that I'd been going over forty in a residential section. The twenty-five had been 2,500 RPM. I hung my head in failure as I climbed into the back seat.

Towards the end of sophomore year, Savannah's mother and stepdad prepared to move from San Jose to Arkansas, planning to take Savannah and her sister with them. My mom suggested that Savannah live with us instead. Since Savannah didn't want to switch schools or live in the Ozarks, she accepted. Everyone on both sides agreed. Aunt Nell gave us a double bed to share while Chris kept the big room, and Mom continued to sleep on the couch. Dad was comfortable passing out anywhere, including the back patio with our rabbit, Clyde, dozing on his chest.

Savannah had a charged, exaggerated way about her. When she got an idea her face lit up as if she'd discovered magic. At movies she ate popcorn in slow motion, her unblinking eyes devouring the story on the screen, her reflexive grip sudden in startled moments. On sweltering days she lay on the floor and lifted a limp hand, calling in a faint voice for something to drink or to be helped up. Her theatricality appealed to my chronic hesitation.

"*Cin*dy," she would say, her eyes bluer.

☑ Other

"Mm?" I'd mumble.

"Listen." She'd unpause a song at the line that had caught her attention. For both of us the world would be dead without music.

Over the nearby mountains at the Santa Cruz beach, the sand warmed under the sun. The water, though, stayed frigid no matter how hot the weather. Like turtles, Savannah and I huddled on our towels. We discussed guys. She didn't know about Rodney. No one knew. I'd done my best to block the whole mess out, though ever-present fear served as a reminder.

Savannah liked Dan Paris, and I had a pitiful attraction to Brendan Hallett, whose locker was next to mine. Dan studied art, while Brendan barely studied. Thinking himself subversive, Brendan snubbed rules, teachers and schoolwork.

One afternoon while we waited for the bus home, Brendan sauntered over, looked into my eyes and asked what our French homework was. I muttered some answer. He walked off, thanking me over his shoulder. Janet and Savannah rushed in.

"Cindy!" Janet said. "When a boy talks to you, you don't just stand there looking down. Oh *well*." The next day at our lockers I turned to Brendan and said,

"Your haircut looks really good," but it came out in a whisper he ignored. Savannah spoke with more confidence to Dan, but he never asked her out.

When she first moved into our apartment, she used polite speech and manners. Something shifted. One afternoon she sneered at a poem I showed her, claiming she created better, deeper poetry. Another day she pointed out that my family was lame. She thought my mom was using the child-support check she received every month to buy food for everyone, instead of using it to take care of Savannah as agreed.

"I doubt it," I said. "She likes buying things for you. The sewing machine. Shoes." Savannah wasn't listening.

"Life is lame," she concluded. "Nothing matters." Instead of thinking she was showing her true colors, I thought this temporarily angry girl would go back to being my friend — the sooner the better.

☑ Other

A shy boy at school, Jason, got up the nerve to ask me out. He became my first boyfriend. I found him boring and unattractive, but safe — the opposite of Rodney. Savannah dubbed Jason The Radish due to his round head and pinkish face with understated chin. His strong shoulders and arms (from wrestling) were his best features. We didn't laugh much together — a bad sign. But I liked escaping a few hours a week to his nonalcoholic house to watch music videos and kiss.

After dinner one night I found Savannah staring at the ceiling from our bed. On her stomach sat an empty saucer stained with the film of melted chocolate ice cream. She looked heartbroken.

"What happened?" I asked.

"Food," she said. "It's food. Ice cream is supposed to be a good thing." Her eyes teared up. "I remember my family tried to have good, normal things. I can't stand it." This unexpected darkness contrasted with my evening plans of dinner with Jason.

"Hey," I said. "It's OK, food *is* a good thing." I smiled even though she had reminded me of the ruined dinners I'd known all my life. I went into the bathroom to get ready.

Ducking back into the room to grab shoes, I noticed a jagged piece of saucer on the rug near Savannah. Now curled on her side on the floor, she was slashing at her wrist with another shard.

"It's not *working*," she complained, glaring at the bloody scratches in her skin. Two things occurred to me at once: an urge to keep a self-destructive friend alive, and a thought that suicide had to be one of the weakest maneuvers a person could choose. Death would happen someday. You couldn't say, *Nah, I'm gonna do something else, do it another way.* Stealing the thunder, or just giving up, looked wrong.

I knelt with my arm timidly on Savannah's shoulder and told her that her life mattered, that there were people who cared and would be very affected by her death. I cancelled with Jason and made sure not to mention food for the rest of the night.

The next time I had a date, I went on it even though as I readied to leave Savannah told me she'd hidden razor blades in our room and would use one if I went out. Shooting a pissed look at her — why would you put someone in that position? — I said I'd be back. Jason might have been a boring radish with mediocre taste in music, I thought, but at least he was sane.

Though Savannah never did follow through on her threat, she brimmed with fury. A look on a face, the denial to her of anything she wanted, or the apparent incompetence of anyone could set off a tirade of insults. While my own anger at the Rodney violation would percolate over the years like lava from a slow volcano, she seemed full of suppressed magma.

As tenth grade rolled into summer we got our first jobs, in a mall at a fruit-drink shop that offered a few fast-food items. *How did she do it?* I wondered. Savannah's mood could morph *like that*. She would be in a scowling funk all day, only to brighten up the second she got to work, encouraging people in their choices of grease and chemicals. The sincerely friendly side of her personality swung around like a lighthouse beam. Since we were together most of the time, I had to wait out a lot of darkness for that wash of brightness to come around. I would anticipate her milder moods in the way that someone lost at sea counts on morning to bring the chance of rescue.

"Let's get away from here after we graduate," she suggested in a confiding tone one night as we fell asleep side by side. I cracked open an eye. Flat yellow light from a streetlamp leaked in through the window and onto the sleeping back of Minka, my blue-eyed sealpoint Siamese cat. My parents had rescued her from a shelter and had given her to me. When I named her, Mom decided that "Miss Ellie" was a better fit. She never did call my cat Minka, and neither did anyone but me.

"Where?" I asked drowsily, thinking I could maybe bring Minka with us.

"Traveling. Anywhere. It'll be cool."

"We'll have to save money."

"We'll go to Europe first."

One weekend, while we visited her dad in Santa Cruz, Savannah asked him to give us palm readings. He had once done it for a living.

☑ Other

With a dismissive wave she gestured that I go first. Marv looked at my upturned hand.

"Hmmm, somewhere between six and nine years old it looks like you had an accident and got hurt. There is a square of protection around that." Impressed, I paid attention. "A type of . . . guardian angel kept you alive. Let's see . . . your heart line is doubled here. That means there will be someone you'll *think* is the one, and someone who really will be. Over here, you have a ring of Solomon." He let my hand go and turned to Savannah.

I would worry over this catch-22 in the future. If I thought someone was the one, he wouldn't be. But if the reading were right, thinking I'd found the one had to happen in order for another to become the one. I wondered if Marv might have been getting me back for scaring him during driving practice.

That evening, he brought us to see a fifteen-piece band that covered R&B and Motown hits. Unlike any music I had danced to, the '60s-era-memorializing orchestra had an upbeat, refreshing style. Just as the band struck up, two college-aged women and their dates rushed onto the dance floor. They wore vintage clothes down to belt buckles, hairpins, patterned tights and thick glasses. All four performed old-school moves well. I watched them. Those people cracked open a fissure that allowed in a beautiful light and wooed me to find out what other light existed. I gave myself over to dancing. For a good hour, there was no separation between the music and me. I became the deep, lovely brass notes and the sweet tones of the ladies' voices.

When the last song ended, the room came back into focus. A skinny man with sweat-plastered hair and a tie-dyed shirt stood before me.

"You have an affinity for dancing," he said, pushing up his wire-rimmed glasses. "Would you like to get coffee or something?"

"No, thank you," I said, glancing around for Savannah and Marv. I spotted them putting on their jackets amid the dispersing crowd and jogged over. I hated when anyone looked at my body.

In the morning I made a big batch of pancakes to stave off a sharp feeling of sadness I had woken with. Mom brought a plateful to Chris in his room and returned with a sigh to the kitchen table.

☑ **Other**

"It's his prom tonight," she said, looking out the window. "And the poor guy's nervous." *Yeah, the poor guy's life is so hard.* I glared at her, but she seemed unaware that I was in the room. That evening I heard my brother's urgent whisper from down the hall.

"*Cin!* Get over here."

I found him standing shirtless, with dress pants on, in front of the mirror in his little bathroom. He pushed his wet hair first to one side, then the other.

"What's up?" I asked.

"Can you do my hair for me?"

"Just ask Dad," I said. Chris rolled his eyes.

"Shhh. Will you just do it? Come on."

"Let me grab a hair dryer."

Twenty minutes later, dressed and ready, he stood by the front door while Mom straightened his collar. I felt Cinderella-like on the sidelines. I resented how she looked at him with admiration and pride. Plus I felt indignant about my sixteenth birthday.

I had been sure I'd get a vehicle because, the year before, Dad had given Chris a Honda scooter he was discarding to buy a motorcycle. I would have been glad to inherit the family Pinto. My gift turned out to be a free kitten from a box outside the local grocery store. The tabby seemed a last-minute decision, as Mom had driven me there to buy cake ingredients.

I turned from Chris and Mom at the front door and sought out Savannah, who was watching TV.

"Wanna go tapping?" I asked.

"Why not?" she said. We pulled on shoes, slipped out the kitchen door and hurried to the parking lot of the nearest liquor store. When we saw a customer about to enter, Savannah tapped his shoulder and asked if he would buy us a six-pack. Someone always did. I couldn't stand the taste of hard alcohol, but beer wasn't so bad, and drinking three never brought on that horrible paralyzing drunk I never wanted to experience again. We brought it back home, walked quietly past Mom in the living room, and played a drinking card game in our room until bedtime.

☑ Other

I had stopped letting Dad style my hair also. His knowledge was outdated. Instead I went to the salon in Santa Cruz that Janet preferred, and took to wearing a spiky haircut along with almost entirely black clothing. On weekends we would go to all-ages music shows, and I danced until I forgot about everything.

I didn't know it at the end of junior year, but around that time my mom would lose her job. Dad's painting gigs weren't enough to pay for more than a sliver of household costs. Chris was about to graduate high school and had been accepted to the California Institute of Technology. Summertime spread out ahead, promising blazing hot days, weekend concerts, and barbecues with weird neighbors in the lot behind our four-plex. Mom didn't tell me she had lost her job, but mid-June she opened my bedroom door and announced she and Dad would be moving back to New Jersey.

"You can come if you want," she began. I protested.

"But you said we wouldn't move again until —"

"Though you'd probably be going to your father's old high school," she continued. "And since we'll be staying at Grandma and Grandpa Campo's, there isn't a lot of room. We could fix up the attic and they do have an extra cot."

"You said . . ." *Promised*, I thought. "We wouldn't move again till I finished high school." *One more year.*

"Well." She paused for a moment before pressing her lips into a thin line. "I've gotta be closer to my mother. She needs looking after. We're leaving in two weeks. Everything's going into storage. The cats are coming with us. You can stay here and get an apartment if you don't want to go."

"What about college?" I asked, my pitch rising. Enviously I had watched Mom helping Chris send applications to universities and taking him to meet with admissions officers. She took a deep breath.

"Why don't you go to art school or something?"

Apply by myself? The perimeter of my visual field darkened and the back of my neck went cold. I searched her face for an answer to my silent question and found only deadpan determination. I wouldn't have been more shocked if my mom had flung my door open and rhino-charged me. Did I either want to live at my grandparents, sleep in an attic, (fixed up or not — we had both read *Flowers in the Attic*) — and switch schools again with only one year remaining, or suddenly live on my own? About as much as I wanted to pour bleach in my eyes.

"I'm not going," I said. If my mom was breaking her promise, I decided, I would carry it through. I refused to relocate to New Jersey.

Rarely had I felt like such a fool. I had found out about the move last. Chris had his dorm room waiting in Pasadena. Savannah had already arranged to live with her cousin in the Santa Cruz mountains.

I was stunned, and wondering what the hell had just happened. Dad knocked on my door a few hours after Mom's announcement.

"Cin," he called. "You in there?"

Opening it to his swaying, red face, anger exploded in my brain. I pushed past him and ran out the front door but stopped short. I sat down on the concrete step of our tiny porch, not sure where to go in the deepening dusk. My head hurt. The door opened behind me. Without seeing me, Dad clomped on my hand as he staggered off to look for me.

"Hey!" I complained and went back inside, tears rolling down my cheeks, ashamed to be crying. I sagged onto my bed. Thrown off by the stark news, I didn't quite grasp that I would be getting out of the madhouse. My strange friendship with Savannah would reemerge later, like a weed growing from cracked concrete.

I zombied through the following days. On a baking-hot morning I slouched at Janet's kitchen table where she and my mom called around for potential apartments. Staring at the floor without seeing it, I felt nothing but a dull ache in my chest. I sat motionless (as Mom had wanted me to do as a child), no different than any other object in the room except that I could hear.

"The one we looked at yesterday got rented," Janet said.

"Chris says Dave needs a place," Mom said. "Let's call him." Dave was one of Chris's gaming friends, a nice-enough twenty-two-year-old. At my mom's request, he agreed to share an apartment with me. I was

☑ Other

sixteen. Within a few hours, Mom secured and signed for a one-bedroom we had viewed in San Jose. I would sleep in the living room.

She then drove me to Bank of America to open my first account, silent about the crucial subject at hand except to mention that while I continued working part time, she would send money for my share of rent. I don't remember putting my belongings in boxes. I don't remember the goodbyes. I just remember that by the end of June, my family was gone.

Putting clothes away in a milk-crate "dresser," I paused, forgetting for a moment to breathe. My chest threatened to implode with a crushing shame as I realized my status had fallen below the level of the house cats that my parents had brought on the airplane to New Jersey. *Loser. Absolute loser.* I let an armful of clothes fall to the floor, noticing that my hands shook.

Getting dropped onto the playing field without knowing the rules felt dangerous. I hadn't learned the difference between deposits and down payments, utilities and insurance, responsibilities and obligations. I was desperate for encouragement and loving guidance. Every morning for the first few weeks of waking alone, Dave already off to work, I sobbed into my pillow.

☑ Other

4.

The Wandering

I abandoned the stigmas from the mother home in half rhymes of refuge and refusal — abandoned the world as I knew it. What or who would replace my family was unapparent.

As a parting gift from one of our neighbors in Campbell I got my first car: a boxy '67 Toyota Corona (which was free, but hardly more than a go-cart). From the twin bed I had slept in as a younger kid before Savannah had moved in, only now without a bed frame, the view outside the window offered nothing but a parking lot. The carpet in the apartment looked dull, brown and worn.

The ostrich feather of the underworld goddess Ma'at, the measure against which hearts are weighed, would have let mine crash to the bottom of the bottom. I slept as if I were departed and woke as if on duty for hell, certain to fail the position with a hummingbird's pulse or a wish for love.

Every night before sleeping I would think, *Let there be one good thing. Just one I can think of that happened today. What was it? Something. Janet came over. But now she's in Dave's room and the door is closed.*

Dave maintained a near-constant buoyancy, his rich laugh punctuating his every few sentences. He came home early evenings from his computer-something-something job, his feet springing and his smile quick, as if we were about to sit down to board games with my brother.

"Hey, Cin!" he would greet with pure cheer. Who knows what I mumbled? I now operated in slow motion while Dave remained in the land of normal. As did Janet. They were finding love, every lip smack and murmur amplified and sticky sounding.

☑ Other

"I see you're annoyed," Janet said, sipping Diet Coke on an afternoon like every other. "If I were you I would be happy to live on my own. You can do whatever you want."

"That's not the problem," I said. Janet didn't, and couldn't, get it. Her parents were supportive — practically *and* emotionally. I was pretty sure I didn't matter to anyone. When you don't matter much to at least one person, you're nothing, while everyone else is something.

September rushed up with its blaring *Back to school, kids!* The lack of food in the kitchen tore down any semblance of routine in the lead-up to fall classes. I reluctantly called Mom and told her I was having a hard time.

"Didn't you get the check?" she asked.

"Yeah. That pays my part of the rent and work pays for bills and a tiny bit of food, but I can't buy new shoes or anything else."

"We'll go shoe shopping at Christmas. You can come visit."

"Mom, I feel kind of depressed," I said. I had never disclosed vulnerability to her, and threw down a bid of hope.

"Cindy," she replied incredulously. "You sound like a destitute person." Angry tears rose. My shoulders tightened.

"I am *not* — OK, fine, thanks a lot." A knot formed in my chest.

"OK, talk to you later," she said and hung up. The knot condensed into a mass, refusing to budge for hours. I couldn't tell if my mom considered me a capable person just having a wobbly moment (though wouldn't she have told me that?) or if she had all but washed her hands of me. Pouring shampoo into bathwater to create bubbles, I couldn't get her out of my mind. *She's acting like I should be fine. And I still don't know what to do.*

In an abrupt about-face from fairly challenging classes, I chose Typing, Foods, Photography, and the obligatory Government. Despite efforts to keep my eyes open, I fell asleep during class at least twice a day. In the halls I noticed none of the students looking at the run-down school, just as I had never bothered to. Blackford hosted a program for kids with muscular dystrophy and other

☑ Other

disorders, which created a sense of "facility." I dredged up small talk with classmates in the margins of the halls.

Among Vietnamese, Korean, Chinese and Taiwanese students, I only noticed one who seemed Japanese: Kenji. If he had a desk next to mine he would start conversation and laugh at my sarcasm. Though we shared only brief exchanges outside the classroom (*Hi, how are you? Bye*), I always cheered up when I saw him.

I found home calmer, at least, with no drunken yelling and no blasting television. I loved being "commercial free," yet another kind of soullessness crept in through plastic bathroom fixtures, windows with no sills and the cheapest-possible kitchen flooring. I kept using the "one good thing that day" tactic to fall asleep by and began to wonder: *What am I — or anyone — doing here?* The minutia of scraping together change for laundry, putting toothpaste on a toothbrush, and doing homework buried the answer.

So did my new job as an assistant technician in a veterinarian hospital — one step up from working in a morgue. I cleaned cages and fed sick pets, and had to hold the really sick ones down to be lethally injected. The bodies were stored in a freezer. The smell of disinfectant took up semi-permanent residence in my nasal passages. My childhood dream of becoming a vet faded.

At least the job paid enough — or so I thought until one month the utilities came to eighty dollars each. Seventy-two hours before payday, the utility company threatened to shut off the power unless I paid the full amount (which was now hiked with a late fee). I mailed a check a day before depositing wages. It bounced, bringing penalty fees. I wrote another one, reducing my two-week's salary to $14 and change. I hadn't signed up for any credit cards.

The old man's voice spoke: *Poor folks are bled right dry in this country.* I had to agree. Why charge more to those who couldn't afford a base payment? Why, indeed. I would find this tactic used by every establishment and institution that accepted payment for any service, requested or otherwise. Not having the money meant that you would be charged extra. Over time, more could be collected

☑ Other

from the poor than from those who could pay the first amount and be done with it.

Living in poverty amounted to riding a unicycle on a tight rope and juggling while someone jabbed you with a pointed stick. As much as I wanted to believe the longstanding ideology that working hard and doing your best resulted in a comfortable life, reality threatened otherwise. After school I scrubbed blood off metal tables and hefted groggy Dobermans into bathtubs. Yet I floundered in financial quicksand, even adding in the monthly check my mom sent.

Whenever I called Aunt Nell, who had gotten married and moved farther north, she listened with sympathy.

"You're loved," she would say. "Remember you're loved."

Confused, isolated within myself, I wanted love but needed role models. San Jose didn't seem to have any. The people I found heroic were all dead — painter Frida Kahlo of enduring strength and grace; Martin Luther King, Jr., the fearless leader. Who would replace him? Behind what curtain waited someone who could exemplify muscular wizardry like Bruce Lee? *Chuck Norris, my ass.*

Scornful toward the dull, concrete-lined suburbs, and disappointed, I yearned for the first third of the 20th century, for the kind of greatness or pureness I'd assigned to my grandparents' era. Something had gone awry and now Velcro existed, and strip malls, plastic and more plastic, molded chairs of discomfort in waiting rooms, 50 million types of disposables from Styrofoam to aerosol cans and automobiles that looked like they would crumple in a hard rain. In photos taken before the '40s, even simple things like straight-backed chairs and pairs of suspenders looked elegant. Bathtubs had been designed for human size, and didn't leave people shivering in rapidly cooling waist-high water.

In my imagination I was a promising young woman in the beautiful beaded garb of the '20s, an ambitious girl who would travel the world in style. In actuality I was an automaton. My main circuit included school, work, Burger King, Janet's and the gas station. Photos of me during that first year on my own show a small girl,

☑ Other

head ducked, shoulders hunched in cheap oversized T-shirts. Shocked to see these pictures of myself, I thought changing my appearance would help. I bought vintage garments, favoring lace-up camisoles and miniskirts, that I found on sale or used. I shaved half my thick wavy hair and let the rest grow long — anything to distract from the whipped expression I caught anytime I glanced in a mirror.

With senior year half over and graduation on the horizon, coming up with a plan to make a living by any occupation other than hope would have been miraculous. For the first time, I walked into the student guidance office. The man behind the desk was the calmest person I'd ever seen. If a gunman or a typhoon were to strike, this guy would have just taken a deep breath and suggested the next right action. He sized me up and glanced at my grade record.

"Don't decide yet. I'm sure you can easily get into a four-year state college where you can take general ed while you look into fields that interest you." Within a span of five minutes he had released me from having to figure out my life. Time leaned back on its endless throne. I had no idea how to apply to college, but first things first. The last year of high school rolled toward summer, and I had met new people.

Sandra, now called Sandi, of the nice voice and fondness for horseback riding, went to a different high school but also took photography. She had snapped a shot of me for a portrait assignment. She told me that when her classmate Brett saw it, he wanted to ask me out. She gave him my number. The last time Sandi gave a guy my number, I stepped into a nightmare, so I was wary.

I remembered Brett from junior high: four-foot-something, with a round head and round body, laughing and jumping around. By twelfth grade he had grown taller, thinner, and cute in a boy-next-door way (at least from what I saw in photos). He called and invited me to a movie. We discovered we'd seen a lot of the same films and had a lively conversation on the way to the theater. Sitting in the dark during the previews, he leaned toward me and spoke into my ear.

☑ Other

"I know this is really last minute, but I was wondering if you would go to the prom with me."

"Oh, how about I ... tell you in a day or two," I said. "We did just meet."

"Of course," he said. Later, dropping me off, he said,

"I had a great time tonight."

Anyone asking me to anything was incredible. But prom, *eww*, was for those who enjoyed school. I had gone to plenty of music shows, but a silly dance for students?

Sandi vouched for Brett's good intentions. A feeling of inclusion won me over. I agreed to go and bought an off-the-shoulder black dress with a flared skirt I found on sale. Brett spent most of the event clowning with friends while I attempted to dance. There were plenty of solo dancers, but I didn't know the popular moves. I sensed eyes on me. After a few long minutes I looked and found Amy Mathis staring at me. She was the friend from junior high who had asked if my dad was an alcoholic. I caught her stifling a laugh with the back of her hand.

Face flaming, I stepped off the dance floor and found Brett. He introduced me to several people whose names I promptly forgot. We made it through picture-taking and then he dropped me home with enthusiastic suggestions to meet up again.

He worked at a movie theater with his two best friends, Mike and Tim. Brett wanted to be an actor, Mike a filmmaker, and Tim a painter. Tall Mike had soft blue eyes that looked a little tragic. Tim, half Filipino, kept his curtain of dark hair hanging halfway over his face and shyly looked out from behind it.

Mike and Tim had already graduated high school. I found them approachable, and joined them in activities I had previously labeled boring: driving to hilly lookouts for nighttime cityscape views, going out for coffee, hiking on trails. Brett, chatty and upbeat with dozens of friends, contrasted my ghostlike status. We started dating anyway. At parties he hurried to join the crowd while I hung back, smoking weed with people at the fringes.

☑ Other

When we stumbled into the subject of sex, I realized I had given it little thought since that dark incident at fourteen — even when, making out with Brett one night, he had relieved me of half my clothes. I took off his shirt, figuring most seventeen-year-olds participated in casual acts of eroticism. Ours would have worked much better had my body not tried to repel his. Painful recollections, alive and well, made some key muscles resist instead of accommodate.

"Relax," Brett said. He softly caressed my cheek and kissed my forehead.

"I'll try," I answered, not looking him in the eye. I hoped sex would get easier. As it turned out, easier wasn't much of an improvement. Where I had long known my body to be the most stimulatory, all pleasurable sensation stopped upon physical contact with another. Instantly.

I avoided this letdown by concentrating on Brett's enjoyment. Keeping focus off myself, I learned what did and didn't turn him on — gaining in the process a few helpful get-acquainted lessons with the male body.

One afternoon, Mike called with bad news. He had seen Brett kissing another girl during a trip to Los Angeles they had just taken. Cheating or being cheated on had never crossed my mind. From then on, worry over betrayal would creep into my relationships like a recurrence of bedbugs. I told Brett we were done, admitting that Mike had dropped the dime on him. Although he grumbled and I got indignant, we remained friends, which was fine by me. I could avoid the awkwardness of seeing Mike and Tim without him, and I wouldn't have to deal with sex.

Graduation finally arrived. At the on-campus party held in the gym — not cool, Blackford High staff, not cool at all — I smiled when I saw Kenji and gave him my yearbook to sign. He hugged it for a moment, swaying with his eyes closed. I wondered if he had ever *like*-liked me. Either way, he became one of those fly-by angels who change the course of your life. I am sure he nudged me toward Japan.

☑ Other

The next morning Mike and Brett took pictures at my graduation. Chris came up from Pasadena, and after the ceremony he came with me to Janet's celebration dinner. He got into a lengthy conversation with Janet's dad while Savannah, who had dropped out after junior year, rolled up on a motorcycle. She had bleached her hair and looked tanner and leaner.

"I'm not staying long," she said. After five minutes in the back yard with hot dogs and soda, she breathed,

"I need a beer." Her boots were scuffed, her jacket leather.

Later that month she called to remind me of our plans, now faded, to go traveling. It didn't occur to me to say no, but far from having the funds to cross international borders, I couldn't even cross state lines in style. When Chris learned of our wayward floundering, he offered Savannah and me a room in a house he shared with schoolmates. We sold our belongings and boarded a bus to Pasadena.

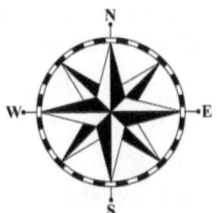

Chris conceded that, as a girl, I'd "had it rougher" growing up. "And," he noted, "I had a way easier time with Mom." Those were two truths I felt glad he had realized.

Welcoming Savannah and me, he didn't charge rent. I had never felt so relaxed as at that house in Pasadena. A wide porch with a couch, protected from view by foliage, promoted lounging in the eternal summer of Southern California. Balmy serenity served as

☑ Other

medicine and recalled childhood vacations to Florida and Puerto Rico.

On our first night, I noticed a hint of the softer, friendlier Savannah. She briefly squeezed my hand before going to brush her teeth.

"This place feels good," she said in the morning as we unpacked.

"I could definitely get used to it," I replied, inhaling the flower-scented air drifting in the window.

"Let's go to Venice Beach sometime," she said.

"Let's go to the grocery store. I'm starving."

We clocked a lot of couch time watching someone's collection of *Twin Peaks* episodes. Curious roommates deemed us harmless transients and let us be. All the housemates were brainiacs. One studied the electron-level properties of metal. Another enjoyed geophysics and another, a Chemistry Major, created nice clean speed piled pure white in a small mountain on his desk. I discovered I disliked amphetamines, preferring substances that expanded consciousness rather than sweat pores. The first time we ate psychedelic mushrooms, the Chemistry student told Savannah and me that we could relax on his waterbed while he went to class.

We turned off the lights and lay back, watching the glowing pinpoint stars he had stuck to his ceiling leave their fixed positions and roam the indoor sky. Between fits of giggles, we made jokes in poorly imitated pirate voices. Sometime after dusk, we climbed out onto an overhang to gaze at the real stars, mesmerized. For the first time I didn't consider myself a mistake.

"I like 'shrooms," I said.

"Definitely," Savannah concurred, zipping up her hoodie.

"Do you ever feel like you've been alive for a really long time?" I asked. She sat up and darted a hand to my shoulder.

"*Yes!* Around two hundred years."

"It's like I'm trying to fit into a world I don't understand," I said. A trace of a smile played on her lips as she put her hand back in her lap.

☑ Other

"I hear ya, sister," she said in a mock working-class accent. Savannah tended to speak like the characters in whatever book or movie she had just finished. After reading *The Grapes of Wrath* she had pointed out how "that there didn't look none too prosperous," and that "they's been mean." This time she had watched *Frankie and Johnny*, a love story featuring down-and-out diner employees.

We applied at various pizzerias and retail stores, while getting unemployment benefits, which I found restful — necessary, even — after working three years without pause. Not wanting to overstay our welcome, we left after a few months. Pasadena had revived my spirits with much needed down time, subtropical climate and the spectral glow only psilocybin could provide.

We headed out in a secondhand pickup Savannah bought. Coast to coast and back we rolled. We had little money and no goal. I loved the open road and sky, especially once we learned to stay off major thruways. Who had decided every road traveler wanted to eat at McDonald's? Off the main highways, all the 30-foot-tall dinosaurs and jackalopes gave way to groves of maples or firs, brookside eateries with local delicacies, and peaceful expanses of meadowlands.

Clouds had giant moods or were towering ships in the earliest chroma of daybreak. We bought a cheap tent and slept wherever we could pitch it. Singing to our favorites while the landscape flew by, sleeping under stars and doing it all again the next day, made for a great escape. Money soon ran out, though — and life, as we knew it, was fueled by money.

Returning to Northern California, we decided to share an apartment in Santa Cruz with Brett's painter friend, Tim. I had gotten a birthday check from my mom, which covered my share of the first month. She had stopped sending monthly checks, but she did give me one or two hundred on my birthday and at Christmas, which sometimes amounted to a godsend.

Savannah found a job at a graphic arts company, and I got hired at a pet store. Her older sister Melissa lived in Santa Cruz too. Their father, Marv, had been there for decades. For me, even without

☑ Other

relatives, the seaside town was a tenfold improvement over San Jose. The beach with its giant boulders, crashing surf and boardwalk lay twenty minutes from home by foot. The university had a political faction that, combined with a still-prevalent hippie element, enlivened the streets. Every few weeks, if there wasn't a protest, there would be a festival. I settled in, nineteen years old and re-convinced that life had much to offer.

Within a year, although I loved Santa Cruz, I'd had more than enough of the minimally waged, forty-hour work week that provided only survival money. Eight hours per day on my feet was exhausting, and all I could afford to eat regularly were potatoes and instant ramen noodles.

I remembered the school counselor saying I could easily get into a state school. The main college in Santa Cruz was university level, so I chose Sonoma State, a few hours north, and suggested that Savannah apply as well. Noting the school's reputable art program, she decided to go. Her sister Melissa joined in the venture, having only completed a couple years of college herself. Melissa had ponderous brown eyes, long chestnut hair and none of Savannah's edginess. After a slew of paperwork we all got accepted. Meanwhile, Tim met a girl from Denmark and decided to travel to Europe with her.

Exiting the highway at the end of August toward the suburb of Rohnert Park rivaled entering an infernal arena of the condemned. In every direction lay miles of low beige hills spiky with sunburnt grass and dead flowers — a raging blaze waiting for one flicked cigarette butt. The occasional puff of breeze smelled of manure. The dorms of Sonoma State huddled together, forming a somber replica of a Disney village, only simpler. No cupolas, steep rooftops or even functioning shutters adorned the thin-walled living quarters.

Despite misgivings we decided to give the school a try. We signed up to share a dorm room while Melissa found a rental in Rohnert Park's "B section." Planners had divided the suburb into mazelike sectors all starting with the letter of their section, A

☑ Other

through M at the time. There was no downtown. Spiraling avenues, abrupt cul de sacs and a head-spinning B-fest of streets — Bonnie, Bobbie, Boris, Beth, Baron, Brenda, Brett and Beverly — conspired to confound fleeing criminals and newcomers alike. At Sonoma State the campus buildings resembled gray concrete prisons. The town ranked among the strangest I'd seen.

Savannah joined the art department while I dipped my toes in psychology studies, choosing from branches at random. Whatever comfort and calm I'd found in Pasadena and on the road had retreated, and though I hadn't done anything to feel guilty about, it seemed I had committed a wrong. Fear came and went, lingering about me like a vapor. I struggled to answer any passing classmate's "Hi," unable to maintain eye contact. If someone looked at me for longer than five seconds, it felt like they had pulled out a giant magnifying glass, and were regarding me as a curious specimen. Though people often told me I looked pretty, I squirmed with uneasiness, certain I appeared somehow disgusting. I'd search my reflection for confirmation, but would find my features appealing enough. The problem was in the sad-yet-eager-to-please expression I couldn't shake off.

My neck and jaw still hurt, too. A visit to the campus health center yielded no results. They couldn't help me, they said, because I had a "preexisting" condition. I found daily aching and soreness "existing" and in need of treatment, but had to put it on hold.

The dorms were filled with perky Los Angeles transplants we had nothing in common with. Two out-of-state students who stood out as much as we did — Jeff, an energetic New Yorker, and Deanna, a gothish girl from Michigan — lived near us. From the moment our paths crossed we spent time with these National Student Exchange schoolmates.

I met Savannah and Jeff for a beer in Deanna's room one afternoon. She studied psychology too, but while I opted for classes like Psychology of Music and Psychology of Film, she systematically took every course that opened the path to a solid career in the field. I had just finished a paper on the history and eventual illegality of marijuana. At the end of an enthusiastic monologue about growing hemp for clothing, houses and medicine, I took a breath.

"That's the most I've ever heard you say at one time," Jeff said. "You're one of the shyest people I've ever met."

"I just have to get to know you," I replied, my face growing warm. I fell into the usual self-monitoring, hoping not to mess up on any level. Worried that I looked in pain or afraid, whatever responses I mustered came out a moment too late to keep the flow of back-and-forth natural. I was sure Jeff and Deanna considered me slow, sure they regarded me with pity.

I couldn't begin to imagine how anyone spoke and gestured normally while being looked at. But almost everyone could do it. It seemed possible that my maturity level had halted at the point when my family left. Or on the night I had met Rodney in the park. *Great. A frightened fourteen-year-old in a twenty-year-old body.*

Before the end of the year, Savannah's dark moods returned. If I didn't want to go with her to do laundry, she would accuse me of neglecting her. If I waited for her in the morning to go to breakfast, she asked why I didn't have more of my own friends. She slung insults at my every aspect, from tone of voice ("stupid") to lipstick color ("too bright") to facial expression ("annoying"). She preferred the company of her art-major friends. I walked into our room one day after classes to find all her belongings gone. I sighed and rearranged the room until it no longer reflected the presence of two.

"Where's Savannah?" Jeff asked at dinner.

"Maybe moved off campus," I said, trying to sound casual.

"You don't know? Were you two fighting?"

"She gets . . ." I began.

"Totally angry for no reason?" Jeff finished.

"So you've noticed. I don't get it. I mean, she can be great. But..." I felt my face go slightly mopey.

"Eh, no big deal," Jeff said. "You should give the National Student Exchange a try. It's just a year, and my school, Hunter, is great. You will *love* Manhattan if you go there. And you're already familiar with the East Coast."

☑ Other

All good points. I'd gathered from a few visits that New York reigned as the city of cities. Though Sonoma County blossomed in the spring, turning from a withered outpost to a fragrant paradise, the school left much to be desired. The psychology instructors were so feeling-oriented that their classes became share sessions. I wanted to learn from my teachers, not commune with them.

I applied to the exchange program, which Melissa also wanted to join because she and Jeff had started semi-dating, and he would be returning to New York. Tall, busty and intellectual, Melissa held Jeff's interest, but her farm-girl style clashed with his urbanity. She also tended to worry over every stage of a new relationship, revealing some insecurities that didn't help. They hadn't gone much beyond weekly hooking up.

The program had room left for two applicants. At the last minute another girl, also named Melissa, applied for the year at Hunter College. This new Melissa was a talkative, bouncy young woman of Asian descent, ultra-confident and cute. An obvious choice for acceptance, she got in and left room for only one. For reasons unknown they chose me, and that autumn I rolled across the country once again, this time by bus.

Californians would often claim that New Yorkers acted unfriendly, insisting that they'd be yelled at if asking directions in Manhattan: "Fuck *off*, will ya?"

New Yorkers, on the other hand, commented that Californians sounded dumb. ("Yeah, like totally, brah. My head *literally* just exploded.") Of the opposite-coast haters I'd met, most had never been to the opposite coast.

My first morning waking up on the city island, I sensed the hum of the metropolis. Sultry September light slanted through a wide window into my dorm room on the ninth floor of a 14-story brick building. The opal sheen of the porcelain sink by the door, the plume of steam slowly rising from a pipe on a building nearby, and even the cooing of pigeons on a windowsill had an Edward

☑ Other

Hopper beauty to it: an invigorating throwback to a quainter urbanity in every facet of my immediate surroundings.

At the end of the hall lived Doug from Long Island, who sauntered everywhere as if headlining at a reggae show. I got into the habit of playing chess with him a few afternoons a week in his ganja-scented room. After a game he would reach for a djembe or some bongos from his collection and teach me basic rhythms.

All the National Student Exchangers met up for pre-planned trips to museums, to the ballet, the opera. I wanted to make friends with girls as well as guys, but kept girls at arm's length because on some level (after Savannah I guessed), they scared me. As if on cue, an outgoing student from my Women's Studies course took a liking to me on first sight and ran up after class to link arms. Though startled, I walked alongside her and glanced over as casually as possible. She had intelligent, kind eyes.

"I am from Japan," she said, tucking a strand of super straight long hair behind her ear. "So I had a hard time as a woman. That's why I study this class. You?"

"I . . . moved here from California. We have sexism, too . . ." I stammered and trailed off, conscious of my arm stiffly resting on her relaxed one.

"We will become best friends and tell everything," she announced smiling. She didn't look crazy — just confident. I made an excuse about having to do laundry, but managed to say it had been nice to meet her. The huge welcome banner she had unfurled overwhelmed me. I kicked myself all the way home. Still, I felt more relaxed than I had at Sonoma State. Manhattan had so many personality types crowded together, eccentricity was more or less tolerated. I acted just less timid enough to be part of the NSE group without anyone commenting on my shyness.

A school loan check came in the mail, a month late. What a deal you had to make with the devil when you signed an agreement with the U.S. government. My full schedule left little time for a job, and the borrowing began.

☑ Other

The Jamaican who taught my first morning class, Philosophy, had an accent so heavy, he might as well have been speaking Thai. At least he gave us a syllabus. We had to study Genesis from the Bible. All Bible believers I'd filed under "misguided," though the idea of a Creator and an afterlife (or in-between lives) sounded possible. Of the characters in Genesis, Cain stood out over Adam, Eve, the Serpent and Abel. I viewed Cain's mark, rather than his murderous crime, as his prevalent feature. I half expected a spotlight to snap in place above my desk and expose Figure A, one such marked individual, for speculative discussion.

Sensitive Cain, firstborn to the parents of humankind, turned to homicide when God refused to accept the vegetables and fruit he'd grown. God favored the offering of the lamb Cain's younger brother, Abel, had slain. Dysfunction appeared rampant from the first. Abel gets praised for murdering a baby animal, while Cain is cursed for doing some gardening. The farmer simply wasn't prepared for deific rejection. He chose to spill the blood of his brother, who had been honored for spilling blood. For Cain's offense, God sentenced him to wander the earth and to be marked in a way that both isolated and protected him — a weird punishment that somehow felt familiar. As I drifted to each of my classes, I watched students casually talking, eating, laughing and walking together. I felt like a stray cat who had snuck into the warm house of a stranger, hoping that if I behaved right, I would be allowed to stay.

Whatever was wrong — the invisible mark that made me feel ugly — stopped me from taking any social or romantic initiative. Most of the students I hung out with were hooking up on a regular basis, and I had no idea how they accomplished it. I planned to practice flirting with Rick Brooks, who lived a few doors down from me. He had sun-bleached hair and a golden tan, playful, mischievous eyes and a smile like a 77-degree day in Hawaii. He always greeted me enthusiastically. The next time he passed my doorway and waved, though, I balked.

☑ Other

"Hi," I replied as he kept walking. Realizing that flirting was way harder than it looked, I shelved the idea.

For four years my parents and I had kept contact through occasional phone calls and visits, which never seemed to further our relationship. Rather, we skirted direct communication by recycling the same batch of small-talk topics.

During my year in Manhattan, I fell into a habit of going to New Jersey every few weekends to see them and to eat homemade meals. They lived separately, because by then they'd gotten a divorce.

After my mom's father died, she relocated her ailing mother to a two-story house she bought, but Grandma had since passed away, too. Aunt Nell, also divorced, had moved into the house. The upper two floors were magazine-perfect with antique furniture, lace doilies, and a bowl of fruit atop a polished end table. Nell had made a studio of the basement with its overstuffed lounge chair, large unmade bed, and warm smell of popcorn. She and I fulfilled our shared movie addiction when I visited.

"What do you want for dinner?" my mom would ask in a tone usually used with younger daughters (which in her memory I may have remained). She kept conversation light and polite, her questions limited to my current school life in New York. She looked much less tired since the divorce.

Dad lived one town over, still at his parents' house, from which Mom had made her departure. As a kid I had enjoyed visiting my dad's parents, because we got to play cards with them, eat late night desserts and sleep on a pull-out couch. Now I braced myself against a drab atmosphere. Where once the kitchen walls, made to resemble stacked stones, had looked modern and gleaming, now they were gray with dust stuck to decades of cooking grease. A more stooped, less genial Grandma Zita paced the dim rooms, wringing her hands. So many years had passed since she had lost hearing in her left ear that she didn't realize the volume her thinking aloud had reached. To people's faces she acted kind and thoughtful as always — even more so.

☑ Other

"Hello, dear," she would burble. "Would you like tea and pie?" After serving it she would turn toward the oven and name-call. "Jackass," she might say, much to my astonishment the first time I heard it. "Taking advantage. Those sons of bitches." I paused mid-bite and it wasn't until my dad chuckled, mirth in his downtrodden eyes, that I relaxed. Swearing grandmas had their comic element, but deep down I felt shaken. Some hidden, unconscious need must have kept me coming for visits, or else I wouldn't have taken regular leave of a city I adored.

My grandfather, scowling and hard-edged, remained the head of a failed house, in which time slowed. One Saturday afternoon while he and his wife shouted their conversation in the kitchen, a baseball game on in the background, my dad sat alone watching TV in the rear parlor. From the dining room in between, where I was doing homework, I could see his vacant stare. He seemed unable to refit himself into the disappearing imprint of the life he had led growing up. He hadn't wanted the divorce, and he clung to false hope.

"I've been over Betty's for coffee," he had mentioned over lunch. "Who knows? She might give me another chance." My father's eyes, red and desperate, would haunt me for years. His body wheezed as he took another drag, another sip. Who did he have? What could I do for him, or say? *I still feel some kind of sad love for you, but don't know how to show it.*

He drunk-drove me that evening to Red Lobster, where he ordered yet another beverage — and where I couldn't get much down. He was mumbling something I ignored until he started to cry in the middle of the crowded dining floor.

"We never should have left you," he said in a stretched and belabored voice, his shoulders shaking.

"It's OK Dad," I whispered, not looking around.

"No. It's not. It's *wrong*. I'm sorry, Cin." His face crumpled. I felt like diving under the table. Just once, I wanted a nice dinner out with a sane father who wore a normal expression and spoke in a reasonable tone. *At least he's apologizing,* I thought, but flushed

☑ Other

with anger twenty minutes later when he refused to give me his keys. I got into the car fuming. *Do I endanger your life?* I wanted to yell. With only a, "Goodnight, Cin," he dropped me back at Mom's dark quiet house and cruised off.

Upstairs on an overhang outside a second-floor bedroom window, I hugged my knees and stared at the constellations in the cold night sky. I did appreciate my dad's apology (over the top as it was), but any real feeling of father-daughter connection seemed as imaginary as the lines between the stars.

I looked over my shoulder into Mom's dimly lit guest bedroom. It was the same with her. The shipwreck of our past lay untouched in its scattered, half-buried state. In her presence I reverted to near-complete silence while she focused on the practical: laundry, shopping, meals. She gave, and I accepted, the basics of caregiving, which I still craved but longed to move on from. A stream of unvoiced words turned into a river of thoughts as I got ready for bed. *I'm only a flash in a series of almosts. I've been waiting to be, loving the idea, anticipating what being will be like, while never actually being a whole person. More like a shadow helplessly watching life's bold displays.*

At school, the freezing East Coast winter in its final throes fooled everyone into thinking that the gray would never end. Ninth-floor residents bounced off walls like indoor cats until, in the first week of March when snow turned to filthy slush and the wind still stung, the whole floor went dead quiet. Groups of threes and fours huddled like refugees in the hallway. One afternoon our residential advisor, Tyrell, gathered us — the five or six who were willing — around the lobby couch. We turned toward him.

"There's been too much *not* flushing the toilets around here," he said. We looked at each other and back at him. "All right now, listen," he continued. "Every one of us shits. And it *stinks* —"

"*Tyrell!*" a girl in a bathrobe interjected.

"And y'all need to not be afraid to let it *go*. Out of *all* of our lives. Flush the damn toilets. And clean up this main area after you

☑ Other

use it." That ended his motivational speech, and the shuffling back to our rooms commenced when tall cute Rick Brooks said,

"Hey! The bathroom could use some love right now. Let's bring in music and beer and warm it up." No one responded, so I agreed to join him.

"Awesome, Cin," he said. "I'll get the tunes." We scrounged beer from our fridges and set up beach chairs next to the showers, letting them run hot as steam overflowed into the hallway. Now and then someone peeked in and shouted over the Beastie Boys or the Grateful Dead's first album.

"What're you doing?" But nobody crossed the doorway, even though we invited them in.

Rick had grown up in Queens, one of New York's suburbs across the East River. His older brother and father were policemen.

"Queens ain't always safe," he said. "I got cracked with a baseball bat once while I was unlocking my car door. Don't know by who. But I'm happy to be alive, you know?" His thick blond hair flopped over his eyes.

"Sometimes," I answered, nodding.

"Hey," he flicked the ash off his smoke into an empty bottle. "I'll bet you . . . a kiss that I can finish this cigarette in one drag."

"I bet you the same thing you can't," I replied. The cigarette had at least three drags. He took a long one, blew it out, and leaned toward me.

"I lost," he whispered.

To a nonsmoker, I realize, that might sound repulsive, but people who smoke a lot can't taste that much. The kiss was luscious. "Let's go to my room," Rick suggested. We turned off the showers and packed up.

Oh Happy Day, the gospel song, should have struck up when we closed his door behind us. We undressed each other. Due to Rick's height and sizable hands, I had expected he would be proportionate. At my double take, he didn't lose his smile, just relaxed and sat back on his bed like a Greek statue holding his arms out. No offense to the larger-equipped, but after Rick I wouldn't have minded never encountering another biggie. No angle or position with him felt in any way uncomfortable. I had a fantastic time.

Hookups were confusing. If you had really enjoyed yourself, why not do it again? And again. But then it would be a thing. A pattern. And getting "feelings" could ruin the carefree allure. Rick and I stayed casual lovers, yet in the future I would find that rare. Most of the time one person would want more, and the hookups would end. But for the rest of that year Rick became my go-to boy for sexual therapy.

By June my thoughts turned back to California. Almost all the exchange students would head back to their original colleges. Aunt Nell had found for me a well-preserved '77 Volvo at a price my school loan could cover. Although I didn't want to return to Rohnert Park, the West Coast beckoned with its relaxed pace, redwood trees and pretty beaches. Glad I would be driving instead of taking a bus, I packed my car and set out to navigate the 3,000 miles.

The skies in Wyoming and Iowa were so gigantic that anything seemed possible. Down from pure white clouds, sun rays beamed against a fierce blue. Because Tom Waits sang from my speakers about leaving behind a broken-down man in Jersey, the image of my suffering dad floated before the magnificent Iowa sky. How he still thought my mom might come back to him ("I've been to Betty's for *coffee*"), troubled me. He had gone from owning three salons and a decent house to slouching alone in a faded room at his childhood home. Clearly, learning to thrive — and not just get by — was key.

I would have preferred to be anything but human, which seemed at times like a sentence: You will serve thus and such many years aware that you are alive, and therefore knowing you will die. You will spend most of that life working, working, working to stay afloat. To avoid becoming a second-class citizen you must make something of yourself. The process got complicated, like the

☑ Other

adventure games I sometimes played with my brother and his friends where we had to memorize books of rules and build characters with certain sets of abilities. Life itself was ten times more difficult, I thought as I rubbed my aching neck. The tightness and pain hadn't gone away. To the sky I whispered,

"I don't want to hurt every day."

The air grew drier through Colorado and Utah, causing my usually wavy hair to go straight. I relaxed a little, too, beholding the open landscape hour upon hour. Miles of canyon hosted giant weathered mesas that looked like ancient statuary enacting myths in layers of yellow and topaz.

One twilight found me blasting the reggae of Peter Tosh. Ready to "legalize it" and keep rolling into the summer night, I glanced at the fuel gauge. It had fallen to the red. Panic clutched my chest as I passed a sign announcing the next amenities lay forty miles ahead.

As I drove into a plain dirt rest area, the headlights lit up two tiny brown faces staring from the back of a white pickup truck. Drawing closer, I saw they were children who looked as if they'd been sitting for hours and were used to it. Up front the parents, it appeared, also sat in the dark. The father got out.

"Hello," he called, walking over slowly, his shoulders straight under a bleached-white cowboy hat.

"Hi," I returned. "How are you?"

"We're doin' fine," he sighed. "We just got evicted though and we're livin' in the truck, for now."

"Sorry to hear that."

"Where're you headed?" His lined face looked patient, his slightly angled eyes steady.

"I'm going to California, but I'm about to run out of gas. I didn't even see. I thought there'd be more stations."

"Well, we can go into town. We'll bring you some back," he offered.

"Oh? Wow. Thank you. Where're you from?" I got out a twenty and handed it to him. He took it and walked back toward the truck.

☑ Other

"Arizona. We're Navajo," he answered over his shoulder. Returning to the driver's seat he spoke to the woman next to him and a moment later, off they drove. The night became chilly. I wrapped myself in a blanket and lay on the ground to stare at the sky, which was crowded with shimmering stars. After a while my back grew sore, but I didn't move. A huge silence engulfed the rest area and the fields around it. I gazed for a long time, wondering if they were coming back. The money could buy shoes for the kids or a couple days' food. I got up feeling naïve and stiff. Sitting for a moment on the trunk as the car bobbed down and up, I looked toward the road, straining my ears.

"Yeah, right," I said after a minute, jumping down. I decided to sleep in the back seat and figure things out in the daylight. Wait. A glimmer of light bounced onto the dark ground. A low hum grew stronger and I felt guilty watching the white truck approach. The wife and kids stayed inside while the father got out with two milk-gallon jugs of fuel and a few feet of plastic hose. And my change. All his movements were unhurried.

"Thank you," I said, looking on sheepishly as he placed one end of the hose in a jug and the other in his mouth. Holding the jug above the gas tank and squatting next to it, he removed the hose from his mouth just before the liquid reached his lips, and stuck the end into the tank.

"That's how you siphon," he said.

Later, grateful and tired, falling asleep in the thin-sheeted comfort of a Motel 6, I frowned in the dark. Accepting the change had been wrong and I hadn't thought of it until right then. I feared I'd always trip over social basics.

Beyond the rise of the Coast Ranges and Sierras, the continent gave way to the ancient and untamable sea. Between the sharp mountains and the crashing Pacific lay California. Scant breezes spiced with wild sage greeted me before I saw the telltale tufts of dusty roadside grass. As a long day of driving waned, a vapory moon ringed with greenish silver raced through streams of mist. I welcomed and dreaded the end of the trip. The accomplishment of

☑ Other

arrival got clouded by the looming *must find a job*. I had noticed that most low-wage positions boiled down to role playing: pretending to be ecstatic about getting someone to buy something, or acting as if the job were the topmost priority in life.

After a few hours of sleep in a parking lot near the beach, I spent the last hour of the trip staring at the ocean as if at a beloved family member. A little nervous, I drove inland. The tiny town of Cotati, preferable to its neighbor Rohnert Park, now represented serious countryside. Meandering roads bordered long-grassed pastures. I'd forgotten the grazing cows, ambling sheep and goats, sauntering horses. Tiny birds swooped, outpouring their songs. Cotati's one main street hosted three lazy bars, a convenience store, a couple of restaurants, and a few scattered shops. The only thing missing was a tumbling tumbleweed. Resident crows now looked gigantic, flapping and croaking from branches on street corners, eyeing passersby. Cotati would take some getting used to, but I felt certain I'd find a direction that didn't include a menial job or school. After sophisticated Hunter College, returning to Granola State (as some locals had dubbed Sonoma State), did not entice me.

I ran into Melissa, Savannah's sister, at a cafe my first day back. She mentioned an available room where she lived, in a house built for migrant workers. Students in this picturesque hovel came and went on a revolving-door basis. A radiator heated the place unevenly, the foundations were crooked and there were drafts. But the yard stretched a quarter acre, and fragrant eucalyptus provided shade. An antique stove had a built-in griddle that was perfect for pancakes. The rent cost next to nothing because the tiny rooms and thin walls offered little more comfort than camping. I moved in.

"I don't think we need all the lights on 24/7." Roommate John sometimes bulldozed with his booming voice. When opposed, he just upped the volume. "The *bills* don't need to be higher than the *rent*. Leave the heat off." If you met John at a loud moment, you wouldn't guess how relaxed he usually was. He spent hours practicing bass, unplugged, while smoking weed. Returning to California's abundance of quality cannabis factored well on the heavenly scale, and I welcomed an in-house smoking buddy, especially one who loved reggae.

We had a constant flow of guests, mostly musicians. I claimed an unused pair of bongos and became resident drummer. On the occasional quiet evening, Melissa and I exchanged tarot readings. We both owned multiple decks. She enjoyed picking apart the minutia of any subject. I had to commit to at least an hour of analyzing when giving her a reading — but it was worth it to get one in return.

"This is really good," she always said, no matter what cards had come up. Then she would ask questions that prompted further development of the good. Using images and symbols, the tarot allowed a look beyond the "veil" of everyday life. A reading could point out the need to correct a minor bad habit, or reveal a huge upcoming change. I kept drawing the "find strength in nature" card.

Sunlight catching in droplets that trembled on leaves after a rain, and giant thundering waves smashing into cliff faces at the beach, demanded investigation into the forces behind nature. I loved that cultures the world over included mythical beings like elves and fairies — not Santa's elves or cute butterfly-winged fairies, but the elves of old Germanic mythology, who wielded magic. Illusions that modern magicians performed, like sawing a body in a box in half or making animals appear from "thin air," entertained. Real magic, I thought, had to be much more powerful. But I'd seen no evidence of wizardry.

One of our short-term roommates, a girl from Los Angeles, had a massage-therapist friend named Eric. I met him when he came by to release the tension in her shoulders. Eric had the warm, inquisitive eyes of a bear cub. He talked about his yoga hour this, his meditation that, and had a tranquility I wouldn't admit I envied. Viewing him as a step closer to the secrets of sorcery, I

☑ Other

decided to make a massage appointment and find out if he would bring the subject up himself. First, I needed income.

I found a job at a much larger pet store than the last. The football-jersey-wearing owner of 49er Pets prided herself on strictness. She wouldn't be caught dead with a soiled cage or cloudy aquarium. To keep up the appearance of flawlessness, she ordered the murder of various animals. When a shipment of fish came in, we underlings would empty the bags into tanks and check for casualties. The owner, short and plump with a brown poodle perm, squinted over our shoulders. If any new fish had even the slightest imperfection, like a bent fin or a slightly stooped back, she'd say,

"Get rid of that one." She never did it herself. "Getting rid" of meant scooping the poor gimp up with a net and throwing him or her into the trash to gasp to death on air. I never carried out these orders. Once in a while she'd notice and tell me in a sing-song voice that I'd "forgotten *some*thing."

I was in charge of the bird room for the first two hours of the day. We boasted hand-fed parrots that we taught to talk. Rose-breasted cockatoos (soft, fluffy and pink) were the snugglers of the bird world, pure affection strumpets. Cocka*tiels*, however, nipped fingers every chance they got. Though it would have been wiser to remain egalitarian with all bird types, I made friends with a South American green and yellow parrot. I swept, changed water and helped customers with the little modern dinosaur on my shoulder. Whenever I put him back on his branch in his pen he'd try to fly back to me, but with clipped wings he would fall slowly to the bottom of the enclosure and have to be picked up again. On one such occasion he stepped onto my arm and said,

"Thank you," unprompted. I decided to increase his vocabulary, calling out a common reggae phrase every time I passed by him:

"*Raaas*-ta-faar-i, the most high." After only a few days he started saying it — shouting, really — on his own. No wonder these birds cost a thousand dollars. Soon he didn't want to be

☑ Other

picked up by anyone else (and would bite whoever tried). Parrots have vicious beaks. This playful two-pound bird refused to be nice to anyone but me. He became a permanent "store bird." Though I had cost 49er the wholesale price of the parrot, they did not bat an eye and let me continue to be the main caretaker of the bird room.

After a couple weeks I'd earned enough for an Eric massage. He brought his table to our house. The aim had been to find out what he might know about metaphysics — the bonus was the bliss of professional massage. As he pressed and worked my muscles, I tried not to drool or let a single ecstatic groan escape me.

"I made a great smoothie today," Eric was saying, kneading my entire left shoulder with two hands. "The persimmons were ready and I juiced 'em with pears and ginger."

"Mmmmm," I said, having no idea what he'd just told me.

"Hey." He sounded concerned. "What's this? Your inner scapula is like a rock." That got my attention. "You need to stretch and relax your muscles. Oh, by the way, I'm gonna meet some friends Saturday for a little goddess ceremony. Are you interested?"

"Mmmmph?"

"Yeah, it's that time of year. Wanna go with me?" I nodded. He asked me to stand and look first to the right, then left.

"Hmm, your range of motion is restricted. I want to talk to you more about that sometime." I made a noncommittal sound, not wanting to hear anything more that might be wrong with me. When he left I looked at my profile in the bathroom mirror and straightened up, noticing how my neck bent a little forward. Straightening proved neither comfortable nor easy, and somehow made breathing more difficult.

That Saturday, I climbed into Eric's pickup with a little flutter of excitement in my stomach. "Goddess ceremony" sounded potentially magic. Eric wore a South American cotton pullover and dark jeans, his shoulder-length black hair in a ponytail.

"You look authentic," I said, and Eric laughed. "You look great," I amended.

☑ Other

"Thank you," he replied, smiling with pleasure. Eric inhabited a layer of reality involving a steady flow of happiness I only dreamt of, putting him at an untouchable distance.

He pulled up to a small house with a huge yard. Inside, women of various ages greeted us. A few were setting candles in strategic positions on the living room floor around an empty iron sauce pot with handles. In a commotion of high voices they introduced themselves. The host, a shamanic-looking woman with long silver hair, offered wine. I sat on a recliner and sipped, looking around. A giant painting of a female figure dominated one wall. She wore swirling robes and an intense gaze. One of the ladies in the room exclaimed,

"Don't you just *love* her?" The tall young woman drew an audible breath, twirling around so that her floor-length dress flared. "I wish she would just *jump* off the wall right now and join us." The zealot's eyes grew large as she turned toward me.

I didn't sign up for this hippie crap.

"I like her on the wall," I said. Ever since I'd grown my hair long and bought a few shirts from a Tibetan import store, people thought I was a hippie, or at least a vegetarian. Certainly, I was against "The Man," too, but I ate meat and didn't enjoy sitting in a circle while holding hands and chanting "om." I had noticed when we drove up that one of the cars parked outside bore a bumper sticker that read:

> IF YOU LOVE ANIMALS CALLED PETS, WHY DO YOU EAT ANIMALS CALLED DINNER?

I wanted to make my own sticker:

> IF YOU LOVE PLANTS CALLED TREES, WHY DO YOU EAT PLANTS CALLED SALAD?

Before the ceremony started, I told myself to stop judging. *You're about to sit in a circle right now. Just chill.* The ritual

☑ Other

involved lighting candles, writing on slips of paper something to be rid of, saying aloud something to bring about, and burning the notes in the pot. Nervous about speaking to a group, I didn't hear what anyone else's wishes were. My turn came.

"Uh, I'd like to be able to speak my mind," I said. The eldest woman responded.

"You have a beautiful voice." I thanked her but had nothing to add. I wrote that I would like to be rid of loneliness. As the papers burned, the smoke carried the negatives away, to be handled by the capable spirits in their unseen realm. Communion came next with several homemade dishes and more wine. The woman who had gushed about the wall painting strode over to me.

"Yay!" she squealed and laughed as she gave me a big hug. My stomach tightened, but I hugged her back. Eric mentioned he needed to get going. He dropped me off back home with promises to investigate my stuck neck in the near future.

I ran up our porch steps and went inside. One of our living-room musicians, PJ, sat on the couch alongside John. Playing guitar with slender fingers, PJ glanced up with a look of half-doubt, half-otherworldliness. He looked like a mix between a Caravaggio figure and an anime character. I sat down next to him and found out that he liked Tom Waits, wrote poetry and loved hiking — all attractive traits in my estimation. By the end of the evening, when everyone else had left or gone to bed, the bluish glow of a full moon shone through the window. PJ said,

"The light looks beautiful on you." We leaned toward each other to kiss, from which our relationship ensued. In the upcoming weeks we hiked to waterfalls, drove miles along forested roads, and wrote poems for each other over a silent agreement of commitment.

I wanted to stay nestled in the span of youth when full-blown adulthood seemed far off, when a year still meant a long time, and where fate held forth its gifts. As the chrysalis dissolved, though, a

☑ Other

point of crossroads snuck up. *Here, already?* And there no gift waited, nor fate eager to relieve its arms of a special destiny.

"Yeah, for sure," I was saying on the phone to Mike, the aspiring filmmaker I had met through Brett and Tim. "But I'd rather go to a university." Mike liked to talk things out on a regular basis, and since I trusted him I welcomed these talks. Because he still lived in San Jose, ninety miles away, our discussions took place by phone.

"Well you'd be doing yourself a favor even if you got a degree from Sonoma State, Cin," he said. In the mid-'90s, getting a B.A. wasn't completely useless. "The clock's tickin'," he added. "And on that note, do you ever think about getting older?"

"Hmm," I said, thinking, *No way.* In accordance with the culture we had grown up in, I saw a cliff-edge separation between people my age and anyone older, which could be broken down like this:

Me and Anyone Who Looked 23 and Under	Anyone Who Looked Over 23
A full-on person ...	... Not important
Someone who mattered ...	... Not worth listening to
Visible ...	... Not quite attractive
In the same world as me ...	... Somewhere odd

By my own illogic, I would reach "older" status in just over a year. I said, "I don't, actually. What about it are you thinking?" Mike was twenty-five and the sole exception to my paradigm.

"About love. About the girl I'm dating and how she views me. It's like this," he said. "Seasons pass over a face, which becomes a calendar marking time. But the heart doesn't see this calendar and looks only with love, with the same eyes it has always looked from."

"Very poetic."

"No, really."

☑ Other

"No, I mean it. That's beautiful. And who cares how much older you are than your girlfriend? Unless she's twelve." I assured Mike that since she wanted to be in the relationship, she liked him regardless of age. "By the way, have you talked to Tim lately?" We nudged each other for Tim updates since he had moved to Europe.

"Not for a while."

When Tim had been roommates with Savannah and me in Santa Cruz, people loved his paintings but he neither showed nor sold. Girls really liked his half-Filipino gorgeousness, but he didn't often date and seemed to be reserving himself for something. When he met a hot, free-spirited young woman from Denmark who asked him to come to her country, he jumped at the chance. Once they arrived she told him she was a prostitute and asked if he wouldn't mind pimping.

"Pretty much," he said, and took off for a little jaunt around Europe by himself. One evening his backpack got stolen — passport, money, and the works. He had reached Amsterdam, and has resided there ever since. When he realized he had no way to return to the States, he decided at last to use his artistic prowess for money by creating huge pastel chalk drawings on public square grounds. He learned that certain images earned more. He did the popular ones over and over to maximize income, but lost his passion for visual art.

Living paycheck to paycheck in Cotati, I didn't foresee that I would someday visit Tim in Amsterdam. At the time of that future visit he would no longer be painting, but instead practicing serious gymnastics. (Much later, when I saw him on my fourth trip to Europe, he would be active in Brazilian dance.) His progress took me back to Mike's question about getting older. The longer one waited to follow one's heart, the less chance of dreams becoming reality.

I hung up with Mike and decided to start following my own heart by driving to Santa Cruz, where I could buy a good drum at a reasonable price. I liked the idea of living in the moment. Thinking about the future stressed me, especially while in a

☑ Other

relationship. I worried that anyone who got close to me would, with little warning, leave. Close was not a safe distance. Still, I hoped for the chance to stay with someone through the decades, looking at each other from our hearts instead of through world-weary eyes.

At a small music store in Santa Cruz I bought a doumbek (a basic African hand drum) and went to a cafe for iced coffee before heading to the beach. In the lot near the sea I noticed Savannah's father, Marv, standing by his car. His hair had turned white, but otherwise he looked the same. He squinted into the distance and reached for his door handle. I jumped out, drum under one arm, and ran toward him, holding down the windblown skirt of my thin blue cotton dress.

"Marv!" I called. He turned as I stopped before him.

"Well, you've changed," he observed, giving the yellow ceramic drum a little tap.

"It's the first of my very own," I said. "How are you?"

"Not too bad. Meeting a friend for dinner."

"Hey, if you have a minute I wonder if you wouldn't mind —"

"Let me see," he said, reaching for my upturned palm. I thought he might clarify the enigma of *There will be someone you think is the one and then someone who really is.* Instead, he peered at the lines and said, "Looks like you'll marry around forty." Using his forefinger to smooth out an area near my middle finger, he continued. "You still have the ring of Solomon, a good connection to the spiritual." He nodded with a finalizing motion and opened his car door.

"Thanks. See you again sometime," I walked toward the beach. *Forty?* That was light years away. How the hell did my palm even know when, or if, I'd marry? And why would it take so long? The roar and hiss of the surf grew louder.

"Hi, ocean."

I heard in each wave the strength of the sea, which could gather in walls and force itself on land, or kiss the toes of wading children with its laced edges. Today the waves looked like rows of exhausted, white-capped soldiers advancing toward shore, each finally collapsing and dying. I propped the new drum in the sand and sat before it, thinking about how life beyond youth was a form of death, especially for women. I'd seen a few old people who still looked good, were fit and had nice skin. These standouts hadn't given in to slouching, grayness, or insanity. Somehow they had vanquished the decades, while thousands around them hadn't.

And you too, ocean. You're ancient, and you're beautiful. Cliffs the color of peacock feathers stretched toward the retreating tide. Driving north along the winding coast highway at sunset, I got excited about meeting up with PJ. We were always glad to see each other, gave one another room to breathe and encouragement, and never brought conflict to argument level. Not a big follower of horoscopes, I still believed that planetary position somehow influenced the destinies of lives and love. In my teens I had read a book called *Love Signs*. The author claimed that each sign had true compatibility with only one other in what she called a "5-9" connection. Sagittarius was my 5-9.

PJ was an Aries — which wasn't the perfect configuration with Leo, but at least the two weren't opposed. I liked his choir-boy innocence, which I attributed to the love for God he'd had during high school. He got to know some things about me — nerdy ignorance of popular TV shows, disdain for the mainstream and overall hesitation — but stayed interested. Yet when a sincere guy fell for me, I could only detect a few muted feelings via thought. *He is gorgeous. We have fun. He's good at guitar and cooking and poetry. So, I love him.*

I got no butterflies, no telltale flicker of warmth when he walked into the room. Instead of seeing those as red flags that warned me that my feelings were numbed toward someone who was good to me, I perceived a series of problems. With him. I thought one day that he needed to open up more and the next that he should be less vulnerable. It went back and forth. He should be more available, less smothering, more understanding, less nicey-

☑ Other

nice. If I questioned my critiquing, the old voice I knew well went something like: *I don't know how to love. Ain't nobody taught me.*

As I pulled into our dirt driveway, a bonfire in the yard lit up John's face in craggy exaggeration, framed by his long hair. He passed a wine bottle to PJ. I waved and headed inside, but stopped at the scent of barbecued meat. I stepped up to the fire.

"You guys are cooking?"

"You got here just in time," PJ answered. I sat next to him, and he put his arm around me. I slipped my hand into his. After dinner, in my room I picked up the small blue box of contraceptives we'd bought a few days before. They were like cough drops that melted inside a woman's body.

I don't often recall specific ejaculations, and it is not with fondness that I remember that one. A tiny click in my mind made me think something had just happened. But it wasn't *that*. We'd used birth control.

"Wow," I said, grinning, looking down. PJ smiled up at me. Snuggling next to him, I forgot Marv's prediction, forgot time, and knew only warmth and PJ's calm heartbeat until sleep enfolded us.

The following Tuesday would be August 1st, an old pagan holiday called Lammas. I'd read about the modern version, and decided to do a "ceremony," which could be as simple as taking a walk in a park to see flowers in full bloom, or a stroll in the countryside to see ripe blackberries on their vines. The point was to compare these with life. Had plans from the previous winter come to fruition? Was there any lack or failure to ripen? The gist was to get coordinated with the surrounding natural cycles.

I stood before the fire pit in our yard. Sunlight, thick and orange, fell in warm patches on the grass. The air stood still. Once in a while the silence broke with the soft clattering of a Eucalyptus pitching down one of its nuts. I focused on the center of the pit where I'd placed plump blackberries picked from down the road, and wild flowers from our yard. I wanted to come home, whatever that meant.

☑ Other

The next morning, I didn't face work with a groan, and I didn't linger in bed. All that week, passing by the yard, I remembered I was seeking the right direction. The fragrant air of oncoming autumn hinted that I would find it, no matter that at work I cleaned iguana droppings and swept up bird seed.

49er Pets sold candy bars for customers. The leftover inventory of Kit Kats, Hershey's and Milky Ways were kept in the storeroom next to the overstock of kibble and Science Diet. For a quarter, the employees could buy the candy. It was stale, but work hunger saw past such trivialities.

On a hot afternoon, I ousted for the second time that day a guy who looked sane but had charged into the store demanding,

"Where are the frogs? I need to touch them." I explained to the well-dressed man that the oils on our fingers harmed the frogs' delicate skin. I informed him that he could look at the frogs, but not hold one. When he attempted to reach into one of the glass tanks, I rushed up.

"No," I said. "You can't put your fingers on the frogs."

He walked out but came right back, striding through the front half of the expansive store. He yelled that the frogs needed him. Startled by his volume, a couple of parrots gave short warning screams.

"You'll have to go now, and not come back," I said with as much authority as I could muster.

"No," he said, stamping his foot.

"I'll get the owner."

☑ Other

He shot a glance over his shoulder.

"Fine," he said, scurrying toward the exit again. "But every last one of you will be sorry when they devour these poor helpless creatures *that I can protect*."

Heading to the storeroom for a breather, I muttered,

"Woah, crazy, relax." I had gotten light-headed with hunger after a long day of showing birds and feeding adolescent rats to our largest — plate-sized — Argentinean frogs that did not need protection. The reject candy bars would be half-melted, but I didn't care. I reached in my pocket for a quarter. Empty. A hunger headache came on as a customer's whiny voice floated back.

"Where is anybody who works here? Can't I get a little help with the bearded dragons?" I grabbed a Snickers.

"Getcha back tomorrow," I whispered to the cardboard box on which had been scrawled:

25¢ please

Daylight still shone when I got home. John, PJ and I took John's car up to Mount Sonoma for a hike along our favorite trail.

"Protect the frogs?" John chuckled as he navigated the road to the trailhead. "What is *really* goin' on?" I leaned my head on PJ's shoulder.

"I feel dizzy," I murmured.

When crossing the creek on the mountain, I usually jumped from boulder to boulder, bounding along the trail when impulse struck. That evening I plodded along. By the time we reached our hillside view spot I was panting, glad to finally sit.

"No thanks," I said to the joint being passed around. PJ's eyebrows rose when I refused the whiskey as well. Tiredness hung on me like full-body chain mail.

"Whew, long day," I said, struggling to focus on a conversation about which bands would be playing downtown that weekend.

The next morning at work, the owner stood next to the time clock. In her high-pitched nasal tone she snapped,

☑ Other

"*Cindy.* Do you know we have a camera in the storeroom?" I blinked in surprise, not fully awake.

"No."

"We saw you steal a candy bar yesterday. We don't tolerate stealing."

"Oh, I was gonna pay. I didn't have a quarter. I have one now." I didn't know if that were true. I'd forgotten the incident.

"Well, don't bother. We've decided to fire you," she declared and stalked away, her arms held out like a guy who wished others to think his back muscles were so huge it was impossible to rest his arms against his body. In slight shock, I wandered out to the sunlight and got in my car. For ten minutes I stared straight ahead.

"But . . ." I said. "They were *stale*. I was in charge of the bird room damn it." To console myself I bought thirty dollars of to-go sushi for lunch and devoured it at home in front of *Caribbean Nights*, my favorite documentary on Bob Marley. I vowed to visit his tomb in St. Ann, Jamaica.

"What're you doing home?" John asked when he came out of his room for a snack. He worked evenings at a cafe.

"I got fired for eating a candy bar," I said.

"Well, you better hit the pavement tomorrow," he said.

"Mmm-hmm."

I wiled the rest of the day away by reading Kurt Vonnegut's *Breakfast of Champions*, a story told as if to an alien visiting Earth for the first time. That night my dreams became extra vivid. Gongs echoed and bells clanged. Rows of dancers clad only from the waist down in bright, loud fabric chanted and clashed their finger cymbals. Elephants adorned in tasseled head cloths bowed and swung their trunks in unison, and the whole crowd of people and animals gathered in a great circle around a pink, writhing smooth-skinned fish that wailed like a human baby.

I woke gripped in fear, balled up on the bed.

"No," I said, turning to the ceiling. "Hell, no. Please, please, please, no. God, no." My period was late, true, but that had

☑ Other

happened before with no issue. Also true: the sides of my breasts hurt like I'd been jumping for hours on a trampoline.

I began a silent mantra in between the please, please, pleases and kept it up all day. *I now have my period. I now have my period.* I wanted to believe the bullet of spermicide had melted enough to do its job. John and I were planning a party for that Saturday, and during the three days in between, I repeated the mantra. On Saturday morning, I greeted the bloodstain on my sheet with relief, and got up to clean for the party.

Feeling too tired to fulfill host duties, I hung back by the hors d'oeuvres until someone set up a standing conga drum.

"PJ," I said after a few songs and a few beers. "Come here a second." I drew him into my room and shut the door. "I finally got it. We don't have to worry." He hugged me, but through the relief I sensed distance.

He didn't like that I had no female friends besides Melissa. Telling him I was uncomfortable letting girls get close felt awkward. As much as I wanted my relationship with PJ to deepen, I had been unable to open up. For the rest of the evening, I kept the drum between me and everyone else, and after the party PJ didn't spend the night.

By morning the blood flow stopped. The soreness, the too-vivid dreams, and exhaustion continued in full force. I bought a pregnancy test. The accursed thing said yes.

No, no, no, no. Please, God, please, God, please, God, please. I went to a women's clinic.

"Girl," said the assistant practitioner, shaking her head as she assessed the colors of the chemical cocktail that would determine the status of my future.

"Really?" I asked, terrified.

"Looks like you've got some decision making to do. If you want an abortion, we do them Mondays and Wednesdays."

"Thanks. I'll think about it, talk to my boyfriend."

I left with a leaden heart, already knowing my decision. I was almost twenty-three, had no job, no idea how to parent, and wouldn't wish a messed-up life on anyone. I knew that plenty of people thought every human embryo deserved to be born, while claiming that aborting the zygotes of cats and dogs was just fine. I believed they *all* deserved to be born, and that unfavorable conditions warranted termination of either. I called PJ. He came over and sat on my bed.

"I thought you had your period," he said, his lower lip trembling.

"It only lasted a day. I made everything take longer because I refused to see."

We couldn't even pretend we were ready for parenthood. In the days leading up the appointment at the clinic, PJ became not only distant but almost hostile. He didn't want to come with me when the fateful evening arrived.

"You don't have to come into the room," I said. "But will you wait in the waiting room?" I felt panic rising.

"I guess," he said, brows furrowed in anger.

"What's wrong?"

"Nothin'."

We remained silent on the drive to the clinic. Once there, PJ said he'd be in the car. Inside, several girls and women sat, most staring grimly at the floor. Each time they called a name and a woman went into an adjacent room, the door closed and you could hear the rumble of a machine. Then the next name was called.

I turned speechless when my number came up and I lay on the table with my feet in stirrups as a practitioner rolled the machine over. She inserted a suction tube and the cramping began. It only took a few minutes to clear out my uterus, but the pain didn't stop — even after she escorted me into another room to lay down. She handed me a heating pad and said I could take as long as I needed. Hot and cold I lay, aching.

I found PJ in the waiting room when I could get up, but he didn't say anything, just tossed aside a magazine and stood up. He dropped me off home and said he'd talk to me later. I couldn't fathom why he would be angry. A breeze shivered through the tops of the Eucalyptus as I climbed the wooden stoop stairs, glancing at the dark empty fire pit.

I'd always thought of abortion as no big deal, just something you did when you weren't ready or able to be a mother. I didn't regret the decision. Yet, I felt sad. I imagined the little unborn soul getting ready for life, such a monumental feat, only to have the whole process stopped.

That night sleep finally backed off, but too far. Dark hours lurched by as I huddled under the blankets. The window of my room faced the eastern sky. I felt nothing as the mango light of dawn bled brightly into the dark. A red-tailed hawk glided in the daybreak at a towering height. Its small wingspan flared as the bird tilted and soared, free to dance in the sky. Where was I? My last paycheck had just been spent. As I dozed off, away fled the naïve hope that the forces behind mundane life were magical.

I awoke wanting to scream. As far as I could tell, my life had just catapulted on a permanently wrong trajectory, a river that wouldn't make it to the ocean. The future, once weighted with infinite possibility, evaporated. My fists clenched as I heard John laughing in the kitchen. I stared at the ceiling. Certainty that he would ask about my job prospects trapped me in my room, seething with worry. I got dressed, chewing gum instead of brushing my teeth, and climbed out the window, avoiding the thorns on the rosebushes that grew beneath it. I crept down the long driveway to the road, taking in the cool fresh air.

A wind had kicked up by the time I reached Tama Rama, a gift store/coffee shop/snack bar run by a sweet round woman named Judy. She allowed locals to run a tab. Her breakfast burritos filled ragged holes in the psyche. She didn't care how long you stayed after you were done. Judy was a mom to everyone. That morning I couldn't bring my eyes to meet hers. I dropped my change, which fell into display boxes of candy or rolled onto the floor and away.

"Oops," Judy offered, picking up stray dimes and quarters and handing them to me. Clutching them in one hand and a hot burrito on a plate in the other, I hurried across the room to a sunlit table near a window.

Methodically devouring breakfast, I noticed some fast-moving clouds roll across the sky. For a moment, a frayed patch of blue remained, framing the sun and brightening the edges of the churning gray clouds that engulfed it. Looking around the room for the first time, I saw a girl I recognized from Sonoma State. Her spiraling black hair held back by a ribbon, she gazed at the season's first rain drops while her boyfriend read a newspaper.

"I wish it would stay like this *all day*," she sighed like a 1930s starlet. Her boyfriend, an artist who showed his work around Sonoma County and had serious prospects, set down his empty cup.

"Thanks Judy," he called out. He gave his distracted, buxom girlfriend a kiss on the cheek before heading out the door. The chain connecting his wallet to his belt loop jangled heavily against his work pants. The girl looked away from the window, picked up the newspaper and began to read.

Recalling the cold stirrups and the sucking machine of the night before, I flinched. My eyes jumped from a rack of pastel-colored greeting cards to shelves of teddy bears wearing glittery outfits to a path of dirty footprints on the checkerboard linoleum. Seeing the paper jolted me with anxiety. The jobs in the classifieds section seemed to mock me, always calling for registered nurses and certified teachers and experienced delivery truck drivers, accountants, hairstylists, programmers, construction workers. My incomplete schooling stared me down. None of the listed occupations were ever anything I wanted to do.

What do you want to be? had always been the question. As if you could really become anything you wanted, which would have been wonderful. Anything at all? I'd like to be a six-foot-two Inuit man who can hold his breath for four minutes and who lives according to the ancient laws of ancestors. Or, a legitimate disciple of the Samurai code, or a dolphin off the Spanish coast. Maybe a flock of cormorants, a giant waterfall, a star going nova.

☑ Other

I looked around, surprised I hadn't noticed the girl leave. In a small voice I told Judy to have a good day — "You, too, hon" — and stepped outside with no umbrella to a gray wet afternoon.

The bookstore-cafe across the street looked safe and inviting. Once inside, I drifted to literature M-Z. Salinger, Updike, Wharton, Yeats. I picked up a copy of *The Jungle*, a novel written in 1906 about corrupt management and predatory lending schemes.

Someone to my left watched me, his constant gaze unnerving. I moved to the biography section and he followed, silent as a tree on a windless day. I glanced over and saw that he wore moccasin boots. A beaded headband knotted somewhere in the folds of his long, sleek black hair. A faded leather belt inlaid with chips of turquoise in the shape of a hawk or eagle cinched his loose brown pants. His face looked withered, as if he had been left in a waiting room for twenty years. His brown buck's eyes drooped and his lined cheeks were sunken. As he watched me, my stomach stirred. *Go away.*

I went outside to roll a cigarette beneath the overhang of the building, trying to hide my pouch of American Spirit tobacco, and he followed again.

"People don't dress like you where I come from," he said.

"Where is that?" I asked.

"Michigan." He offered a lopsided grin. "Do you know what Michigan means?" This time he pronounced it "Mickigan." I shook my head. "It's one of the Chippewayan ways to say wolf, though people will tell you it is from an older word meaning great lake." It was not a good day to be alone, but I didn't want to talk to this man. Yet he had plenty to say.

"I had a vision as a boy of a snake who came into my tepee, but did not bite. Although later I left my tribe to live in a house three states away, the elders who interpreted my vision came to bring me back. They knew I would be a medicine man. When they arrived to get me," he went on without having moved or gestured, "I was down on my knees trimming my lawn with a pair of scissors, wearing a suit and short hair for my computer job. But they had already decided."

I noted his sad eyes and the way his lips didn't quite meet. Time could make a caricature of anyone.

"But you didn't stay with the tribe," I said.

"No, I wanted a wife and a family. I have a daughter with my ex-wife. That's another subject, though. There is something else," he said, now looking like a serious dork who happened to have been born in a tribe. *Lucky bastard.* "A place on Mount Sonoma. My friends have a house near where we like to do our loud ceremonies, by the creek there." Incredible that he had walked away from livelihood as a medicine man.

"I go hiking on Mount Sonoma all the time," I said. "It's that yellow house on the way to the creek?"

"Yeah. We try not to use our drums after sunset so the ranger doesn't kick us out. I can do a ridding-of-negatives exercise for you up there. I've come through some hard times, and I can see on your face you might have, too." Inwardly, I cringed.

"What kind of exercise?"

"Well, we use tobacco," he said. "You can direct energy into it. Cut some squares of cloth, however many you feel is right. Take some loose tobacco and put a little bit in the center of each square. When we go up to the mountain you'll sit down and put these in front of you. You think of the worst thing you've been through, the very worst one, and you direct all that anger or sadness straight into the tobacco. Then go to the next worst thing, the next piece of cloth, and the next. When you're done, tie the squares into bundles and bury them. You can visit them again later if you need to let go a little more."

The man's name was Fred Jack "Ghost of a Wolf" Miles. Seeing that he wasn't a perv (at least, not so far), I decided to accept his offer and agreed to visit Mount Sonoma with him the following week. Back home, I returned to bed and slept a dozen hours. The next day I pulled on job-hunting clothes and went for the easiest available position — a deli clerk at Cotati's main grocery store.

☑ Other

The hiring manager looked bulletproof. She had a tough stance and a leathery face. After making sure I had full-time availability, she hired me. Motivation low, I trudged home, wondering why PJ had retreated in anger.

"John," I said before even taking my jacket off. "I'm employed."

"Whoa," he said, smiling from his seat on the couch. "Who was worried?"

"Just thought you should know." Over the next few days I cocooned in my room. After my first deli shift I tried to enjoy dancing to a local band with John and a few of our house musicians, but couldn't quite shake my morose feeling. If anybody could tell, no one said anything.

As offered, Fred Jack arrived to bring me to Sonoma Mountain on the agreed day. He drove us up in his faded yellow Volkswagen Rabbit. After a ten-minute walk along a trail from the parking area, we stopped at a spot where a willow hung over a tiny pond.

"That's where my friends live," Fred Jack said, gesturing toward a house thirty yards away. I nodded. He placed a drum he'd been carrying onto a large rock and motioned for me to sit.

"I made this drum from the wood of a dead tree and the skin of a cow I knew," he said, and crouched next to it. "Got your squares and your tobacco?" I nodded again. "I'm going to sing two songs before you do the exercise. The first is for everything here: the animals, the trees, the water, everything. The second is about the entire life of a woman, every woman, strong in youth and wise in old age."

The first crack of drumbeat echoed off the mountain like rolling thunder. I flinched and looked around. Unheeded, Fred Jack chanted in a growing reverie. He went into the second song, starting with a lively beat, sitting bolt upright. I watched as his straight shoulders slouched and his strong chant faded to a croak. By the end of the song he looked like a crippled raven with closed eyes, rocking to his own heartbeat.

"Wow," I whispered. He blinked a few times and got up.

☑ Other

"I'm going to walk a ways away. You stay here and do the exercise." He disappeared into the tall grass.

I hoped he wasn't watching as tears squeezed out of my eyes while I directed raw feelings into little piles of tobacco. First in went the worst-feeling incident of my life — the rape. I sensed only revulsion where the beginning of a healthy sex life should have been, and realized how young fourteen was. I sent a lump of sadness rolling into the tobacco.

Because it was recent, the abortion became the second-worst of the terrible things. I wept for the almost-born who would never have a birthday, and how we would never meet. I remembered to let anger flow into the tobacco, too. I was angry at myself for not having made more of my life, and angry with PJ for ducking out.

I moved to the next worst: being deserted at sixteen. That was a tricky one. I almost felt mistaken in believing any part of me should still be heartbroken about having been left on my own. My mom had said, when we briefly discussed the incident by phone once, that I was "thrilled" to stay in California. My heart knew otherwise, but I got confused by her logic. She said that since I had chosen to stay, I was glad. She told me the story of losing her job and of being such a wreck that she couldn't make good decisions. I still felt abandoned. *That's how you look at it*, she had said. *But I told you what happened, and I don't know what else I can say.* Scar tissue had formed around a wound that flared up with unexpected intensity. Anger struck out like a snake biting the tobacco on the square of cloth before me.

The last of the worsts: the car accident when I was eight. Remembering that the hospital staff hadn't x-rayed my neck, I figured the untreated injury caused all the aching, restricted movement, and muscle knots in my neck and shoulder. Living in physical pain compounded the emotional pain, resulting in suppressed rage. I knew better than to let the anger out on others, which left me stuck with it. Trying to direct rage into the tobacco didn't work, mentally push as I might.

☑ Other

I tied the pieces of cloth into bundles. Startled by a crackling of leaves, I thought Fred Jack had returned, but saw a deer stepping up to the opposite bank of the pond. The deer watched me bury the bundles and only sprang away when I stood up. Fred Jack waited by the car.

"A deer came up," I said, crossing the parking lot to him.

"That means something," he said. "It depends. But it's good." He drove me home. With a quick self-conscious thanks I hurried inside. No dramatic turn of emotion occurred, but I noticed after the tobacco bundling that I had renewed appreciation for my housemates and my tiny room in the countryside.

The weather turned hot when spring arrived. Lying on the couch with a book, I glanced toward the open front door and saw a pale blue sky framing PJ's cautious face as he climbed the porch steps. I wanted to jump up and hug him.

"PJ. What's up?"

"Just coming by and see how you're doing," he said, eyes down, long lashes casting tiny shadows on his smooth cheek.

"Not too badly," I said.

"Our friends are one big group," he said. "And there's no way we won't run into each other. But otherwise . . ." his face clouded. "I also came by to tell you we can't go back to what we were." I let that sink in for a minute.

"Why were you so angry?" I asked. "That day." Hazarding a glance, I saw his eyes had gone round and soft.

"I wasn't sure if it was even mine. You know. Ours."

"Are you serious?" I asked, offended, and he nodded. On impulse I rushed to my room, slamming the door, but the thin plywood merely hissed across the carpet and shut with a *whump* against a cushion of air.

Sitting motionless, I listened to PJ's car receding and then silence. Feeling alone and hating it, I reached for the phone and called Mike, the only friend I could totally open up to, but he didn't pick up. I felt frustrated — he always said something encouraging or had some way to cheer me up. I didn't leave a message for fear of sounding choked up.

Sometimes the world continuing without interruption surprised me — the sun still spanning the sky, the mail still being delivered. I wished I could call *Halt!* and catch up with reality before going on so I could do things right. With horror I realized that living meant being present for every waking moment until death.

I gave myself a "what to do" tarot reading. I got the "Ruin" card and the challenging "Hanged Man." *Great.* Flanking those were "The Sun" and "Judgment."

Ruin was represented by swords, a matter of the mind. Ten swords urged a change in negative thinking, easier imagined than done. The Hanged Man hung upside down in order to greet life with new eyes. Aside from literally hanging upside down, I didn't know how to get the reversal of perception.

"Free music and free food," John called from the living room. *Oh yeah* — a fundraiser for the Bird Rescue Center.

"I'm going," I shouted. A few others would be joining us: Eliot, an Iowa transplant, his hippie friend Mark, and Jim, a winery employee/hiking enthusiast. On the ride I thought about the tarot reading. *The Sun, the sun . . . promise of rebirth, joy in living, shared warmth. Judgment, day of reckoning, assessing past actions before leveling up can occur.* Ken parked at the event site.

Inhaling the aroma of spring grass, eyes closed, waiting for a band to begin, I heard a dog's jaws clamp onto a Frisbee and then closer, the gurgling of a bong.

"This Great Horned Owl almost died," an amplified voice announced further off. I sat up.

"Be back," I said as I walked toward a small platform. Perched on a Bird Rescue advocate's arm, a striped owl stared out at the few people who had gathered.

"These birds can lift three times their weight, straight up from a standstill. Their vision is far better than ours, and their hearing

☑ Other

too." Except for its piercing eyes, the Bruce Lee of owls looked nonchalant. The musical act on the larger stage started warming up with complex keyboard runs and playful saxophone banter.

"This one isn't ready to be let loose yet," the man said. "He was born at our facility and hasn't learned the art of hooting. Without it they'll die." The owl's head swiveled until its gaze landed on the man's face. "But the hunting instincts are in the core of their brains — an area that is still part of our human brains today." His voice rose a few octaves. "Folks, thank you for coming out this afternoon. We have more info at the booth right over there."

The band struck up and I wandered back to the group, who were now dancing. I began to move and sway too.

"That owl is amazing," I said.

"What owl?" John asked, his gaze half-lidded.

Spinning and shimmying, I exchanged elated grins with people. The weight of the past couple months dispersed.

The next day at noon, the phone roused me from sleep. It was Eric reminding me that I had a massage appointment. Thank God(s). I needed it, and around Eric I always felt relaxed. I imagined that in his free time, he sat on huge cushions eating sumptuous meals with other tranquil people, having enlightened conversations.

I had loved Eric's house from the first incense-scented inhale. The rooms were open and bright. Fruit just picked from the yard rested in and around a massive ceramic bowl on the kitchen table. Eric knew how to find affordable quality, and in turn offered body therapy for whatever a person could afford. As he led me past a heavy rectangular mirror in a hallway, he said,

"One of my friends thinks that mirrors show the other side. The land of the dead."

"So those are our ghosts?"

"Guess so." He smiled and opened a door to the plant-filled room where the massage table sat. A fountain plashed in one corner. Eric stepped out while I undressed and lay face down under a clean sheet. After a moment he returned.

☑ Other

"Cindy," he said, concerned, as he kneaded my neck and shoulder. "You have muscle spasms, even more than last time." After a few minutes he said, "Hey, did you get whiplash a long time ago? This looks like a delayed complication."

"I was in a car accident as a kid," I said.

"You're going to have to do something about this or it'll only get worse. It's beyond what I can help."

"I definitely want to," I said, filing full treatment under *Someday*.

I kept dancing and hiking — certainly for pain-reducing endorphins, but also because nature and music held the power to transport the mind away from the body.

☑ Other

5.

Perseverance

The dance floor of the Elbo Room glowed orange and blue. Located upstairs in an old building in San Francisco, it had a bar at the back and small tables strewn at the edges of a huge space. John and I drove down on Tuesdays for low-cover-charge music.

While John wandered toward the stage, I leaned against a thick beam and drank a syrupy Long Island iced tea. It was way too sweet. Thirsty, I turned to the guy in my periphery and asked for a sip of his beer.

"Sure," he said.

"Thanks."

His name was Jordan Lee, and he looked how I wanted to feel: utterly at ease. The tilt of his head as he brought the bottle to his lips, and the way his free arm hung loosely at his side, reminded me of a graceful tree in a carefully tended garden. We turned our attention to the Charlie Hunter Trio. At the set break, he told me he had ditched his last semester as an architecture and art student at the University of Michigan.

"I got back from traveling on a fellowship," he said. "And graduation stared me down. I bugged out. My parents don't get that the pressure is way too much. They're *so* Korean. They're both doctors." He rolled his eyes. "So, do you live around here?"

"Sonoma County," I said.

"I've been driving up there every Thursday, my day off," he said, eyes on mine. "Looking for new places to hike."

"I can show you a good hike this Thursday," I offered.

"Perfect."

The day after next, an hour before Jordan's arrival, I prepared a calming infusion of the herb skullcap. I'd be alone with someone

☑ Other

I didn't know *and* found attractive. I sat on the couch, sipping and breathing. Right on time, I heard an engine outside. My heart beat faster.

"Cindy," John said, looking out the window and shaking his head. "There is something wrong with this picture." A small cinnamon-hued Porsche sat on our unpaved driveway. I remembered Jordan telling me his parents had helped him buy the car.

"What," I said. "It's cute."

No one we knew could afford such luxury. John believed that people should work for what they owned. He grabbed his bass and headed for his room. Stepping onto the porch, I grinned at the sight of Jordan standing next to his car, his eyes closed, his face in a serene Buddha repose. Overhead, sparrows twittered on swaying Eucalyptus branches.

"This is awesome," he breathed. "I love your place." We got in his car and drove to Mount Sonoma. We hiked the steep creek strewn with boulders, cold water rushing down between.

"I grew up on Lake Michigan," Jordan said, stepping carefully on a wet rock, an arm out for balance. "This is different, but beautiful." I liked when a guy didn't reserve the word *beautiful* for complimenting women.

"I love it," I said. "See over there? The fat moss looks like green snow."

"Hippie," he joked.

"That's what living in the country does to you."

Reaching the top of the creek, we walked to a sloping field scattered with the last flowers of Indian summer. We sat in the warm shade.

"What's your astrological sign?" I asked, knowing the answer before Jordan said it.

"Sagittarius."

My "5-9" connection.

"Oh, cool," I said. "I'm a Leo."

☑ Other

"I'm glad we met," he said, glancing at my hand. "Since I got to California there hasn't been anyone I can really talk to. For some reason I think I'll know you for a long time."

Enough said. Sitting next to Jordan on the blossoming hillside, all nervousness disappeared. My neck and shoulder felt less painful, and life seemed a little less complicated. Jordan let me drive the Porsche back to my house and, to my delight, invited me to San Francisco that Saturday.

"Thanks for today," he said.

"Of course." He gave me an appreciative look before backing down the driveway.

By the next day, though, doubts had snuck in. I had no career plans, no solid goals, and hardly any money. I didn't study art, architecture, or any school subjects. I was a loser who'd had an abortion.

"Don't worry about it, Cin," Mike said over the phone. "Just enjoy yourself. Come with me to a party Friday. There'll be Frenchies and other cool people." A devout Francophile, Mike was convinced he would find his future wife in France.

The party took place in a long, boxcar-shaped apartment filled with Europeans who worked in the acting, advertising, film, or music industries. I wore a T-shirt and faded jeans. Men and women in tight designer clothes looked right through me. While Mike discussed his last epic trip to France, I filled up on cheese, sliced baguettes, and red wine. No one asked what I did.

Mike's San Jose apartment, where I awoke in his guest room the next morning, felt like a sanctuary. French doors separated the kitchen from the sun-drenched living room. The smell of pancakes and coffee led me to a nicely set glass table near a tall window. Over breakfast, he asked,

"Why don't you move in here with me? I won't ask much for rent, and we can inspire each other."

"San Jose?" I said. The very words evoked images of struggling on my own as a teen and Savannah's attempt at suicide.

☑ Other

"Hell yeah, Cin. This is downtown, the hip part of San Jose." I laughed.

"Well, San Francisco it is not," I said. "But I really like your place." Mike had the top floor of a hundred-year-old redwood house. I knew he would be a great roommate. "I will definitely give it some thought."

I got a message from Jordan confirming our weekend plans in the city, and thus began our Thursdays and Saturdays. Every Thursday, I would bring him to a new hiking place or to the ocean. Every Saturday, in San Francisco, we would go out for drinks or join his roommate in a painting session.

I adored their apartment. Sitting before canvases with brushes in our hands felt like floating in a gondola. I loved staying overnight under Jordan's down comforter. His reaching for me and caressing my shoulder or waist didn't trigger unwanted memories, unlike the well-intended touches of some other guys. I loved his hands, gentle and steady and warm. The way he looked at me, with tenderness and admiration, made me feel beautiful and important.

I should get a degree, I thought. But from where? I would start researching. While Jordan spent the holidays back in Michigan, I baked and cooked for various parties.

Eric, the massage therapist, invited me one Friday to a reggae show in Berkeley.

Inside the club, antique lamps gave off shimmery yellow light. A long mirror lined one of the walls. The band started. I was thinking about what Eric had said — that mirrors showed the "other" side — when he leaned toward me.

"Look at all the dead people dancing in the mirror." He winked.

"Happy ghosts." I stepped into the crowd to join the dance.

The following week, when Jordan came back from Michigan, I took him to the forest to see gushing waterfalls.

☑ Other

"I love California," he said. "And I'm glad I left Michigan, even though my parents aren't happy about it." They liked that he had chosen architecture, but insisted he go to a prestigious school. To stall, Jordan had fled to the West Coast.

Mulling over Mike's suggestion to move in, I weighed the exploding beauty of springtime in Sonoma County against his energetic inspiration. San Jose lay about the same distance from San Francisco as Cotati did, so visiting Jordan wouldn't be a problem.

I called Mike to tell him yes. Jordan invited me out for a "change is good" dinner.

"Wanna drive?" he asked when I got to San Francisco.

"Absolutely." Taking a scenic route to the restaurant, I parked briefly at the Marin Headlands. The sweeping, lit-up Golden Gate bridge and cityscape lay below.

"Five minutes of luscious view," I said. "We'll still make our reservation."

"Cin," Jordan said, turning toward me. "I think..." He gently took my hands in his. I knew what he thought: that everything clicked. That we got each other, that we believed art could revolutionize. I had told him my dream of traveling the world, and his response had won me over. "That's exactly what I want," he had said. "No one telling me how or where to live. No one deciding my future." Now in the car, he said, "I think we both know." I nodded.

"We should go to Jamaica," I said.

"Yes." His face lit up. "This is so great. We're actually doing this, Cin."

Jordan helped me move to San Jose once I was packed, ready, and had said all my goodbyes. Glancing at him in my rearview mirror as he followed me in his car, I wondered if he would propose or if we'd just set a date. I thought about asking him myself rather than waiting. Since we both agreed that we "knew," the risk of rejection disappeared. It would be fun planning the setting and approach. At Mike's house, walking up the front steps,

☑ Other

I got my new keys out and leaned over to kiss Jordan's cheek. He hesitated at the tall front door. He looked almost fearful.

"What's the matter?" I asked.

"I have to call my parents," he mumbled, frowning as if he'd just remembered something horribly important. We stepped inside.

"What's wrong?"

He folded his arms, closed his eyes and said nothing. He looked like a stubborn warrior. I sat next to him, and he rested his head on my lap. Stroking his forehead, I told him everything would be all right and that he could phone his mom and dad.

"I gotta go," he said.

"What?" I exclaimed.

"I can't do this," he said as he stood up. He walked toward the door.

"Don't leave," I said, panicking.

"I'm sorry, Cin, I have to." He didn't look at me.

"Please Jordan," I said. I had no idea what had just happened, but I knew that reaching the point of begging meant "too late." Without another word, he left.

I heard Mike on the phone behind his closed door as I paced the room, stunned. My ears burned. My hands froze. My heart was like a car that had been suddenly thrown from fourth to first gear while going 80. It helped to rest my head in a square patch of sun on the living room rug. I flashed back to the first morning I had woken in the tiny San Jose apartment after my family had left. *They don't want me. They don't want me.*

I got up and walked out to the trunk of my car to grab my bike. Too dazed to drive, I pedaled to the train station and loaded it on a rack. I sat throughout the hour-long ride with my head tilted back, eyes closed and palms upturned to the heavens.

Oncoming darkness and fog shrouded the San Franciscan streets. When I could no longer pedal up the steep hills, I walked the bike. *I shouldn't go after him like this,* I thought, remembering the Hanged Man card and Ruin. I pushed on anyway through gray

☑ Other

silence, glancing at street signs. Jordan answered my knock with a look of surprise.

"That's what I would have done, Cin," he said, stepping back to let me in. We hugged. Relieved he hadn't turned me away, I didn't ask any more questions. In the morning he told me we'd talk when he got back from work.

There was a place in Golden Gate park where, I'd heard, people gathered to drum. The fog rested on the city so heavily that droplets coated the ground as I pedaled toward the park. My front wheel caught in a streetcar track and slid, the handlebar ramming into my ribs. I continued, though it hurt to breathe. The fog lifted and the sun beat down. I made a left slowly into the park. Passing two scruffy men smoking a joint on a bench, I heard one say,

"It looks like your wheels are turning backwards." I emerged from a grove of trees at a field where two girls with drums sat. One told me to wait about half an hour for a lot more, so I set my bike in the grass nearby. I sat, protecting my aching ribs with one arm. There were a couple of families at a short distance, picnicking and throwing Frisbees. Taking off my hoodie and covering my face to protect it from the sun, I lay back in the grass, half-dozing. I heard rustling next to my head and a voice saying,

"So, it's come to this." Thinking it might be someone I knew, I sat up and revealed my smiling face only to be shocked by a pair of crazy eyes.

"I came here for you," said the homeless-looking man, his teeth caked with tartar, his face lined, yellow crumbs around his mouth. He pushed me back down, and I found to my horror that I could not move. I flashed on a second memory, which flooded my senses: the night smell of the park, cool grass beneath me, Rodney's body on mine. My limbs refused to obey. *I can't move. I cannot move.*

"I traveled through the corn field," the man babbled. "And you are the goddess who called me." He slid a hand over my abdomen and up, at which point I shut down, floating, no longer feeling.

☑ **Other**

Why? I thought. *Why doesn't anyone do something?* But the picnicking families, of course, must have assumed that I wanted this crazy homeless man to touch me. My inner voice rose to a howl.

Overwhelmed with shame, I clumsily managed to push the man away. I sat up. My ribs protested.

"You've had enough," I said, and stood. The man, wearing a filthy woven blanket, held his arms out for a hug. Disgusted, I got on my bike. After going only a few feet, fury kicked in. Full functionality returned to my limbs. Wanting nothing but to kill this man, to rush at him with rage, I turned around, but he was gone. Shaking, walking my bike out of the park, I could not believe I'd let that happen. It was impossible. I told myself I knew better. As I made my way along, I didn't raise my stare from the sidewalk.

Jordan's apartment would be my safe house. He had given me a key. I let myself back in to wait, not caring that my ribs still hurt with each inhale or that death looked like a reasonable option. Soon enough, Jordan would come home, hold me and listen. I would release the nightmare feelings.

I must have drifted to sleep on the couch because the front door opening startled me. Jordan saw my face and rushed over.

"Cin, what happened?" he asked.

"I'm shocked that it did, but a crazy guy in the park..." I looked down and gestured toward my body.

"Come here," he said, drawing me close. "You're OK now."

In novels and movies, the devastated girl buries her head in her man's shoulder and weeps. He remedies the pain with assurances that everything will be all right: exactly the comfort I craved. I began pressing my enflamed cheek against Jordan's warm shoulder. To my surprise, he backed away.

"I can't," he said.

If our relationship had unraveled the day before, this moment shredded what remained.

"I'm going," he said. "Back to Michigan."

☑ Other

"But we're . . ." I started. "Our plans. And traveling."

"I know you want to go around the world. I can't live like that." He directed his eyes toward a corner of the room.

"Since when?" I asked.

"I need to get my degree. And then go to grad school." I looked at his shut-down face, hating him. *Love doesn't turn to hate so fast. I thought we both "knew."* The old man's voice chimed in. *You remember? One you* think *will be, and one who* will. *Simple. And you didn't even see it coming.*

Before tears could well up, I turned to grab my purse, breathing lightly to ease the pain in my ribs. I stumbled into the hallway, reaching for my bike. The blood in my veins ran cold. I couldn't get out of that apartment fast enough. Heading toward the train station I realized, the way people do when they are trying to find their way around a deserted island, that I'd gone in a huge circle. San Jose was the familiar tree reminding me that I was lost.

I shed several pounds over the next few weeks. I slept twelve hours at a time. Though I was a prime candidate for therapy, without income I couldn't afford it. The question that ran through my mind most often (*What am I doing here?*) became *What the hell am I doing here?*

Ever patient, encouraging Mike assured me I had talents, skills and worth. I felt grateful. Plenty of people fell through the cracks to nothing and no one. They ambled along the streets every day, cut from whatever lifeline they had previously held. Hanging onto my own thin thread, only changing every few days out of the various T-shirts I slept in, I lost track of the calendar date and resorted to taking long, comforting showers.

"Cin," Mike called through the bathroom door. "You alive in there?"

"Be right out," I answered, turning off the soothing water and noticing how hungry I was. None of the items in the refrigerator were mine. I bit a bullet and called my mom to ask for a month of living expenses, which she reluctantly and with tsk-tsking sent.

I took a trip to Sonoma County to briefly escape urbanity. Country roads acted as medicine for my bruised spirit — until I saw a pair of twirling red and blue lights in the rearview mirror.

"Miss, your tags are not current," said the officer who had pulled me over. "You'll be getting out and walking, and I'll be taking the car." A new law had gone into effect that week. Police were confiscating all unregistered vehicles instead of ticketing the owners. I'd ordered the new tags, thinking that if I got pulled over, I would just pay a fine.

As I trekked to a bus stop near the highway a few miles away, I felt like giving up. *No job. No boyfriend. And now, no car.* I'd shoved away memories of the homeless man's face, but that night it leered in dreams where his crumb-flecked mouth zoomed toward me. I woke up feeling as though someone were watching me. Someone with a weapon poised to strike.

In the living room, I clutched a cup of warm coffee, my eyes darting to the shadowy corners of the room. I killed several hours by watching one TV drama after another.

"Mike, I promise to get a job soon," I said from a prone position on the couch later that evening. I would not become a burden to my friend.

"You should wait tables," he replied. He had been making decent money as a waiter for years while working on becoming a filmmaker.

"How do you carry all that stuff — you know, balancing it all?"

"Practice here for a few days." He jumped up and grabbed a cork-lined tray from the kitchen. "This'll be easy. Put some water in wine glasses and walk the tray from one room to another. Set them down and then put them back on the tray. Pick it up and bring it to the kitchen. Once you master that, it's just a matter of greeting people and writing down orders. Trust me."

Something about spending what pittance I had on the cheapest possible interview-worthy clothes really pushed my "bitter"

☑ Other

button. I was glad I only had to wear them once. I got hired at my first interview, at Carrows, a family restaurant chain. I received a 12-by-16 laminated menu to study, an employee manual and a uniform. Women had to wear an unbreathable beige shirt with puffed-out short sleeves, and a heavy polyester knee-length skirt, nylons not included. The guys got to wear pants.

"Can I wear pants?" I asked.

"No, the ladies wear skirts and the men wear pants," answered the interviewer, a vacant-eyed woman in her 40s with a dirty-blond bun.

Nylons were a pet peeve of mine. Though skin-colored, they didn't look anything like skin. Worse, on hot days they trapped sweat, which made me itch.

"I got a job, Mike," I said after taking three buses home.

"Congrats, Cin. I knew you could do it." He handed me a cold beer. Getting ready for work himself, Mike had put on a thin cotton shirt and black dress pants. He looked extra gracious and happy — he'd started dating a perky redhead who shared his passion for photography.

"See ya tonight. Oh, there's a message for you on the machine." As soon as he left I pressed play.

"Hey, Cin, it's me," Jordan's soft, steady voice said. "Call me. I'm really sorry." He paused. "I made a huge mistake." I picked up the receiver, put it back down, picked it up again and dialed the Michigan number.

"I'm glad you called," said Jordan. "As soon as I got here I realized I messed up. I'm so sorry."

"It's OK," I said, though that wasn't true.

"I'm relieved," he went on. "I miss you so much. I've told everyone here about you. And already worked out a deal with my advisor. I had a ton of extra units, so I'm doing a special project and I'm gonna graduate in a couple of weeks. I'm coming back."

"What about grad school?" I asked.

"That can wait a year," he said. "We can figure out where we want to live before then. I can't wait to see you."

☑ Other

"OK," I said. "I miss you, too." I paced the room, grinning.

"I gotta go now but I'll call you in a few days. Remember," he said. "Jamaica."

Whether I forgave Jordan or suffered from the gratefulness of the rejected, I found myself transformed into the twin of mythic Pandora, who let loose blessings instead of evils. On my first day of work I acted accommodating, patient, friendly, enthusiastic, and appreciative. Neither the cheesy getup, the eight hours on my feet, the paltry tips after special requests from customers, nor the multiple bus rides home could deter me. I went to bed happy. Not only had Jordan admitted his mistake, he had rearranged his life to be with me.

Or had he? A few days passed, then a few more, with no call. I phoned him, but his mother told me he wasn't home.

"He's at his friend Stacy's," she said.

"Thanks." I stared at the dusky orange sunlight reflected on the living room wall. The rest of the room looked dreary and neglected. First thing in the morning after a fitful sleep, I called again. Jordan answered this time. He sounded nonchalant.

"I didn't hear from you," I began. "Uh ... weren't you gonna call me?"

Silence.

"Hello? Jordan?"

"Cin, it's not going to work."

"*What?!*"

"Yeah, I thought it could. But ..."

"But what?" *You pile of shit.*

"I'm not coming back. I'm applying to Columbia."

I slammed the phone down. A few times. Pandora's twin repacked her treasures and hightailed it. No time to mourn — I had to work a lunch shift. I jumped into the shower. The cascading water couldn't douse the flaming ball of embarrassment that consumed me. *You fool.*

☑ Other

At Carrows, I was working behind the counter when a lone man at a booth by the front windows asked for coffee. I lifted up a full pot, dragged my feet to his table, sighed audibly, and poured.

"Damn it," said the man, startling me. He shoved his newspaper aside. "You don't look glad to be doing this at all."

"OK. Yeah," I said, straightening up. "You must come here a lot." I tried to smile. If I wanted to survive my new job I needed to pay attention. Losing one more thing, I was certain, would be one too many.

I started bicycling the nine miles to work because it was faster than taking three buses. I soon discovered a downside: pain and tension flared in my neck and shoulder. I'd never followed up on Eric's suggestion to have my neck checked. On my salary, I could afford acupuncture or chiropractic, but without health insurance, physician visits remained way outside my budget. I made an appointment with a Dr. Foo. She had been trained in her homeland of China. During a consultation, she frowned after prodding my back.

"You carry the trays *a lot*?" she asked. "You have muscle spasms."

"Old car accident," I said.

"OK, lie down."

Placing needles partway in at strategic points, she told me to relax and that she'd be back in ten minutes. Within that short time, massive streams of tension shot out the ends of the needles. My body went limp. Unexpectedly, I began to cry. Dr. Foo reentered the room.

"How are you?" she asked.

"Emotional," I mumbled.

"What? Can't hear," she said.

"Crying but fine," I answered. She removed the needles painlessly, and rubbed my back as I hid my face.

"Let it out," she said. "You need to always just let it out." Her kindness, for some reason, brought more tears. That outpour happened only the first visit, but the incredible release continued

☑ Other

with each treatment. I figured a longer time would help even more, and asked Dr. Foo to leave the needles in for more than ten minutes. She looked skeptical.

"Not usually a good idea," she said, but obliged and left me face down in the room for half an hour. I started feeling weak and dizzy, and feebly knocked on the wall.

"Doctor Foo, please come in here. You were right."

After she removed the needles, I could only move in very slow motion. Any attempt to go faster than a 150-year-old tortoise caused an agonizing ache deep in my bones. Inching home from the bus stop, I felt ridiculous taking one gradual step after another.

I had told Rachel, an acquaintance from Santa Cruz, that I would meet her at the train station that day. We used to meet up for coffee. Rachel had a stopover on her way north. I could make it. Getting on my bike in slow motion, reaching for the handlebars and grasping them in slow motion, I managed to get my feet onto the pedals after a few minutes. Once I got going, I could maintain a fair speed. I pedaled toward the station.

What happened next made me wonder if I had somehow entered hell. From a side street, two boys looking no older than fourteen sped in on bikes to either side of me. Both reached forward to grab at my body. *Why today?* I thought as I tried, with great effort, to kick at them, yelling,

"Fuck off! Get away from me! Fuck *off*!" But my slow kicks missed and one of the boys pedaled closer, running a hand from my shoulder to my breast to my waist, and down to the seat while I cursed and flailed at him. He said,

"I don't care, I don't care," in a taunting voice. They pedaled away and I thought, *I must be in hell.*

Flushed with anger, I arrived at the station to meet Rachel.

"Hey," I said, hoping I didn't look anguished.

"Hi," she returned, her auburn hair pulled back and her bag heavy on her shoulder. As we began to walk away from the platform, I kept silent about the boys — instead I described the

☑ Other

acupuncture and its effects. Rachel's face turned sympathetic and she suggested that we go to the cafe in the station. We talked for an hour about new movies and books.

"Good to see you," I said, waving slowly goodbye. Hoping the strange condition would disappear by the next day, I climbed back on the bicycle, and kept a wary eye out on the ride back.

At home I prepared a ham sandwich while listening to the radio — early '30s jazz. I sang along with *Gimme a Pigfoot* by Bessie Smith, wishing I could cheer up. Rachel had looked really happy. Everyone else's lives seemed way better than mine. I could swear I had a "Kick Me" sign around my neck, except it said "Touch Me." *No. No more crying. Just finish making the sandwich.* Pulling crisped bread from the toaster, I scowled over the DJ's decision to follow Bessie Smith up with amateur, studio jazz. The news came on.

The announcer detailed how the Pentagon had just spent $14 billion on a new naval ship, which took money "from schools, student work programs, and proper heating in subsidized housing for the elderly." The music came back on, as if all that were acceptable. Even KPFA, a station known for its decrying of injustice, was rolling out scheduled programming right after reporting national-level offenses.

The U.S., I had noticed, used its vast riches to dominate other countries, fueled by an endless supply of consumers and a stockpile of people that the government and military considered disposable. I ground pepper on the sandwich and opened a bag of pretzels. If school work programs and heat for the elderly could be sacrificed to build war machines without public protest, who would stand against even worse? I hated enforced expansion. Before sitting down to eat, I switched to NPR.

". . . a reading of The Ugly Duckling," the host was saying before a vaguely familiar voice came on.

"The Ugly Duckling tells the story of the exiled child," said Clarissa Pinkola Estes, the guest author. "But it also shows how that child can find the way home." As if my heart had strings, her

☑ Other

words struck a deep chord. "Even someone motherless who feels like an awkward outsider, or tormented pariah, can still be accepted and loved. Even that person does belong somewhere."

Could I actually belong? I would consider that a miracle, but now felt I had something to strive for. The author, who had instantaneously given me more hope than I'd dreamed possible, urged the lost and forlorn to never give up, ever. She assured listeners that their lives could be mended. I had read her book, in which The Ugly Duckling and several other tales had been examined, and decided to read the entire work again.

The following morning I woke relieved to move at a normal pace without my bones and joints hurting. I did laundry, straightened, dusted, vacuumed, scrubbed the kitchen and bathroom, and did dishes.

"I'm taking a trip to Missouri," Mike told me over lunch. The windows were open to scant breezes alleviating the June sun.

"Not to France?" I teased. A little wistfully he said,

"Not just yet. No, I'm going to Missouri. I haven't seen my parents in a while."

"How long will you be there?"

"A month. You'll have the place to yourself."

"Anything I need to know?"

"Yes," he said, holding up a key. "This is the key to my car. If you have an emergency and you really need to, you can use it. Otherwise, do not touch this key."

"Sure."

I had felt hobbled since my car had been impounded. A chance to operate a vehicle was too tempting. San Jose's summer temperatures had risen to the 90s, and I told myself that biking nine miles over melty asphalt was something of an emergency. Not two days after Mike left, I started driving his car to work.

One afternoon, I was running late and annoyed that I needed to buy a pair of nylons when I backed out of a parking space too fast. I heard a sickening grinding sound as Mike's car crunched against the Jaguar in the adjacent spot. I made a split-second

☑ Other

decision to keep going. No inspection of the damage, no note. I knew that was wrong, but I was horrified: the car I'd dented was a *Jaguar*.

"I am sorry, I am so, so sorry. God. I am so sorry. Really sorry," I said aloud, as if Mike and the owner of the Jaguar could hear me. Wishing it so. At work, time crawled.

Driving the car home amounted to dragging the body of a victim I'd killed. Worse, I noticed that a piece of the front bumper had fallen off, subtle as a face with one eye. I went back to biking, and avoided looking at Mike's car.

What to say when he got back from his trip, how to say it, what could be appropriate and how to approach the issue — all of that frightened me. I worried I would lose my closest friend. No matter what I thought, fear took over: *If you let your guard down, you will be abandoned.*

"Hey Cin," Mike said the evening of his return, after greetings and the guilt dinner I'd made. "I was wondering if you could help me out. Did you notice anyone bumping into my car? It's been damaged." My heart thumped.

"No, I don't know," I said. Another bad decision.

"Did you see the piece of bumper anywhere? You've been here..."

"It's been parked right there. I don't know what happened." My skin went cold. He sighed.

"If you remember anything, let me know."

That night I lay in my bedroom, staring at the ceiling without seeing it. *He'll hate me. Gotta fix this.* For some reason I thought of my dad, who was still living at his parents' in New Jersey. Grandma Zita had passed away of Alzheimer's, leaving just him and Grandpa. Mom had told me Dad quit drinking, had no friends and watched TV all day. Maybe I could help somehow.

That is some displaced intention, girl. By the morning, I'd decided. Greyhound had a cross-country special for $99.

"Hey, dad," I said on the phone. "Would it be OK if I came out there for awhile?"

☑ Other

"Yeah," he said. "You all right?"
"I'm fine, just want to save money."
"When're you getting here?"
"In four or five days."
"See you soon."

I packed a few bags. Without looking Mike in the eye, I told him I planned to stay with my dad in Bloomfield.

"Cin," he said. "Are you sure you don't know anything about the car? Why are you leaving?"

"I want to save money for a trip to Europe." He sighed again. That evening Mike drove me to the bus station and sent me off with a sad smile and a knowing look. For perhaps the thousandth time, shame engulfed me. I tried not to notice that all the waiting passengers looked like they were going to funerals. Riding across the country on a bus with narrow seats and locked windows was a torture reserved for the poor, and I felt deserving of it.

I climbed into the chair that would be my home for the better part of a week and chose a book to read. Alone with my mind, its usual stream of thoughts and images sharpened. I saw a dragon's face, with rolling eyes and gnashing jaw, licking its black lips with a forked tongue, as if gloating. I tried to think of soothing images, but the leering face remained. If I could somehow right what had originally gone wrong near the beginning of my life, I intensely hoped as I drifted into an escapist's sleep, maybe I could start over as an unbroken person.

☑ Other

My grandfather opened the door of the old gray house I knew well.

"What are you doing here?" he asked. I peered over his shoulder to my dad.

"She can come in." He beckoned and nodded.

"Why isn't she with her mother?" Grandpa asked.

"She can stay in the front room."

"Jesus, Mary and Joseph," Grandpa growled and threw his hands in the air. "She should be with the mother." He plopped into a kitchen chair and faced the baseball game on the tiny television he kept above the silverware drawer.

"I didn't bother telling him you were coming," Dad whispered as he took my elbow and guided me to the unused front bedroom. "Put your stuff away and have some dinner."

I ate alone, while Grandpa went off to bed and Dad watched a movie in the back room. That night I read myself to sleep. When I walked bleary-eyed the next morning into the kitchen to make coffee, the first thing Grandpa said was,

"So you're gonna clean the bathroom and the kitchen today? And look for a job, right?" I glanced to see if he was joking, but his icy stare said otherwise.

"It's good to see you too, Grandpa," I said. He didn't smile.

"Your father is out getting bagels. Ask him to bring you to interviews. You're not loafing like the gypsies." He waved his arm toward a window and I imagined the neighborhood when he and my grandma had first moved there, with stark distinctions between immigrant groups. He glowered at me, made a dismissive gesture like *To hell with you*, and shuffled off to his room. I wondered what I'd gotten myself into.

Dad returned with a dozen bagels. Quitting drinking had done nothing for his appearance. Once he had looked red and saggy —

☑ Other

now he was ashen and puffy. Instead of subdued rage, he wore an expression of grief. It would prove true that he did little other than watch TV. He saw a doctor once a month and took milk thistle to help his liver. He had his own ruin to contend with, but he welcomed me and offered what he could.

Next to the single bed in my narrow room sat a dictionary on a small stand. *This won't be so bad.* The first week I jotted in a journal, keeping the windows open to the humid warmth. Evenings, I went on firefly-seeking walks in the neighborhood, which looked a little fairytale-like with its sidewalks draped crookedly over massive tree roots.

I loaded my arms with books from the local library. Re-reading favorites — *Dubliners* by James Joyce, *The Waves* by Virginia Woolf — I compiled wordlists to expand my vocabulary. Glancing up from an open dictionary, I noticed Grandpa looking stoically into the room.

"Buffo," he said, using the Italian nickname he had given me when I was a child. (*Boo*-foe.) "What're you doing?"

"I like looking up words," I replied, pen in hand. He just shook his head, turning away to his teacup on the kitchen table.

He had been right that I would need rides to interviews. The bus system was a mystery. New Jersey's roads were a tangled network fashioned along river valleys by early colonists. When I landed a job waiting tables at a steakhouse a few towns over, I knew better than to argue with Dad over driving me to and from every shift. Being a forced passenger fit my vehicular crime, I supposed.

Just outside my room, Grandpa often sat watching baseball. When I got ready to leave for work — the uniform this time including a long-sleeved white cotton shirt with a full men's tie — if I hadn't put my hair up yet or tucked in my shirt when I walked by him, he would say,

"Don't you have any respect for yourself?" I chalked it up to old-school standards. He had been a bartender for 22 years. In his day there must not have been any casual last-minute readying before stepping onto the establishment floor.

☑ Other

    I decided on a day off to do some of the cleaning he had asked for. As I scrubbed shower walls, he paused, with one eyebrow raised, in the bathroom doorway.
    "At least *one* of you turned out all right," he remarked.
    "Who?" I asked, swiping at the tiled wall.
    "Your brother. A good job, a fiancé, but what've you got?"
    "I'm doing the best I can, Grandpa."
    "Well I can see that," he chuckled and walked out of view.
    Dad kept to the back room. No longer a hairdresser, no longer a housepainter with drinking buddies, and no longer drinking, he had become a hermit. His goals, if any, remained secret. My mom told me that he still tried to see her (though she had been with another man for years), and that sometimes he asked for money. I wondered what kept him going.
    Denial keeps reality at bay, but for how long? Until a quiet Sunday afternoon, alone at home with no one to talk to, I hadn't thought much about the reason I had left California. Picking up the kitchen phone and dialing Mike's number, I pushed away the fear that gripped me.
    "Hey, Cin." He sounded pleased that I'd called.
    "I have something to tell you."
    "What's that?"
    "It was me."
    "I know."
    "What? How?"
    "There was a witness who reported the accident and described you. I got a letter from my insurance company. I just wanted to give you the benefit of the doubt, in case it wasn't you."
    "You're way too nice, Mike. I'm really sorry."
    "It's OK. I've dealt with it. I forgive you."
    "Glad you don't hate me."
    "Never."
    Fleeing to New Jersey now seemed a ridiculous overreaction, especially since the plan to help my father had failed. He and Grandpa were the ones helping me. I made it true that I was saving money for Europe.
    I had Thanksgiving dinner at an aunt's on my mom's side. While my extended family wanted to know what I was doing with

my life, Mom showed concern that I dressed nicely. She rarely asked questions I associated with mothers:

How is _____ going? How's your love life? What's new? Instead:

"Let's give Uncle Lou a ride. We can look at his gem collection. He loves that."

I suppressed a thought that my mom didn't know what *I* loved. We stopped by to pick up Uncle Lou, who showed us his basement full of gorgeous stones, all catalogued and stored in tiny drawers.

"I'm saving to travel," I told my curious relatives over dinner. "Twenty-five won't be too old for a youth hostel, will it?"

"Not at all," said Uncle Chuck. "Hey. You should visit the Blarney Stone."

"See the family in Italy," urged Aunt Helen.

"Go to Amsterdam," cousin Lori said with a wink.

I started getting excited about going overseas. Meanwhile, I killed large blocks of time in my little room by exercising, reading, and journaling. Grandpa sometimes interrupted with charming proclamations.

"I found your *dope*," he said as he slammed a hand-rolled cigarette onto the dresser.

"Grandpa, that's tobacco," I said, showing him the American Spirit pouch. His face softened.

"Oh," he said. "Does that give you pep, too?"

"Yes." I couldn't help laughing. Tobacco might offer pep, but did little for boredom. The only remedy for that was New York City, seventeen miles away. A bus went straight there. Manhattan bustled around the clock with multiple cultures enlivening an island of brick, iron, glass and steel. Graffiti decorated the buildings crowding the Lower East Side, while towers rose over the vast green park of the Upper West. If I brought a drum to Washington Square, within minutes someone from Africa would come over and show me beats. At the Metropolitan Museum of Art, viewing their immense collection cost whatever a visitor wanted to pay. On any day, New York offered authentic Russian, Irish, Greek, Filipino, Puerto Rican and dozens of other cuisines.

I spent hours reading in the city's giant main library. While researching the history of religion, I was delighted to learn that

☑ Other

women hadn't always been considered inferior to men. In Celtic culture, women could be warriors and courageous leaders. Unlike their counterparts in other parts of the world, they maintained status when married — they could legally divorce husbands who became impotent, obese, or showed preference for other women (or men). Along with respecting women, the Celts considered the natural world sacred. I imagined that somewhere in the UK, I might find people who still thought that way.

One night I couldn't sleep. Bouncing around the country and the globe, goalless, seemed like running from adult decisions. I got up around 3:30 to make a cup of tea. Dad stood in the kitchen, reheating half a roast-beef sandwich and drinking the leftover coffee he had put in the fridge, still in a French press.

"How ya doin'?" he asked.

"Can't sleep," I said, opening a cupboard.

"Me, neither," he said. "So, what're you gonna do, that psychology stuff?" It took me a moment to remember I'd studied psychology for two years. "You really believe in that?" he added.

"I liked studying it," I said. "But I dropped the major. I'm not sure. That's part of the reason I'm going traveling."

"You'll be all right," he said. "So you have Thursday off, don't you?"

"Yeah."

"I'm gonna make linguini and a pot of sauce. They got real ripe tomatoes at the Shoprite." My dad had always liked to cook. That Thursday he made a ragout with seasoned beef, chopped sausage, roasted bell peppers, and a bit of red wine. This last ingredient didn't bother me until a week later when he made another pot of sauce with more wine. I wanted to call him on testing his recovering liver, but there was still an elephant in the room (and by then, an old one.)

The third batch was wine-soaked. Two days later, I stopped short at the doorway of the back room where I'd planned to watch a movie. On Dad's couch-bedside table sat a wineglass drained of all but one red drop. *Back on the sauce.* Old memories flooded in: shattering glass, thundering crashes, and *Fuck you, Cindy* in an angry shout up the stairs. I walked to the front porch where he sat smoking.

☑ Other

"You're drinking?" I asked, breaking a lifelong silence. He looked unsurprised.

"Yep."

"Why do you want to kill yourself?" I asked. "Not very noble." We had never had this conversation, and I expected an answer.

"I never claimed to be noble," he said, taking a drag.

"You know what this did to our family." I stormed into the house. We didn't speak for the rest of the evening. The next day I woke with a pinch in my neck. I tried to withstand it, but the sharp pain, on top of the usual aching, was too much. I dialed a chiropractor and made an appointment.

Doctor Lemongello x-rayed my spine and scanned my nerves. He found excess pressure at several points.

"How did this get so bad?" he asked. "Looks like an old whiplash accident. It's going to get better. I'll adjust you today, and want you here twice a week for a month or two."

"I'm going to Europe in two weeks," I said.

"Then you need adjustments every other day so we can start retraining your vertebrae. I know you're in pain. I'll work out a deal with you."

The quick spinal manipulation made a loud crunching noise, but helped. If Lemongello and Doctor Foo could have been in my life at the same time, I believed, my spine and muscles would get back to normal.

Packed and ready with a ticket to Paris secured, I sat in the kitchen penning a list of places to visit. Grandpa approached and said in a bright voice,

"Cindy, I get you now." I looked up, surprised, and he went on. "You were made for traveling and art, like a celebrity." His whole face was transformed by his smile.

"Thank you, Grandpa," I said, my faith in humanity revived. I would be leaving that evening. Dad offered to drive me to the airport. I looked at the wineglass in his hand and said no thanks. Suddenly Grandpa growled,

"Joey, you can't even take care of your own family, for cryin' out loud. Will ya take a look at yourself? What are you doing?

☑ Other

Jesus, Mary and Joseph," he shouted and Dad turned to him with a hostile glare.

"You never knew shit about taking care of anybody," he yelled. "And you know it." Dad looked at me. He had aged far beyond his years, his dyed hair still styled and sprayed around his purple face. "I never told you and Chris what to do," he said. "Not after growing up in this fuckin' house."

"Cindy," Grandpa said with his hands held forward, palms up. "Whatever you do, don't live like your father." Dad's body sagged and sighed like a great sack of dough. His eyes flared, circled by folds of sallow skin. He turned and shuffled to the back room. I followed, wrought with seeing his brokenness.

"It's gonna be all right, Dad." That's all I could come up with. Just a gesture.

☑ Other

6.

Acceptance

On the plane, my chest heavy, I considered a beer and then decided against it. I leaned my forehead on the cool window. Outside, the ocean was an edgeless expanse reflecting a red and purple sunset. A huge orange moon had risen. I could see the face in it singing or crying. One star appeared near the moon as if to admire or console.

In Paris, curved streets hosted curved buildings with no shortage of gargoyles. I found the French quick to use English as long as I started off *en Francais*. Paris remained easygoing among a frenzied modernity, with a refreshing *Be what you are, we don't mind* air. I saw plenty of solo travelers at my hostel, at cafes and museums. After two weeks that included a visit to Pere Lachaise (the most beautiful cemetery I had ever seen), I went to Scotland.

I had hyped the possibility of finding paganism alive and well. Envisioning desolate foggy hills strewn with Celtic crosses and ritualistic standing stones, I took a ferry to the island of Arran and found desolate foggy hills strewn with sheep. Reality came into focus against a backdrop of forgotten history. My most pagan moment there: I sat on a hilltop, eyes closed. It seemed that the wind coursing over the sloping field lived a life as surely as the stockbroker on Wall Street did — I just didn't know where to corroborate that. Notions of finding living remnants of a vanished society deflated as I walked down from the empty hills.

Scottish patrons at a cozy pub drew me in with their *Hello, wee lassie* and delicious beer. Visiting the cultures of the world, I thought, could be a life choice beside work or school. Earning money for a journey didn't have to involve slaving away in a nine-to-five, Monday-through-Friday existence.

☑ Other

Whenever I felt good for more than a day, a critical voice would say, *You're a mess. You don't know what you're doing and you're a very strange girl.* I would stare into a mirror and agree I looked weird. Pushing gloom away, I made Amsterdam my next destination. One step off the train, one look at the old Dutch city, and I fell in love. Strolling along sparkling canals, I stopped at a grocery store for fresh fruit, cheese and homemade bread to bring to my expat friend Tim.

He lived in a squat — which sounds "squalid" or like camping, but was actually an elegant four-story apartment building with electricity and running water. Though the whole block was slated for demolition six months from then, the city allowed squatters to live there.

Tim looked younger and more relaxed than he had in the States. His second-floor room was clean and spacious, devoid of drafts and more importantly, rent free.

"You just would not find this in America," I said. "So, working on any new paintings?" Tim shrugged, flicking his long hair behind his shoulder. He showed me a percussion set he had built.

"Let's do gymnastics," he suggested as he tipped forward to walk on his hands across the floorboards.

"Nice," I commented, standing up to practice cartwheels. That afternoon Tim loaned me a bicycle (important for easily navigating the city's spiderweb layout of streets). Women in long skirts cycled with children riding sidesaddle on the back rack, bumping over criss-crossing tram tracks with ease. Men in suits pedaled casually along. Public bikes sat unlocked for free use. America's car-dominated, dangerous-for-bikes roads now seemed uptight.

Tim invited me to stay as long as I wished. My heart swelled, full of thanks. His gesture made the city even more lovable. In public squares, buskers plied their songs or magic tricks. Handcrafted traditional gravies and soups lent archaic tastes to modern palettes. Tall Dutch houses with steep, red-tiled rooftops shone brightly under the sun.

Wandering for hours in the Rijksmuseum, craning to view gargantuan Rembrandts of vast darkness and subtle, rich highlights, I looked at one last painting before the museum closed. Circa the 1500s, an artist had created an exact likeness of an Amsterdam canal. A small

☑ Other

bridge overlooked low wooden boats shaded by trees lining a through-way of tiny glittering waves. Outside, a block from the museum, I stood on a little bridge over a canal that, except for the cars to either side, looked exactly like the painting, even after 500 years.

"Lasting beauty is in the design of this whole city," Tim said over our dinner of tomatoes, tahini sauce, melon, sharp cheddar and soft bread with a crispy crust. "By the way," he said. "Hide the rest of this cheese. Sean from upstairs will take it. And he'll just say you were wrong not to share it with everyone."

Sean, another American who hadn't gone back since arriving in Amsterdam, remained perma-stoned, asking people all day long to play backgammon. Over a game, he told me some English friends of his would be going to Spain. He could ask them to take me along.

"Sure," I said.

"They're going in a few days, though," he said. "You really want to leave Amsterdam?"

"No, but I have to budget my travel funds."

"Roger'll be by here in a bit, and I'll let him know. They'll take you, but you'll have to meet them at the stacks."

"The what?"

"Ask Tim — he knows them. It's a squat settlement." That Friday, Tim rode with me to the end of a tram line and told me to keep walking along a dirt road until I found the stacks.

"Ask someone if you don't see it," he suggested. We did the Dutch three-kiss goodbye. I couldn't help smiling at how contented he looked.

Along an unpaved track I walked for about an hour before starting to worry. Relieved to see an approaching cyclist, a young, athletic blond woman, I called out.

"Do you know where to find the stacks?"

"No, sorry."

"A lot of people live there. It's close by," I tried, but again she said no. When I swore, she laughed. I feared missing the departure.

The road continued around a bend. Through tall reeds peeked a hovel made of corrugated tin. Beyond it sat more homemade structures, trailers and tents in a large dusty lot — very Mad Max. I asked the first

☑ Other

person I saw, an unshaven, rather wobbly man in a sweaty shirt, if he knew a Roger, Sarah or Michael.

"You'll find Sarah just in that caravan there," he said, pointing to a small white trailer. A skinny girl with short fuzz for hair except bleached bangs, neo-Nazi style, answered my knock. She said I must be Cindy and invited me in. I watched as she wrapped pills in plastic.

"Don't worry," she said. "These aren't for plugging."

"Hmm," I replied. "Think I'll walk around while you're taking care of that." I found a folding chair in a shady spot and sat down, annoyed that Sarah had told me not to worry. The pill wraps were the size of large Tootsie Rolls. If they *had* been for plugging, would she have expected me to volunteer my rectal cavity? A train ride through France to Spain started looking a lot more comfortable, but maybe I was overreacting. After all, these folks were offering me a venture off the beaten path.

Roger, also a bleached blond, would be driving us in a square truck, pulling Sarah and Michael's trailer over the Pyrenees to the Spanish village of Tarragona. With a watchful eye and hard-set jaw, Roger seemed the type who acts jovial enough until you do anything on a long list of offenses.

Michael, Sarah's boyfriend, led their mission to fund a trip around Spain by selling ecstasy and acid. Michael sported a glinty stare, a wife-beater and combat boots. His Rottweiler, Gunther, would accompany us. I had to remind myself these were Tim's friends.

I needn't have hurried. Roger and Michael took four more hours to get ready, which I wiled by journaling.

The windowless back of the truck offered no view, but when we left I didn't squeeze up front with the tightly knit trio. Gunther the Rottweiler and I leaned against each other for back support. I'm sure he was as stoned as I, with every inch of the vehicle's interior hot-boxed by the spliffs in rotation from the moment of departure.

My three English companions asked few questions of their passenger. They chatted about who said what at which party, who fought whom where, and their favorite topic, drugs. As we made our way to Spain, the number of substances we imbued kept rising. Early the next day, after a breakfast of crackers and cheese, vodka and hash made a pleasant pairing. Valium chimed in. When we pulled into a huge grassy lot alongside tents, cars, vans and trailers at the site of a three-day performing arts festival in Tarragona, Michael doled out speed to wake everyone up, and topped the entire medley with uncut ecstasy.

The air bristled. Along intimate passageways between old stone apartments, a crowd of Spanish villagers and some foreign visitors flowed like an endless serpent with hundreds of eyes, arrayed with a living collage of mouths singing and drinking beer. A trapeze and a tightrope had been set up in a field where the performers, lithe, strong and dressed in black, swung and leapt and balanced. The festival remained enthralling even as the drug effects wore off.

Late into the night, I got swept into a crush of revelers chasing three harlequin-costumed figures on tall wooden stilts. Just behind them but ahead of the throng, a jester dragged a wheeled black box that threw sparks. The crowd snaked around stone corners and under archways through the warm night until the figures threw themselves, dramatic and bat-like, against an ancient building, ending the parade.

Though dawn approached, children and elderly villagers still joined the adults in the streets, linking hands and dancing steps in unison. People ages seven to seventy thrust their hips and shuffled their feet, laughing into the sunrise.

I yawned repeatedly as I walked toward the encampment area, falling in step beside Sarah heading back to her trailer, now parked next to Roger's truck. I needed nothing other than a long, deep sleep, but the truck was locked and Roger missing. People without tents or vehicles had gone to sleep all along the ground, as well as on top of his truck.

"Here he comes, love," said Sarah with a weary smile as she disappeared into the trailer. Roger's pace quickened when he saw people sleeping on the roof of his truck.

"Oy!" he shouted, climbing the back ladder. Before any of those dozing could respond, Roger lifted one by his clothes and threw him off the tall truck. He landed with a dusty thud and a surprised grunt. The others scrambled to jump down.

☑ Other

"And you," Roger said, turning to me. "You get one more snooze in here, and that's it. You're out tomorrow." I stood open-mouthed at the violence, exhausted and not about to argue.

At 2:00 p.m. when we woke, Roger reiterated "off limits." An hour later, a girl from the nearby mountains showed up. She knew Roger from a previous visit. She spoke little English, had intense blue eyes and wore a flowered dress. They went inside and locked the truck's door, pulling the curtains shut.

It was the last day of the festival, and already most of the campers had gone. I took my time washing up at a long, outdoor porcelain sink. Rain began to fall and Sarah invited me into the trailer to wait out the showers. We played lazy hands of poker with Michael, sipping tea and speaking seldom, while various people knocked on the door looking to get out of the rain. A longhaired Irish guy with a pretty German girl stopped in for chitchat. They were on their way to France. Later an American dropped by.

Gunther greeted each new arrival with wags and licks, then lay back down just inside the door. The American, a juggler from Colorado, looked very happy to run into another American. He sat by me with a boyish smile.

The trailer didn't have a bathroom or electricity. Candles lit up the table but not the corners of the room, and when I got up to step outside, I accidentally kicked Gunther in the nose. He yelped, causing Michael to demand why I had abused his dog. Everyone looked at me like I'd done it on purpose.

"Sorry," I said and went outside to relieve myself. When I got back, Roger followed me into the trailer.

"Maybe Sarah and Michael will let you crash in the caravan," he said, relaxed after a day with his Spanish girl. But Michael still looked angry.

"You can sleep outside," he said.

The juggler offered to sleep outside as well.

"Here," Sarah said, avoiding my eyes and handing me a blue tarp. Rain still poured steadily.

☑ Other

"Thanks," I sighed, taking it and heading back out the door. In the wet and emptied field, I spread the thin plastic tarp on the ground, my volunteer companion arriving just after.

"The English," he said, "suck. They are *so* inhospitable." Bonded by circumstance, we curled up together on the tarp, wrapping it around ourselves. Raindrops hitting the plastic felt like the pins and needles of a waking limb. Cold shadows lurked in the murky distance. *I'm spooning with a stranger.* My mind tottered between wariness and gratefulness.

"Thank you," I murmured into the crook of his elbow.

When morning broke, I gazed at his sleeping face. I caressed his forehead lightly and smoothed back a strand of his wavy brown hair. He barely opened his eyes.

"Good luck with the juggling," I said. "I'm gonna head out."

"Goodbye." He smiled and closed his eyes again. I knocked on the back door of the truck to get my pack from Roger, and headed into the village. Bits of feathers, colorful cloth, and spent pyrotechnic material littered the slate ground. Bread makers were baking fragrant loaves and brewing strong coffee.

"Train station?" I asked a baker as she wrapped a warm roll in paper and handed it to me. She pointed to a white building in the distance.

Two hours till the next departure to Barcelona. Leaning against a sunbaked wall, my body drooped. *Thrown into the rainy night by drug dealers.* I was relieved when the train arrived.

Ah, Antoni Gaudi. I love how you improved humanity by designing houses, buildings, and churches as sculpture. Thank you for putting bird nests in spires, for a curvy rooftop of turquoise fish-scale tiles, and for pillars shaped like bones. A daylong stroll through Barcelona blasted the English-dealer-trio fiasco into another dimension.

Over the city, majestic clouds marched and whispered Catalonian curses on the Spanish. The desk clerk at my hostel gave out free beer, while a military band paraded the Catalan flag through the streets.

"Australia?" he asked me.

"America," I answered. He looked surprised, frowning a little. I turned to the windows. Firecrackers popped somewhere down the

☑ Other

block. Outside with locals, I sipped my San Miguel and also frowned as I reflected on my home country. In a scant 200 years, America had gone from "Oh, beautiful" to "Oh, trashed." The national parks and open countryside still looked stunning, but were now trapped by a lacework of highways, oil and coal refineries, and chemical manufacturers. Having crossed the U.S. by land several times, I'd seen miles of clear-cut mountains and small mountains of garbage, as well as oil-choked estuaries and gargantuan quarries where the ground looked like an open wound.

The government back home promoted fear — of drug use, of immigrants stealing jobs, of terrorists — and at the same time carried out a violent agenda. To me, the U.S. was like an adolescent with a gun, flexing its killing power but failing to build character. Meanwhile the most basic provision, health care, was getting expensive. Another essential, education, had gotten so underfunded that public schools were falling apart in the richest country in the world. I shook my head and refocused on the mild autumn day in Spain.

After Gaudi-tastic Barcelona, the larger city of Madrid looked bland. Worse, I'd almost run out of money. Two months in Western Europe had flown by, and my only plan for post-return involved figuring out how to reduce living costs. I wanted what I'd found in Europe, where people were allowed to be people rather than work-and-consume bots.

My flight out of Madrid departed at ten in the morning. I arrived at 8:00, voucher in hand. I had bought a stand-by ticket dirt cheap. I stood before the drawn window of the ticket office. Not moving to get a drink or even use the bathroom, I got anxious around 9:30. The office still hadn't opened. By that point, a line of sighing, muttering people had formed behind me. At quarter till ten, the window blind shot up and a uniformed man with a just-woken face stared out. I held forth my voucher.

"Hmm. I think there is no room left. Maybe tomorrow." He shook his head.

"Well, can I try?" I asked. My bank card hadn't been working at Spanish ATMs, so what money I did have was inaccessible. I didn't want to spend the night at the airport.

"Here," he said, stamping the voucher, "but there is nothing for you." An uproar of complaints rose as I sprinted to the check-in counter. The ladies there shook their heads.

"No room left," a smiling clerk told me. She took my bag off the weigh-in stand. The urge to leave got so strong that I began to pray. A surge of emotion swirled in my torso — and an odd sensation of vertigo without the confusion. Just then, the check-in lady beckoned and nodded. I rushed back over.

"*Si*, yes there is one seat. Here." She took the voucher and rushed me through the check in, pointing toward the exit.

The plane sat on the tarmac. I ran. A flight attendant closed the cabin door behind me and I hurried down the aisle, sinking into the one empty seat in the last row. The prayer didn't raise religious feelings in me. Actually, I was a little nervous that there might be a God who could see me. At the same time, I felt glad something extraordinary had happened.

Accustomed to hosteling, I booked a bed in New York City for a few days. I wandered the city's streets, cafes and museums, losing myself in the pre-Christian, Greek-and-Roman section of the Metropolitan Museum. After a couple months of not understanding what people around me had been saying, random conversations in English stood out. Behind me, a child spoke.

"A big lady."

"What?" a man's voice answered. "Well, why's that?"

"Cause a big ol' black lady could beat anybody in the whole world."

"Who told you this about who's beatin' who?"

"You said I could be anything I want when I grow up. You lyin'?"

I wanted to hear the answer, but the voices drifted off. Turning around, I saw a vastly overweight woman wiping something off the mouth of her vastly overweight son. Outside, the dusk sky glowed with the burnished bronze of autumn. On Bleecker Street a van sat double

☑ Other

parked, its two back doors open where a gray-haired man hunched over something in his hands. Yellow letters painted on the side of the van read: The Being Philosopher. The man looked up and nodded as I passed.

"Hello," he called. "And how are you?"

"Pretty well, thanks," I said, relaxed around the vagabond. "What are you doing?" He showed me a dirt-encrusted crystal.

"I mine these, clean and sell them." He gestured toward boxes of unearthed crystals in his van.

"Do you make enough?"

"Why, sure," he said. "This is my livelihood. And this," he placed a hand on the bumper, "is my home."

Aha. I would find a vehicle outfitted for habitation. I wouldn't be forced into overpriced housing. I headed west yet again, once more traveling by bus to save money, and called PJ from the station in San Francisco. He had sent me a birthday card mentioning that since I had left, he realized that knowing me made his road somehow smoother.

"Hey, Cindy, what's up?" he said.

"Just got back from Europe. I'm not sure where I'm moving, but I'm thinking of buying a van. To live in."

"Come up to Cotati. You can stay with us for now. I'm living with John, Elliot, and a couple other guys. I'm pretty sure Scott wants to sell his VW bus."

"No way," I said, trying to remember who Scott was. "Are you sure I can stay there for a bit?"

"Of course. You'll have to couch it, but yeah."

I knew John (my old roommate) and Elliot from the music-jam days, but I'd only met brothers Randy and Scott once. Randy kept busy diving for abalone, biking long distance and gardening. Skinny, fierce-eyed Scott always tried to prove himself as capable as his brother. He had rebuilt the engine of the dark green 1966 Volkswagen bus that he indeed wanted to sell.

"This," Scott said as he led me through their half-acre back yard, "is Sampson." The curved bus came with a closet, shelves, a collapsible table and a cushioned backseat that folded down to a full bed. The

☑ Other

windows had snap-on curtains that filled the interior with golden yellow light when the sun shone, and hid it from peering eyes anytime. Scott was asking $1,100. Having only a quarter as much in the bank, I searched for a job.

PJ came out of his room one morning with Jeanette, a girl I remembered from parties. He introduced her as his girlfriend. With her wide brown eyes and rich voice, Jeanette reminded me of Natalie Merchant, the singer of 10,000 Maniacs. She gave me a warm hug and wished me luck with everything.

At every Sonoma County restaurant, the waitstaff was a permanent fixture. Server positions opened about as often as tidal waves struck. Bussing down to San Francisco, I spent a full day dropping resumes, despite the hour-and-a-half commute. A week of no replies convinced me that I had failed. On the eighth day, though, the manager of an Italian eatery in Fisherman's Wharf phoned and asked when I could start.

Three nights a week, after a seven-hour shift, I waited at 2:00 a.m. for a bus that got me back to Cotati by 4:00 in the morning. Knowing I would own Sampson in a month made the exhaustion worthwhile.

Sometimes I went to parties or out dancing, but avoided the housemates' nightly drink-fest, which only brought my father to mind. When I updated him on my new address and phone number (he didn't know how to email), he began sending letters every week. Still angry that he was drinking again, I left them unopened. He called early on a Sunday morning.

"I don't know why you're so pissed at me," he said.

"Dad, I just need some space."

"I'm all the way on the other side of the country," he said.

"I know. I just need some space and time." I was pretty sure he was unfamiliar with that concept. "Just please don't contact me for a little while."

After a long and trying shift full of undertipping European families on vacation, one of the delivery drivers gave me a ride to the bus stop. Desolate, windswept Lombard Street looked empty except for three slouched figures waiting for the bus. All-night drunk they were, but without any predatory gleam.

"He's German," said a short man with an unshaven face. He was pointing to the tall, swaying man next to him.

"Thanks," I called to the delivery driver, waving. He looked doubtful for a moment before motoring off. The drunk German, who wore metal-sided boots, an open leather jacket and no shirt, also waved to the driver. A blue pentagram had been tattooed on the middle of his forehead.

"She's pretty," he observed and reached to pat my head. I aimed a lit smoke at his bare chest, halfway in jest.

"Don't start with me," I said. The other two, one sprawling on a car bumper, nodded in agreement.

"You catchin' a Golden Gate Transit?" the short one asked. The German said,

"You live in San Anselmo?"

"Where's San Anselmo?" I turned to the other men.

"I live in San Anselmo," answered the third, a long-haired man with a deep scar on his cheek. "In the hills. *Above* George Lucas."

"You look like," started the German, facing the one who lived in San Anselmo. "I mean you sound like that guy in *Dances With Wolves*. Got the grass?"

"You got a paper?" The German staggered toward the other two, straightening a crumpled rolling paper with his fingers. He walked back to me and pulled a disposable razor from his pocket. He let a smile widen his dirty chin.

"I'll shave," he offered. His eyes softened and glazed. "Look!" He pulled the sleeve of his jacket up, exposing a white scar perhaps three inches long.

"Tried to off yourself?" I asked, feeling suddenly tired. *C'mon, bus.*

"About seven times," he stated. I noticed his tattoo again, dully separate from his smile. The short man pushed himself up from the curb where he'd further slumped. Pulling a harmonica from his pocket, he held up a finger at me to wait. Playing fast sloppy blues, he shuffled back and forth on the sidewalk while the German and the man from the hills searched their clothes for the grass. The music maker fell over, still playing. I took his outstretched hand to help him stand as the bus pulled up.

Taking a seat at the very back, I fell asleep at once, waking at my stop in Cotati and dragging myself home. Under the covers on the couch, I dropped off immediately. Around seven that morning, I heard what sounded like one of the speakers buzzing, but as it got louder I realized the noise was coming from inside my head. As if that weren't strange enough, the distinct buzz became a growl, exactly like that of an angry panther or tiger, seemingly sourced from the center of my head. As the snarling snapped me awake, Elliot stepped into the living room.

"Your dad just called again," he said. "He's driving to California."

"You're joking," I said. *I tell him I want space, and he charges across the country.* "Thanks for taking the message, El." I got up, made coffee and opened one of my dad's letters.

> Cindy
>
> I knew your stay in New Jersey was only temporary, but I was real glad you were here. I believe you are seeking some kind of enlightenment and all I can tell you is, the answers are within. You are the only one I can talk to about this kind of stuff. We are on the same path. Betty told me when she married me that two should become one, but she never understood that there are not two, there is only one life individually expressed. -Dad

There is no right or wrong, no good or evil, I remembered him saying. I now understood that he got a lot of his ideas from people who borrowed from Eastern religions. A person of understanding, according to Hinduism and Buddhism, is not swayed by the opposites of beauty and ugliness, pain or pleasure. This made sense, in that being objective could reduce drama — but Dad's booze-addled version of religious themes didn't put us on the same path, I thought. I didn't want to see him until he could respect my request for breathing room.

☑ Other

During the few days it would take him to drive across the country, I helped PJ and Randy pick vegetables and herbs from the garden. Listening to them debate the merits of soils and discuss upcoming music festivals, I yearned to be more carefree and have closer friends. Instead I was underemployed with a pursuant alcoholic father. When he finally called, my guard was up, my chest heavy and tight.

"Cin, I've been driving around San Francisco for two hours. I can't find my hotel for some reason. Can I come up?"

"No," I said, feeling guilty. "I told you I wanted space." A long silence followed.

"OK then," he muttered. "Guess I'll visit Chris down south."

"Talk to you later," I said and hung up. I pitied him, and our broken family.

The next bus ride home from work ended my short tenure at the Italian restaurant. Sleeping on the back seat again, with one arm draped over my backpack, I woke to find it open and a hundred dollars in cash missing. Whoever had taken the money had found my glasses first and tossed them aside, where they had broken. I'd slept past my stop and had to walk a blurry, cold twenty minutes home. I stumbled along the sidewalk, angry, mostly at myself.

"No more late night buses home from the city," I said to Judy, who was preparing one of her comforting breakfast burritos.

"Hon, you can work for me. I'm here seven days a week and could use a couple off, and at busy times you can help me too."

"I'd love to, Judy."

The job was easy, but better suited a high schooler — not what I'd imagined for my future when I left Sonoma County for New York City. One morning, a regular glided in on tall boots, shaking out his mane of hair.

"Hey," he said as I poured a large coffee and handed it to him. "You wanna take over my job milking goats for fifty a week? It only takes half hour a day."

"Where is it?" I asked.

"Just up Sonoma Mountain Road a ways."

"Sure," I said.

☑ Other

At the cold early hour of six, I learned how to lead lactating goats from their pen to a milking stand, lock each one by the neck and coax milk from their udders. I loved the clear, fresh smell of the air and that the goats warmed up to me after the first week. The extra money put me back in new socks and better meals, but didn't advance my goal of buying Sampson. As if in reward for being a good sport, I soon found a better paying job at Lagunitas Brewing Company. A friend of Elliot's put a word in for me there when he heard I worked for almost nothing.

I took a position in the bottling room, gave back the goat-milking job and told Judy I'd found work. The constant flow of bottles to boxes to pallets demanded focus, and the noise of the machinery kept conversations to a minimum, but I enjoyed the hard work.

A month went by without word from my dad, giving me time to reflect. His relentless communication attempts had been disturbing, in part, because I had sometimes acted the same way. Whenever I'd liked someone who wasn't interested, I would try to get his attention by contacting him repeatedly — never a good idea.

Every day some part of me regularly summoned a vulture pack to tear off hunks of self esteem. At least once a week, I had nightmares where a leathery creature flapped around and drained away all sweetness. I'd tried (and failed) to banish this interior villain by thinking, *Just leave me alone.* Sometimes I caught myself gazing enviously at strangers who looked completely free of bad dreams and low self-worth.

I perked up when my savings reached the point where I could buy Sampson and begin a year of living rent free. A gym provided showers; a camp stove, flames for cooking. The bus was so old that seatbelt laws did not apply, which was handy because there were no seatbelts in it. I viewed moving into a vehicle not as dereliction, but as liberation. I could sleep next to the ocean or at the edge of a tranquil field. I could be home right after a long concert or long day of work. Having no rent or bills meant I could afford a good chiropractor and regular massages. Relaxed muscles meant less anxiety. In appreciation for hosting me, I cooked a huge meal for PJ, Elliot, John, Randy and Scott, and cleaned their entire house.

☑ Other

In April, as rain tapered to a soft mist falling on acacia and magnolia trees, I bought a camera and took Sampson on day trips to waterfalls. Soon the soft breezes of summer arrived. I'd wake, nice and warm, and just muse for a few minutes while looking at the travel photos tacked to my corkboard ceiling. July and August meant long lazy beach days and group dinners featuring barbecued oysters.

Anywhere I went, I had my home. I was back to loving the road. By the time autumn blew in, I easily acclimated to the cold. As the rain played songs on my metal rooftop, I'd bask in the simple beauty of candlelight.

An email arrived from my brother, saying our mom wanted me to phone her. Dad was not well.

"Grandpa said Joe couldn't eat anymore and looked sick," Mom told me. "*Sick?* Cindy, he looks like a walking corpse and he's terrified. He's all puffed up, his hands are black and he's jaundiced. I told him, 'We gotta get you to the hospital,' but he didn't want to go. He just asked me for money. Can you believe that?"

"That sounds horrible." A chill rippled across my skin. "I should call him."

"You should do it now."

I shivered as I dialed Grandpa's house, as if I had the jaundiced body.

"Dad," I said when he answered. "How are you?"

"Not too bad," he replied. "The last ten years have been shitty, but I'm all right." He told me it was muggy as hell out, and that Aunt Nell checked in on him once a week.

"Take care of yourself," I urged. "And Dad?"

"What?"

"I love you," I told him for the first time in my life. He went silent. "Talk to you again," I added.

"Bye, Cin," he said in a thick voice.

A cheerful Guatemalan lady from the brewery invited me to her fiftieth birthday party. She lived on a twisting road just outside nearby

☑ Other

Petaluma. By the time I arrived, the revelers had been drinking all day and supplies of beer and tequila ran low. I volunteered to drive a few of the birthday lady's friends into town. The road doubled back on itself in a couple places, but I didn't mind the trip. Word got around of my willingness to make runs to the store. I ended up going twice more throughout the evening, wishing I'd learned Spanish instead of French.

After a few plates of chiles rellenos and caldo de res, and an earful of marimba, I set out to make one last trip along snaking road. Because I had driven it over and over, I was a little careless. Approaching a turn too fast, I braked hard — and the top-heavy Volkswagen flipped. With no seatbelt to hold me in place, I gripped the wheel and braced my brewery-hardened arms in a don't-let-go-no-matter-what way. The view through the windshield became a swirl, just like in a cartoon, and I yelled,

"NOOOOOooooooo."

Suddenly I was crouching on the inside of the overturned roof. The driver side door was above me at a sickening angle. Glancing around, I saw that the heavy seat/bed had been torn from its metal moorings and thrown against the back window. If I had been wearing a seatbelt, I might have ended up dangling sideways from the driver's seat.

My coworker Herman, who had been driving behind me, yanked open the door and gently helped me up. I floated from the wreckage, happy to be alive and that I had suffered no more than a burning ache in the lower right side of my back.

"I can walk," I exclaimed to Herman as he escorted me to his car. Delirium faded when I turned to look at Sampson. The bus lay upside down in a ditch, the entire front passenger side crushed like a Coke can.

Herman called Jeff, a mutual acquaintance. Jeff offered to take me to the hospital and invited me to recuperate at his place for a few days. His familiar, bearded face looked extra concerned when he saw me, but he mustered an encouraging grin and ushered me from Herman's car.

I viewed the stark medical room and the unsympathetic doctor from a dreamlike distance. He prescribed rest and painkillers for a torn muscle. Managing to catch a few hours of sleep on Jeff's couch, I felt grateful when he ran a hot bath for me in the morning. His home, as

☑ Other

with the first Cotati house I'd lived in, hosted regular live music sessions and frequent guests. Somewhat in shock, I stayed out of the loud garage and lay on the couch letting my back muscle repair. Everyone had ups and downs, but looking back at my life, the ups looked fairly tame while the downs were nothing short of devastating.

"My life is in ruins," I said to Jeff when he came to check on me.

"There is nothing you can't come back from," he said with a sad smile. "You survived. You're doing great."

I called Chris and then my mom to let them know I could be reached at Jeff's. I kept the story of the accident brief and told them I was all right.

Jeff drove me to the site of the crash, where police had hoisted the bus out of the ditch and were preparing to tow it away. They let me gather what belongings were salvageable. The dilemma of losing my home/vehicle ratcheted in the extreme direction when I got replaced at the brewery. Huddled under a blanket on Jeff's couch, I breathed despair, tasted despair and looked through the eyes of despair. Air felt as heavy as water.

Why did I attract catastrophe like a magnet? Maybe karma played into it. What kind of monster had I been to rack up this many setbacks? Or maybe they were tests. But why so much testing?

Why was a human question. Cats and dogs might ask *what, where,* or *when.* (*What is this over here? Where is my dinner? When are we going for a walk?*) But only people wondered *why.* I wanted to know the reason behind what seemed like a curse. I was convinced that not only had I wandered into hell, but that I was stuck there. Evidently, life could turn into a puzzle that became difficult to solve.

Jeff told me I could stay with him until I found a place of my own. Judy at Tama Rama again offered me a few days of work per week. Blessings within the curse. School now looked like a shining opportunity ushered in on a chorus of angels. Not Sonoma State, though. If I had to go into education debt, it might as well be at a university. I wanted to go to Santa Cruz, where the campus had respected professors and views of the ocean. I called their registrar's office. The clerk told me I'd already had my chance at a four-year

☑ Other

school, but if I really wanted to attend the university I should take classes at a junior college for a few semesters, get all A's, and apply to transfer.

All was not lost. Signing up at the local junior college would be easy. For the first time in a week, I felt better. The apples growing in Jeff's yard were fat and ripe, perfect for pie making. His two dogs, both half wolf, accompanied me while I chose the best ones. The next morning I woke filled with joy.

"I can do anything I want," I said aloud, heating a slice of pie for breakfast. The phone rang. It was my mom. She sounded like she'd been crying.

"He passed this morning," she said.

"Dad?"

"Yes. Nell and I are at Grandpa's. I think it's hardest for him, outliving his son."

"Oh, Mom, I'm sorry."

She told me about the final days of my father's life. Drunk, he had broken his femur bone when he fell down a flight of stairs at home. He dragged himself into Grandpa's truck and drove toward a hospital, only to crash into a bench. He spent two days on dialysis and in traction before succumbing to kidney failure.

The rest of the phone conversation remains a blur. Afterward, digging through my bags, I pulled out another of my dad's letters.

Cindy,

Like I said, it seems you are trying to find yourself. Buried deep is a special pressence, it's damn near impossible to find but it is atainable. I've been trying for 25 years. The only piece of advise I have to offer is don't discuss truth with anyone who is not on a path. The place to find answers is in your own conciousness. You asked why I still mess with booze. I don't claim to have risen above the human scene yet. I still have old habits. I don't know exactly what to expect when I die. Not to sound bragadoshis but I have no fear of dying,

☑ Other

because it's not death, it's making a transition from one state to another. I know I am not a good role moddle, but I loved you since the day you were born and always will, no matter what you think of me. I wish you happiness.

Love, Dad

Usually I cried as silently as possible. Jeff approached at the sound of my ragged sobs and pulled my head to his chest. He had overheard the phone call.

"It gets easier," he said. "With time. My father died, too. All I can tell you is that in time it'll get better." For the next few days I breathed deeply and slowly, drank cup after cup of tea, and watched comedies.

A package weighing several pounds arrived from my mother. Inside I found a plastic bag containing my father's cremated remains. "Ashes" did not describe what was left after a human body burned. The heavy gray soot looked like powdered stone strewn with bits of bone. The package also contained his death certificate and a letter to my grandfather, which, my mom's brief note said, came from one of Dad's first girlfriends. The note didn't explain why the remains and the letter had been sent to me. I guessed no one wanted to be responsible for what was left of Joe. I filed the box that contained my father under *Deal With Soon* by placing it far back on a high shelf in a closet. I opened the letter to my grandpa.

Dear Mr. Campo,

You probably won't remember me, but I am the lady who came up to your house when I heard about Joey. I asked for a picture and you were so kind to give me one. Thank you so much. I only wish I could of seen and spoken to Joey. I really cared for him. It has been 41 years since I've seen him, but I never forgot him and never will. We would go ice skating and he used to come and see me at my house where we would sit outside in the freezing cold, but lord I didn't mind just being with him. I've had a terrible ache and feeling in my heart for a year now — I was always thinking of Joey, I kept feeling something was wrong, and God above, it was.

He will be missed. When you care for someone in your teen years, sometimes the feelings stick with you even after decades, you always have special memories of that one person, and to me Joey was that one person. I just wish I had the chance to tell him. He might not of even remembered me — who knows? Well Mr. Campo I am truly sorry for your loss, but Joey is home now, no pain, just peace. You know, I've been searching for him for such a long time — looking on the internet, looking everywhere I could possibly think of, asking people we knew and when I finally find him God has him, but I now know that he is happy.

Sincerely yours,
Josephine Davenport

Time for a long walk. I washed my face, pulled on a dress that suited the warm weather, slipped into sandals, and headed out the front door. Josephine, emotional and religious, was the opposite of the intellectual, secular woman my dad married. Josephine's searching and her terrible feeling in the year leading up to his death haunted my every step. I felt like a ghost, as if the family created by Betty and Joe was never meant to be.

After their divorce, Dad had carried a ten-year torch for Betty, but Josephine triumphed as Lady Liberty compared to that. I considered sending her the remains, then realized that might be strange. They couldn't stay in the closet. For seven straight nights after I stored them, I dreamt of my dad. In one dream, he and I stood in an attic near my sleeping mom as I pointed out the window to a towering ocean wave. In another, we were driving cross country and yelling at each other. On the eighth morning, I pulled down the box and asked Jeff if I could borrow his car.

From a small bridge over the Russian River where it emptied into the Pacific, I let the ashes fall into the water. Most of the remains fell straight down with a *whump*, but an unusually strong wind carried a

☑ Other

little cloud of my father and sprayed it against the living room window of a nearby house.

Sorry.

That night the dreams stopped and the feeling returned. *I can do anything I want* — a weight lifted. But it seemed odd that my father could have limited my life from three thousand miles away.

In quick succession I found a cheap car — another old VW, but his time a bug, low to the ground and safe — and a cheap place to live in the hills of Sebastopol. A couple was renting out a tiny addition that sat 25 yards from their house. The wide deck made the propane-fueled kitchenette and miniscule shower bearable. Thanking Jeff, it occurred to me that I now had a long list of people who had helped me. Jeff hadn't judged me, but I felt ashamed to have become so dependent with so little to give in return.

"Absolutely no problem at all," he said.

I found a used bed that came with sheets and blankets. No other furniture would fit in my one-room home. In every direction, I saw an early-pioneer landscape of grass, shrubs, trees and sky — beautiful, but isolating. I hadn't been thinking about tending my grief, only of securing shelter and a car. The triple whammy of losing my father, my job, and Sampson pushed me back into a pit that I had spent a long time climbing out of.

I convalesced by sitting outside. What at first seemed like complete silence revealed an orchestra of tiny sounds: the rustling of squirrels and lizards, the distant whistling of a red-shouldered hawk, the clattering of falling pinecones. Panic always intruded on the peacefulness. I could not remember any time of stability. Paring each morning down to a thickly brewed cup of coffee in the sun allowed, at least, a measure of calm.

During my next shift at Tama Rama, people stopped by to offer condolences. John's girlfriend Maya came in, followed by PJ, then a cute regular from Taiwan. Each walked behind the counter and took my hand or gave me a hug, murmuring heartfelt words, resulting in my intense effort to keep from crying in public.

☑ Other

A week remained till school registration. I never, ever wanted to hear the words "job hunting" again. Working for Judy would no longer be enough, and until I secured yet another position, not even basics like Band-Aids figured into my budget.

I took the number off a flyer in downtown Sebastopol requesting a pamphlet-maker for a man who taught Native American workshops. Tom Toohey sounded glad to hear from me. He interviewed me in his home office, where he and his wife exchanged glances and hired me after only a few questions.

"We have a sense for what Great Spirit wants," explained Tom, who looked like an ex-Hell's Angel. His softly rounded wife had kind eyes. I accepted the position, though the under-the-table wages wouldn't be enough to cover body treatment. Without it, the pain in my neck and shoulder increased, expanding to my temples and lower back. Specific stretches helped a little. Sometimes I wondered how I'd make it through the day. Regardless of the glaring setbacks, I signed up at Santa Rosa Junior College and took the math and science I'd skipped during my two years of college.

I filled the rest of the schedule with literature and Latin. I now felt lucky to be privy to millennia of knowledge distilled down to reasonable portions presented by trained instructors.

To get financial aid, a student had to be on the verge of homelessness. Living below poverty level, I qualified. Perks. Sweet, precious perks — though if I did get into UC Santa Cruz, I would still have to borrow tens of thousands of dollars.

I'd forgotten the stability and structure of a day of classes. Rescued from the maw of directionless doom, I took to schooling like a butterfly to a field of asters, sitting at the front in class to better absorb lectures.

At home I started a deck garden. Gardenia and lavender gave off soothing scents while red succulents and yellow sunflowers gave color. I taught myself the rudiments of herbal medicine, and learned to make lotion and balm. As much as possible, I turned the little place into a sanctuary. The trees, deer, land and sky around me felt like family, and I worried over the destruction that climate change would bring. I worried, too, that the younger George Bush planned to run for President. His dad had done enough damage.

"The way this country is going, I'm not sure I want to stay," Mike said one afternoon over the phone.

"You've been talking about living in France forever," I replied. "What's keeping you here?"

"I don't know French, don't have residency, and what if I can't find work?"

"Plenty of people move overseas without those, and you can always teach English."

"I have too much debt to pay off." Mike's credit card damage made me extra glad I'd never gotten one.

"That doesn't have to stop you," I said.

I understood wanting to leave our mismanaged country — but despite the government's valuing of corporations over citizens, the high income tax and corrupt leaders, I didn't want to go. Having been born "on U.S. soil," I felt stubbornly akin to its natives, considering myself part of the country itself before being part of the governed populace.

"I might declare bankruptcy," Mike said. "And I don't believe in that true love shit anymore."

"What do you mean?" I asked, catching some of his sadness in my voice.

"It's bullshit and I know I'm not going to find it. Whatever. I'm OK with that."

"Mike, you deserve a woman as kind and wonderful as you. Don't worry. There's real love in this world." *You have no proof of that.* "How could there not be?" I had never heard Mike sound cynical, and it rattled me.

"Yeah, yeah," he said. "I need to make dinner. Talk to you soon." I went to bed early. The next day I had a double of school and work.

My new employer, Tom Toohey, had been a Drug Enforcement Administration thug before teaching his Native American workshops. Sitting in his office, he told me his story. As an employee of the DEA, Tom had worked with a squad that raided suspect homes in search of drugs, taking people out "when necessary." Sometimes the planned raid

☑ Other

would get cancelled last minute, and the strong-arms would have to lay low for a few days. On one such occasion, Tom attended a powwow in Arizona and went into a sweat lodge. Afterward as he sat on a stone, a native man approached him.

"A tall Navajo will come up to you," the man told Tom. "And he will say that Grandfather wants to see you. When he does, you go with him." With that he walked away. Tom forgot the prediction until a few months later, when another raid got delayed. He went to another native gathering, where he avoided lodges but sat near a drum circle. A tall Navajo man made his way over to him.

"Do you know what he said?" Tom asked me. "Grandfather wants to see you. Exactly that. So I went with him." The Navajo led Tom to a truck and drove them along a two-lane road. After nearly an hour, Tom wondered why the hell he had accepted a ride with this large silent stranger. But he still had his DEA gear with him, bulletproof vest, gun, and pager, so he decided not to worry. Eventually they rode up beside a hogan (a small eight-sided structure), and the man told Tom to go inside. Grandfather, who sat in the hogan, held up a hand for Tom to stop. He made him leave all his thug accouterments outside.

"Well, I sat with this little old guy for a few minutes while he told me he'd been waiting for me, that he wanted me to move onto the reservation and learn from him and the other elders. While I took it all in, my pager went off outside, and Grandfather said, 'You can go back to that, and them, or you can stay here with us.' So I stayed. And they taught me. Now I teach."

Tom handed me a spiral-bound booklet full of lessons once passed down through oral tradition. He offered to answer any questions I had. When I asked about the native perspective on reincarnation, he said most believed in it. The elders had told him that each person was born in the location and to the parents of his or her choice, with a planned main purpose and two side tasks. If you died without remembering your plan, they said, well, OK — but figuring it out the next life would be even harder.

I got the specs to make a brochure for his workshops, and saw myself out. Aside from a massive bull skull over the mantle, their house

☑ Other

looked average suburban. Despite Tom's cycle-gang appearance, I accepted his stance as a teacher of native culture. Encouraged that elders on a reservation had taken a white man under their wing, I went home grateful for the glimpse beyond the mundane world — something I hadn't thought about in ages.

I remembered the bundles buried on Sonoma Mountain and how Fred Jack said they could be revisited. A few moments of quiet in the gorgeous woods couldn't hurt. When I got to the parking lot of the nature reserve, though, I found that the trails and creek I loved so much had been commandeered by Sonoma State and were now off limits. A ranger stood watch at each trailhead. I drove back down the mountain and into Cotati.

At The Eight Ball, I spotted John and his cute brunette girlfriend.

"Cindy," she called, halfway rising from her chair. "Come sit with us." I brought a pint to their table. Later, when PJ and Jeanette showed up, we all moved to a back patio.

I didn't really hear the conversation, even as I participated in it. My gaze drifted off the patio to where huge tufts of dry grass glowed blue in the moonlight as I realized that I was the only single person at our table. On the drive home, the dark roads through the hills lost their usual charm. I crawled into bed, cold and wishing I had someone to hold.

A flyer on a campus message board announced a presentation on happiness at North Light Bookstore/Cafe. Instead of dismissing the peddling of happiness, I read the flyer with interest. Even if you had chronic depression, it said, stuck emotions could be released.

A perfume of fallen leaves spiced the chilly autumn air outside North Light, making the warm, coffee-aroma-permeated interior even cozier. With a latte and biscotti on a table before me, I surveyed the other attendees: a few students with binders on hand, and a man I had often spotted smoking outside the biker bar downtown. In his 40s or 50s, he kept his shoulder-length hair loose and always wore the same beat-down leather jacket. His face looked like a textbook definition of "sad."

☑ Other

The speaker, a hippie-ish man of thirty or so, began by telling us he had learned to meditate through a guru. With that, my attention wandered. I regarded people with gurus as followers, going along with someone's made-up agenda.

"I had never meditated," the speaker was saying when I tuned back in. "But the method was so simple and had such powerful results, I went with it. One moment I'd be focusing on my breath, and all of a sudden barely able to handle the massive energy coursing through me." He made an expanding circle with his arms. "At first I thought I would explode ... really explode. But my guru pointed out that there were no exploded corpses of anyone doing this type of meditation, anywhere."

Like television news, he delayed getting to the real story. Sipping my latte, garnished with nutmeg and chocolate, I realized I had expected him to just tell us how to release depression, anger and fear. Keeping still long enough to concentrate on the breath and allow energy to ebb and flow sounded like a lot of work. My right hand moved to massage the tight muscles of my left shoulder.

"Walking meditation, lying down meditation. It all works," the man said. *How about massage meditation?* I glanced at the sad-faced man, who listened with rapt attention. It got a little harder to breathe as I sensed through the usual blocking of pain how much my past injury still needed help. Restless, I got up and made my way out. At home I did extra stretches before laying down, stiff and sore, hoping to sleep.

I imagined a life without injury. There was no way things wouldn't be easier. I couldn't resist spending a chunk of my first paycheck from Tom on a professional deep-tissue massage, and got rewarded with one day of utter relaxation. At school, my classmates smiled and greeted me. Later I arrived in good spirits for work and showed Tom a pamphlet I'd finished.

"Now we just need to print and distribute these, and find a space to rent," he said. After I tended to the business of locating a workshop space, he invited me to ask questions about the teachings.

"What's the main focus of the workshop?" I asked.

"Different for each participant," he explained. "We all go through phases at different points in our lives. For you, I'd say start with learning to be at cause, not at effect. You are responsible for all your actions and words, so don't let other forces direct you."

"That sounds good, but how do you do it?"

"Every living thing deserves respect," he answered. "From the tiniest insect to the planet-sized being called the earth. You are included, and you start by respecting yourself as a being who belongs here." To my dismay, the word "belong" brought tears to my eyes.

"So," I said, bending over my notebook. "To be at cause I need to be ... nicer ... to myself?"

"Energy can't be created or destroyed, but it can be directed. You want to direct energy in a way that allows you to create your life how you most want, and not be at the mercy and whim of just any old person who comes along. You may have had damaging image-makers," he said, by which he meant parents. "But you can still design your life by your higher self."

I feared I would never be like girls whose voices reflected self-esteem and brightness, who looked great in their new accessories: a nice purse, exotic earrings, fashionable boots that made a satisfying *tok tok tok* sound. They reminded me that my pockets were my purse, and that my accessories were bought at thrift stores.

Focusing on the world's problems detracted a little from mine. I was surprised that few people commented on how corporate oriented America had become, as if there were no other way to run a country than catering to the wealthy. And few batted eyes over record-breaking temperatures becoming the norm.

When I opened my front door on the morning of December 25th, I saw Easter lilies blooming on the hillside. Northern California had very mild seasons, but this was unusual. It made me uneasy. As a child in New Jersey, I had loved knowing four set seasons. Each started by a certain point in the year, stayed in character for three full months, and then ended. Winter stayed freezing cold until the season finished, with no sudden warm days. When the March thaw came, everyone knew the cold would end with no unexpected April snow. Spring remained mild until summer, which did not linger into October. I missed the assuring routine of seasons. My practice of calming and motivating myself with a cup of coffee on the deck didn't work.

I went inside to look up free therapy in Sonoma County. The next day I made the first available appointment — three months from then.

Wind shook the wet branches of trees as I drove over to PJ and Jeanette's new place. They had moved into a house in rural Cotati. Inside, red light from a wood stove glimmered on blue walls. The mellow tones of musician J.J. Cale thumped in the background. PJ greeted me from the bench of an upright piano.

"The place looks really nice," I said.

"Still have a lot to do," he said. "But by spring it's gonna be sweet." I hugged Jeanette, her embrace quick but warm, and we three settled in to a game of dominoes.

"John and Randy'll be over later," PJ said as I passed beers around. I loved the company, wood fire, piano, and colorful warm house. When I glanced at a wall rack that held jars of hot sauce, a twinge of longing poked at my heart. Bright labels stated the hot sauce names: Not Cool, Jump Up and Kiss Me, Ass in the Tub. I yearned to co-create a welcoming home with clever and delicious items. *Don't be envious*, I reminded myself. *Your turn will come.*

In the weeks leading up to therapy, I researched trauma, relieved to find that rape victims often froze up when their memories were triggered. Playing dead hadn't been the best response to the molesting transient in Golden Gate park, but it wasn't something I had done on purpose.

I really needed therapy to help with all my past traumas, though when my first appointment finally arrived, I felt irritated. A stranger was going to put me on the spot, staring and taking note of every emotion that crossed my face.

The counselor greeted me with a grandmotherly smile and blinked over her bifocals. I relaxed, but hesitated when she asked what had brought me in. I hated when anyone saw me cry, which cut off sharing the reasons for coming in. I could have told her that everything had become too much — my dad dying right after I'd wrecked my home on wheels and lost my job; suffering from an old spinal injury and having no health insurance; loneliness and worry about the future. Any of those could bring on the tears. No way would I mention the rape or that my parents had left me when I was sixteen.

"I don't think I choose boyfriends very well," I said.

"Daughters who have unresolved issues with their fathers often pick relationships that bring up the same difficulties," she said. "With children of alcoholics or addicts, as adults, if you put them in a roomful of strangers they will make a beeline — it's uncanny — for the one person who will be most like that destructive parent. You follow a script, and people your life with those who mimic your family members because you unconsciously want to fix the issues." That made sense. I saw her four or five times over the next few months, but never talked about my deepest problems.

"I feel ugly sometimes," I admitted one session.

"I'm going to suggest something," she said. "Take off your glasses." Since contact lenses were expensive, to make them last longer I wore them only once or twice a week. The therapist had never seen me without my cheap pair of glasses. I removed them.

"Your eyes are really quite beautiful," she said, as if unmasking the pretty-behind-those-glasses girl who blossoms and is loved because she switches to contacts. "I think you're just fine," she said with a radiant smile. I thanked her and made that the last session.

Focusing on finishing undergrad college, I finally sent an application to UC Santa Cruz. During the two-month wait for an answer, I got scared, even though I had managed to get A's in all the classes I'd taken the previous two semesters. Santa Cruz was the only school I had applied to.

When the bulky envelope arrived at long last, I tore it open and read the acceptance letter, running to tell the good news to the first people I could find: the couple I rented from.

☑ Other

Finding a room posed no problem in the college town of Santa Cruz. Former boyfriend and girlfriend, my two new roommates were blond, tanned and healthy looking. They kept a clean house and didn't drown the home in partying. During my first week there, on the way back from grocery shopping, we noticed an enormous vehicle at a gas station.

TERRORIST RESPONSE TEAM

had been printed in bold lettering across the front of the giant truck. The words

NUCLEAR, BIOLOGICAL, CHEMICAL

were repeated all around the top edge. On the back, under a giant coil of wire and a hook, a sentence read:

IN THE DEFENSE OF OUR COUNTRY, THERE ARE NO RULES

My roommates and I looked at each other with either raised or furrowed brows, united in the disturbing reality known as post-9/11 America.

Activism in Santa Cruz had turned from the frequent, loud protests I remembered to occasional, tame marches carried out with the city's permission on pre-agreed dates. Those who still cared about whether or

☑ Other

not there were rules governing the defense of the country were getting outnumbered by those succumbing to a screen-absorbed lifestyle. It was a bit creepy.

Screen life gave people a tailored version of reality while the Bush administration made decisions that hurt the nation. I wanted to do something about it, but had to focus on my own challenges first.

I'd be reaching for a cereal box in the morning and notice how afraid I felt. When entering a full classroom: afraid. Stepping up to a cafe counter: afraid. Through tense muscles, my voice wisped out like a geisha's. I struggled to keep from turning resentful. Life wasn't easy to begin with, but to go about it in fear was an ordeal. At least I had chosen the right school. The azure expanse of ocean visible from the UCSC campus wasn't its only picturesque feature. Between buildings separated by hills, giant redwoods towered and ferns thrived.

My attempts at greeting classmates were met with flat stares until I finished one of the first assignments in Short Fiction. A tall girl with thin brown hair and huge eyes, who had never returned a nod or hello from me, ran to catch up with me one morning on the treelined path to class.

"Hi," she said, out of breath. "I liked your story." I turned slowly.

"You refused to say hi but now you do because you like something I wrote?" She nodded.

"Meet up with us later if you want," she said.

"Thanks," I said in the "don't really care" tone that was popular with the in crowd. After classes, I casually joined the group trip to a bar. Over a second round of drinks, a few poets and I decided to form a weekly group. Going to feedback sessions would be way easier than actually making friends.

I was a little older than most UCSC students. Of course, this made me feel afraid. I wished the culture weren't so youth-glorifying. It didn't help that as soon as a body matured, the breakdown process started. *Hello, tail end of my 20s.* I searched my reflection for tiny signs of aging, and yanked out two gray hairs. Since old people were often considered little more than living rubbish, the beginnings of aging on anyone looked awkward at best, and like a hideous forewarning at worst.

☑ Other

I still went dancing fairly often. Most club goers were in their early 20s, as if following an unwritten age limit I had never noticed. When I invited a few aspiring poets from our group, they shied away.

"Oh, I don't go to the clubs anymore," one guy said. "I'm old."

"How old?" I asked.

"Thirty-one," he answered with a sigh. "I feel stupid out there."

"You shouldn't," I said, remembering New Orleans and its wide age range of revelers.

David, a confident classmate who favored brash, slam-style spoken word, mentioned a free workshop at school. I joined, thinking it would be like the feedback group, until I found out that it culminated in a stage performance.

"I don't think so," I said at the second meeting.

"C'mon, Cindy," David said. "It'll be fun. I can play guitar as background for your poem, if that helps."

"That might be better," I said. "I'll give it a try." David held up a hand to high five.

Looking over my poetry, I fretted. I didn't write anything like the style of my peers, who lashed out in savvy, politicized rants. Slam poetry ruled as *the* performance method at UCSC, featuring demanding tones, arm flinging and mock anger.

I chose a piece that I hoped might be good. David brought his guitar to the next workshop and strummed a melody, pretty but haunting. I practiced to the music.

"It works," he said. "You're good to go."

Of the eight poets scheduled to perform, I had the shortest piece. The emcee told me to go first. I hesitated for a split second, took a deep breath and walked onstage, thankful that David sat on a stool behind me. Beyond the footlights, indistinct faces floated. I spoke in rhythm with the music, no slammy angst, and made it to the last verse:

☑ Other

> The lizard with its four feet
> that could not give a hug,
> made involuntary gouges
> in its attempt at human love.

After only a moment of abysmal silence, mild applause filled the room and the next poet jumped onstage. I joined the audience. After the performances, a workshop mate approached me.

"My friend just told me he thought yours was the best of the show," she said.

"I'm so glad someone liked it," I said. We flagged down David and headed through the warm June night to a pub. Excitement filled the air. We were nearing graduation. I felt exhilarated to have performed onstage, and noticed I could now maintain eye contact without getting nervous.

I knew better than to expect my mom to attend my graduation, but I imagined that one of my relatives might say, *Well, Cindy, we had our doubts, but you did it. You put yourself through college. This I've gotta see.* That didn't happen. And since the ceremony was at 7:30 in the morning, I didn't go, either. The degree would have to be enough.

☑ Other

7.

The Question

Sometimes I wanted to grab a merchant by the collar and shout, *Why are we both a party to this?* People didn't need to buy, buy, buy in order to have good lives. On the other hand, after prolonged bouts of going moneyless, I loved shopping as much as anyone.

I found myself back at poverty level after graduation, at a time when President George W. Bush handed out rebates of a few hundred dollars. I fell under the radar and didn't receive a check. By the end of the summer, thankfully, I found an assistant-editor position with a newspaper of art and entertainment. Though the pay wasn't quite enough, I did get free tickets to all kinds of events. The chief editor expanded my job duties to include the reviewing of plays, but didn't offer me a raise. At local theaters, choice seats were reserved in my name — granted, they were usually folding chairs with a piece of paper taped to them, but I took whatever prestige I could get. I loved sitting at a desk in the skylighted newspaper office, where I felt that I mattered.

After spending a full month's salary on everything from hygiene to auto care, I didn't have enough for groceries. I went to churches for dry-goods handouts. I volunteered with Food Not Bombs to get a regular supply of fresh produce.

Newspaper staff sometimes were treated to press dinners at bistros that served expensive dishes and specialty wines. One evening I'd be enjoying sumptuous food, and the next morning I'd be boiling government-issued oats with nothing to flavor them. Taking leftovers from press dinners was an unacceptable faux pas. Most of my meals included saltines.

☑ **Other**

At a gallery opening on a hot October evening, the topic of clean air came up. After making a sweep to look at paintings of perpendicular lines, I joined a small group of locals who were discussing a new oxygen bar. Santa Cruz had become choked with traffic. I had a plan to start filling my room with plants that would provide as much oxygen as possible.

"I'd love to visit places with clean air," I said.

"There's none left," replied a tall thin woman. She looked to the man standing next to her. He added,

"Well, maybe at the most uninhabited spots on the planet, but otherwise, no, there isn't any. Or totally pure water either." The woman shook her head, sighing into her plastic cup as I drifted to the next room. Cruising from painting to painting without really looking at them, it occurred to me that the earth didn't seem the best place to bring a new life. Almost all of the people I knew in Sonoma County had found spouses and started families. Bringing a baby into a world with toxic rivers and disappearing wildlife didn't feel respectful. Besides, passing on any genetic markers of the distress I'd endured just felt wrong. But I understood the urge, as well as the expectation, to make a family. I couldn't blame anyone for having children, but hoped there were enough men out there who didn't want any, either.

Playing darts on a Friday night, I got ready to go home when an acquaintance from school suggested that everyone come over to watch *Fight Club*. Following his car, I noticed a telltale red and blue flashing in my rearview mirror. I pulled over.

"Do you know why I stopped you?" asked the stocky blond officer.

"No."

"Your tail light just went out. I'm going to write you a fix-it ticket." I nodded. "And I'll need you to step out of the vehicle." I got out. The policeman told me to tilt my head back, close my eyes, stand on one foot and announce when 30 seconds had passed. He said not to start until he finished explaining, and asked if I understood the test. I did. I followed the instructions without swaying or setting my foot down, and finished in 28 seconds. He then asked me to walk heel-to-toe along the yellow line on the road, which I did without wobbling. He pulled out a breathalyzer. My breath measured .08 percent — the lowest amount of alcohol in the blood that made driving illegal. The police would often let a driver with a .08 level slide, but with a warning. The officer who pulled me over said he was going to arrest me.

"What are my options?" I asked.

"No options."

"I'll walk home right now," I said. "I don't want to go to jail."

"Neither do I," he said. "Gotta obey the law. Turn around and put your hands behind your back."

"Please," I said.

"Turn around," he said again. Not that it excused my actions, but almost every adult I knew, East to West Coast, drank and drove. Even designated drivers would have one or two early in the evening.

Rigid with anger, I let the policeman cuff me. At the station, my purse, shoes and jacket were taken. When the officer on duty opened the holding cell door, I saw a woman crawling on the floor inside. She wore a sleeveless black body-suit, inside out. The legs reached mid-thigh like an antique bathing suit. I hesitated.

"Go inside," the officer said, nudging me. The bright cell reeked of urine. A calm but weary-looking pregnant woman leaned against a half-wall that only partially shielded a filthy metal seatless toilet.

Both women were barefoot, which made my socks seem luxurious. Locked in, I sat on a bench and stared at the floor. The crawling lady got up and reached toward me, making a sound like *You OK?* while I leaned away. She never stopped moving, swishing words around in her mouth. When she veered too close, her rotten breath lingered. Sometimes she rushed at the wall, only to stop short and begin tracing the peeling paint with a forefinger, exclaiming over what she found there. The other lady asked me if I spoke "Espanish." I shook my head.

☑ Other

Now the mumbling woman shivered in her stretchy black outfit, rolling the short legs up and back down as if maintaining important details. She had been cute once, and her hair, glossy and dark, remained beautiful. I glanced — mistake — at her eyes, which were bloodshot and saggy, like a basset hound's.

Earlier, at the bar, someone had said, "But you can't ever be *too* empathetic, can you?" I had answered that you could. Seeing signs of a possible future you in the person you were empathizing with was too much empathizing. The pacing woman approached the dirty window of the cell door.

"Can ya bring me a blanket?" she called. Then she yelled, "Asshole!" before running to flush the toilet. As the industrial, loud sound subsided, she rushed at the wall again, but this time she didn't stop. She whacked her forehead. Cupping her eye with her hand, she whimpered,

"Fucking wall. When did they put that there?"

I could no longer detect the urine stench but knew it was there. On the bench, I leaned against the chilly wall. My eyes closed. After what seemed like hours, I passed in and out of semi-dreams. A voice said, *Give it up already.* Another said, *Don't give up.* Both sounded reasonable. The first voice said, *Do you know the atoms of your body were once part of a star?* The other responded in a hiss, *I wasn't no star, and don't tell me I was.* The first voice just nodded. I heard little pieces being torn off a leaf. Red eyes caught the early sun, but that was impossible. Nor did the room reflect starlight. I opened my eyes to the windowless gray walls. After a guard barked at a wailing, sobbing woman in another cell, he opened the door to ours.

"Who's Ann?" he asked. We all shook our heads. He left, only to return a few minutes later.

"Cindy?" he asked. I said yes. "Come with me." He led me to the center of the jail's main room and took my fingerprints.

"What's your middle name?" he demanded.

"Ann," I said. He gave me a sideways glance.

☑ **Other**

"My *middle* name," I said. "My *name* is Cindy." He remained silent. "How long do I have to stay here?" I asked. I hadn't felt buzzed or drunk even when I'd gotten pulled over.

"You got two hours."

"Why?"

"I'll restrain you if I have to," he threatened. I noticed a black metal chair equipped with straps, in view of all the cells. *What a nightmare factory.*

Around 8:00 in the morning, when they released me into the fresh air and sunlight, I knew only one thing: not being locked up was the best possible aspect of being alive. No matter that I had seven days of community service to perform, a $1,300 fine, and a suspended license for six months (which wouldn't even go into effect right away.) I cruised the sidewalk, soaking in every detail: seagulls landing on rocks in the San Lorenzo river; the breeze on my face; joggers and cyclists huffing along in their shiny clothing; a fat orange cat in the window of a bookstore that wasn't open yet. My car sat where I had left it. At home in my large room, I burrowed under my thick feather comforter and slept till the afternoon.

Six days later, Friday night, I got a phone call from David, the slam poetry fanatic, asking if I wanted to shoot some pool. In regular Friday mode, I agreed. David told me that he had just spent all his money on bills. He asked if I would bring him a beverage. Sneak-in drinks were not a new concept. Living on a student's budget meant cutting corners. David's request didn't surprise or bother me. I felt glad to help him out with half a small bottle of whiskey I had in the kitchen.

At the bar, I poured the whiskey into David's empty water glass, and put the bottle back in my pocket. The evening was unmemorable until later. After a few games of pool, I ran into a lawyer I only knew from that bar. I usually found him fun to talk to, but that night we got into a stupid argument about my not wanting to go on a date with him. By the time he left, David had, too, and I stayed to allow the alcohol to leave my system. I watched after-hours chess games, smoked cigarettes ... and waited.

☑ **Other**

No helpful warning shouted from my subconscious as I approached my car. I felt fine. The bar sat less than a mile from home. The short drive involved a sharp left turn, and the lane lines didn't match up from one street to the other. You had to look carefully to stay in the lane. Not that time.

A police car jumped on my tail in seconds. Again I was asked to step out of the car, when all hope disappeared. There were two officers this time. One patted me down, finding the empty whiskey bottle. He laughed, confiscating it. They skipped the regular tests and went right to the breathalyzer. I could have cried when it showed .09 percent.

Back in cuffs, back to the back seat, back to the station. My heart beat hard as the policeman herded me into the same cell. Again the jail stench. My stomach kept flip-flopping. Two nice, well-groomed girls greeted me without sloshing their words or bashing their heads against the wall. One gave me a hug. After a couple of hours of paralyzation — *What will they do with me?* — I strained to understand why I was reliving this nightmare again. At that point, as I saw things, the matter wasn't whether or not I was an idiot, but how much of an idiot was I? I kicked myself for not anticipating that spot as a trap. One DUI now looked like a winning lottery ticket.

The fake potatoes that they brought us for breakfast made my mouth burn — not from heat, but more of a chemical burn. They were a strange shape, like tiny perforated rectangles. After the girls were let go, I awaited my release. When the cell door opened, an officer told me that in light of receiving two infractions within a week, the D.A. had decided I posed a danger to society. She decided that I would stay in jail four or five more days. I couldn't breathe.

"But I have a deadline," I said. "I work at a newspaper. I'll get fired."

"If you want out, your bail has been set at $20,000," the guard informed me. "A two-thousand dollar, non-refundable fee will release you." He slammed the cell door. I picked up the in-cell phone and dialed my brother collect, my face hot. As fast as I could I said,

"I-got-a-DUI-and-there's-bail-but-if-I-can-borrow-two-thousand-dollars-I-can-get-out-and-avoid-getting-fired."

"Sure," he agreed without question or judgment. I heard Cathy's voice in the background. "Hold on, Cin," Chris said and muffled the phone. After a moment he returned.

"We'll do it. But I'm about to go to work so Cathy is coming down. What's the address?"

Oh, why her? To my shamed eyes, my sister-in-law looked like an angry rubber puppet that day. She arrived with both her kids in tow. We sat in silence while she drove me home. She dropped me off with a terse goodbye.

I lay beneath my comforter again, exhausted, stomach acid churning, sensing a lingering fluorescence and detention grime. This time I had a court date for the sentencing.

I've slipped. I've failed. I could hear my inner villain laughing. *Thought you could get away?* This time I took all credit. *My fault. This is completely my fault.*

I was grateful that the part-time hours at the newspaper were flexible. My hands shook as I got ready for work. I had barely slept and it showed. Halfway through the afternoon, the chief editor got up and crossed the room to my desk.

"Come with me for a minute," he said. I'm certain terror flashed across my face. I followed him outside.

"Is everything all right?" he asked. "We've noticed . . ."

"Um," I said, smoothing down my hair. "I'm just sleep deprived. Sorry. My pieces are written and I'll have everything in and done on time."

"Good. I wouldn't want to have to give you an official warning about anything." As we headed back inside, I envied how untroubled he looked.

A familiar sense of inferiority had returned — as if it had smashed through with a claw hammer. Court sentencing was for criminals. That people liked and cared about me didn't matter.

☑ Other

Anything shady I had done, I believed, turned that fondness to loathing.

One section of Pacific Avenue, not far from the newspaper office, hosted a year-round faction of people who played music, juggled or read fortunes for spare change. One of these was a guitar player named Elvis. With dark eyes, a petite frame and toffee-brown skin, he looked nothing like Presley.

He lived in a VW bus that had the same "barn" doors and double windshield as Sampson. After work I spotted his bus parked on the avenue. Living on the fringes of society, Elvis sidestepped the usual conversational mores. I could speak freely to him without having to explain myself. He set his guitar aside.

"Have a seat, if you want," he offered.

"Thanks. How's everything?"

"Not bad, not bad. I'm going to visit my daughter Persephone in about an hour. Long day?"

"Yeah," I sighed. "Elvis, how much of our own realities do you think we create? If any."

"A lot. But let me back up. I believe what we experience is more about what we expect, and accept. I was struggling for a few months, to the point where I almost lost my bus over stupid parking fines. I got all caught up in it and angry. Why would I create such a bad situation for myself? I realized I didn't believe I deserved even a little stability, and expected disruptions that fit in exactly with how Persephone's mom views me. Seeing that, and adjusting my expectations, all the negativity evaporated."

"That sounds so easy." I stared at the pedestrians and cars passing on the street. Elvis picked up his guitar.

"Good," he smiled. "Then everything's gonna be all right."

I arrived grumpy and tired for my court appearance at 8:00 on a Wednesday morning. I had told the manager at work I had a dentist appointment. The judge, a dour white-haired man, called my name.

"You are here . . ." He ruffled through some paperwork. "For a second DUI. In light of the proximity of the two, you will complete forty-five days of community service, pay a second fine of $3,220, and your license will be suspended until you complete a year-and-a-half of alcohol awareness classes, which will cost you an additional $1,500. And you will attend thirty AA meetings." He glanced up, looking bored.

Holy shit. It took all the restraint I could muster not to shout that I didn't even drink that much. I headed for the exit when the bailiff approached and told me that I needed to submit forms to the criminal department downstairs. The fines totaled nearly $4,500, not including the $1,500, plus $157 for each arrest.

"I have to pay for my own arrests?" I asked the clerk at the window of the criminal department. She didn't bother to answer.

At home, I made a meal of canned tuna with mayo on tortillas, and sulked in my room. The mere thought of the huge fines made my heart beat hard, so I tried not to think about them. Mike called. After the full-length version of the story, he said,

"Oh my God, Cin. I drove home after two drinks last night."
"People do it all the time," I said. "And AA meetings? Really?" The *Once an alcoholic, always an alcoholic* motto made the organization seem questionable to me. Although, one Cotati friend swore by the program and had said he wouldn't be who he was without it.

"Maybe it'll be interesting," I said.

"Good luck."

If I thought a visit to an AA meeting would convince me that the program didn't promote powerlessness, I was wrong. Meeting goers, looking either desperate and fidgety or lofty and self-satisfied, perked up when members volunteered their drunkalogues of how alcohol had damaged them. I felt much more damaged by the condescending treatment from officers and court clerks than by alcohol.

Let's just get these out of the way fast, I thought. At meetings, speakers liked to say that if an attendee didn't replace alcohol with the twelve-step program, drinking would kill that person. While it must have been true for some, I doubted everyone in AA had reached the same stage of addiction. The third meeting seemed the

☑ Other

least alcohol-oriented, more like "a"A, but the constant self-labeling grated on my nerves.

During the part where quotes were read aloud from the Big Book (aka the AA bible), the leader asked me to participate. Since there were only women present, when I got to a part that read "he" I changed it to "she." The leader admonished me in front of the hushed group.

"You don't do that. Ever. You don't change a single word of the Big Book. Do you understand?" I avoided her glaring eyes, and nodded without mentioning fascism or blind allegiance.

To prove to the court that I had attended all thirty meetings, I had to get a signature from an organizer at each meeting. I asked a woman next to me if she knew about the process, and she told me the court didn't bother to match signatures to names. Later that day I gathered several types of pens and pencils, and created a list of signatures for the remaining twenty-seven "meetings." I shook off AA with relief. One line in the Big Book actually read, *I'm better off if I don't try to figure things out.*

As for community service, each eight-hour day became nine when adding in the mandatory lunch hour. At the start of every shift, we criminals met a crew leader at one of Santa Cruz County's jails, then went to a site. Most of the work involved picking up litter or sometimes landscaping. The county was so small that most sites were already litter-free and clear of weeds.

On Day One, while waiting for the crew leader, a clerk told me to work on an area around an oak tree in front of the jail. The dirt had been raked so often, it looked like a Zen garden, only sad. There was nothing to do, yet I had no choice but to drag the rake through the thin dusty soil until the leader arrived, fifteen minutes later.

We parked at the ocean. The leader sent me and two others off in three directions to collect litter. There was none. I put on earphones and set some music at an enjoyable volume. Walking cliffside by the sea was more than all right with me. Within minutes the ranger on duty caught up with me. Her mouth rapidly formed words. I removed the earphones.

☑ Other

"No music," she said.

"Oh, I didn't know," I said, putting them in my pocket. "You are not allowed to bring a music player to the worksite," she repeated.

"*OK*, I understand."

"Follow me." She made a quick call and had the crew leader drive me back to the jail for reassignment.

"Our officer at Natural Bridges says you have an attitude problem," the clerk said. My mouth fell open. "You won't be returning to that location. For today, you'll work here." I spent the next six hours circling the jail grounds, carrying a metal grasper I never used.

Other sites did need work, such as cutting and hauling away branches, weed whacking, and digging out stubborn invasive plants with a shovel: blistering labor, especially on hot days. Gloves felt suffocating, so I didn't wear any. My hands took a beating.

Each crew had about ten people. The leader I worked with the most treated his crews well — he usually stopped for coffee and morning snacks on the way to the site, easily killing half an hour. Having done community service himself (for a triple DUI) in his past, he knew what we were going through, and assured us that our time would be over before we knew it.

Other things the system didn't allow us to do involved working in pairs or having extended conversations with crew mates. Even during lunch, we weren't permitted to have books, phones, journals or any personal items, nor allowed to work through lunch. I felt like a wild animal trapped in a simulated habitat.

I stopped meeting up with friends altogether. *Off to the rock piles,* I'd think, slathering sunscreen on my face, neck and hands. Months passed in a way that felt like straining, shoving, pushing with all my might against a boulder that, whenever I checked on progress, had moved only millimeters. I lost count of how many shifts I'd done. One morning on the way to a site, the leader got a call from the main station.

"Cindy," he said out of the side of his mouth as he held his phone with his shoulder. "Today is your last day." I let out an

☑ Other

involuntary whoop. "Didja hear that?" he said into the phone, as if the clerk would care.

We arrived at a field overrun with dead brambles and wild, weedy grass. "Here." He beckoned, pointing toward a huge mess, and to the largest hand-pushed lawn mower I'd ever seen. "Clear that area there and you can call it a day."

He fired up the machine. I would not be mowing grass, but dead bushes and spiky weeds. Leaning forward with all my weight got the mower moving. It pulled me forward until it hit a jutting root or a rock.

"You've got to be kidding," I said. *Just get through it and you're done. Done!* I kept reminding myself, sweating and groaning until I mowed the last row of debris. The consequences to my neck and shoulder were severe, but I was free of the burden of hard labor.

With AA meetings and the chain gang checked off, just the fines and the suspended license remained, but those troubled me the most. Even if I made an extra few hundred a month, it would still take years to pay them off. It bothered me that the $4,500 would go mostly to the court, not to road safety reform. And charging an extra $1,500 for anti-alcohol classes prioritized cash flow over recovery.

I did feel relieved not to go to gas stations anymore. By that time, 2003, even children knew that burning refined oil caused the planet harm. I wished America would quit using fossil fuels. Despite harmful carbon emissions and diminishing oil reserves, though, politicians still rushed to suck out every last drop.

Throughout the '80s and '90s, the year 2000 had hung like a megalithic banner heralding The Future. People would say, *Wow. I'm going to be 25 when it turns the year 2000.* Or, *I wonder how much hover crafts'll cost in the year 2000?* The changing of millennia seemed to mark a different world entirely, as if every aspect of life would alter as soon as 11:59 p.m. on December 31st, 1999 became 12:00 a.m., January 1st, 2000.

Despite the crazed hype of near-Armageddon, the buying of emergency water and batteries, and decades of *What will life be like*

☑ **Other**

in the year 2000? — nothing had happened. At least nothing monumental. Yet with the rise of programmable everything from coffee makers to electronic pets, something was definitely lost.

I came to believe that before everyone had a personal phone and computer, the nation was less fragmented. People held conversations without a screen filtering the exchange. I didn't like seeing in-person discussions about important events get replaced by a stream of posts about a celebrity's latest scandal or which bar had the best happy hour.

Meanwhile, and to me this was much worse — civil liberties were eroding. Civilians used to be protected by law from constant monitoring, and you could feel that crucial degree of imperturbability wherever you went. The newer, surveilling nation was not a free nation. I very much valued the level of freedom I'd known until then, so this development made the future look dismal.

So many machinations had crept in. In the past, the idea of identification cards linking to databases struck most people as a serious, preventable invasion of privacy. Now, almost no one protested the widespread use of personal information, even though data mining would inevitably lead to misuse of that information. Not long ago, the idea of putting barcodes on newborns would have been considered Nazi-like. I was surprised that anyone thought safety could be guaranteed through scannable babies.

One thing stayed the same, though. People needed a lot of money just to get by. I had to step it up. I tried to get a job waiting tables, but I didn't have recent experience. In a college town, plenty of applicants had that requirement. Lacking another skill anywhere near as high paying, I got discouraged — not only with restaurant jobs, but with moneymaking in general, and finally, with the purpose of life. No matter how I tried, or what I achieved, serious difficulty always came back.

Biking home, balancing a laden grocery bag on the handle bars, I thought, *Don't give up. Don't give up,* amid a towering wave of hopelessness. On my days off I got into the habit of climbing back in bed with a book, a cup of coffee, a plate of crackers and a jar of

☑ Other

peanut butter. I tried to gain a positive viewpoint. For some reason, a quote attributed to Jesus popped into my mind:

> If you bring forth what is within you, what you bring forth will save you. If you do not bring forth what is within you, what you do not bring forth will destroy you.

What I had not "brought forth" was doing its job pretty well. The haunting question floated in. *Why are you here? What do you mean to do?*

I had no idea. Debt, coupled with family tension, battered my mind. Chris told me that Cathy had decided I could no longer babysit their kids. The most recent time, when I'd brought my young niece Kendra to Big Basin State Park, took on heightened importance. I wistfully remembered looking in the rearview mirror as Kendra held a stuffed buffalo out the window so it could "fly." Telling Chris I didn't drink all that much would be useless. He and Cathy didn't drink at all. I zoned out on documentaries and romantic comedies, trying to forget about my life.

"Cin, what do you think?" asked Mike during one of our thrice-weekly phone conversations. "Should I just move to France? This is getting expensive." He had fallen hard for a sexy, intelligent, unemployed French artist. He flew to Paris to see her every few months, and paid for her to come see him.

"For the zillionth time, yes. You should be there already, enjoying gruyere cheese and grottos where you can discuss film and painting ideas over glasses of Bordeaux." He laughed.

"But you don't understand," he said. "My debt. Wanna know much I owe?"

"Yes. I have a feeling it'll make me feel better."

"About twenty-five thousand."

"I was right."

"If I stop doing the smoke work, I'll have no way to pay this off." Mike had landed a lucrative job video editing using a machine called a smoke that few others, at the time, had the skill to handle. "And I

☑ **Other**

still don't speak fluent French. Where the hell will I work over there?"

"Who cares how long it takes to pay off?" I asked, mindful of my own hypocrisy. I didn't want to stay in debt for one more second. "You can learn French by having to speak it when you move there. Your girlfriend can help you."

He kept hedging. By the time we hung up, I kicked around an idea of how to make more money while expanding my own horizons: teaching English overseas. I considered Japan. Back then, most Japanese English schools covered a new hire's airfare and work visa. And they didn't require an expensive teaching certification, just a college degree. Over the next few weeks, I narrowed my choice down to one: Kumano Intercultural Center, a conversation school in Shingu, Japan.

Rory, the American who answered my inquiry call, sounded delighted that I was phoning from Santa Cruz, which happened to be a sister city to Shingu. He asked for my resume.

I don't remember a word of our phone interview except the part where he said, "Let's drop the formal discussion and continue this conversation when you get here." He told me I'd be sharing an entire two-floor Japanese house with one other teacher for less than $200 a month. *Whew.*

I liked the food, anime, and sometimes the fashions of Japan, but my mild interest was dwarfed by the Japanophiles I had met here and there. The most dedicated of them wore only bright, well-pressed manga T-shirts, kept organized collections of bootleg recordings, watched every obscure Japanese film twelve times, and studied the language. The only thing Japanese about me was that, for some reason, I gave a slight nod when passing lone strangers in public. Once I moved to Japan, I would find that the passersby nodded back.

I had a month to kill before the job started, which gave me a housing problem. My lease was expiring, and the roommates wanted someone to commit to at least six months. After frenetic searching, I

☑ Other

found a landlord who would let me rent a room for just the one month.

Jeremy, one of the housemates at the new place, occupied its large front bedroom. He was a fairly accomplished voice actor, and he aspired to be an accordion player. He was so gorgeous, he could have been Johnny Depp's cousin. I was attracted to him, but I tried to keep things platonic, knowing I'd be leaving the country. Late one night, he was sitting in the kitchen as I was washing a few dishes.

"Do you want to watch a movie with me?" he asked.

It took all my willpower to keep my eyes on the screen as we sat together on the couch. After the movie we talked and laughed until we got too sleepy to speak. We pulled a blanket from the closet so we could curl up next to each other on the floor.

In the morning we went downtown for coffee. While we warmed our hands on our cups in the crisp sunny air, Jeremy looked above me.

"Do you enjoy rooftops?" he asked.

"They're one of my favorite things."

"Let's go," he said. We ran to a metal staircase that zigzagged up the side of a building. From the top, Santa Cruz looked like a quaint village with emerald green mountains in the background.

A first kiss, and a second and a third, were inevitable. Over the next few weeks I tried to stay detached, which only intensified our chemistry. We discussed reconvening in San Francisco, maybe sharing a house with other artist types. Even saying goodbye, we smiled.

I had always thought that flying to Asia from California meant heading straight out over the Pacific, which would have been a little scary. In reality, the plane hugged the coast up to Alaska, down Russia and finally landed in Japan. I boarded a train in Narita.

Tired-looking businessmen smelled of cigarettes in the plush glow of a silent car. The darkness outside hid Japan from view. I felt excited, but kept thinking of Jeremy. I missed a connection to

☑ Other

Shingu and had to call Rory. He offered to pick me up, even though it meant a three-hour round trip over mountains at dawn.

Rory had pale skin, auburn hair and a friendly manner. I'd be staying at his house for the first few days. After a tour around the bottom floor, he showed me up a massive staircase to a thin-walled bedroom. Opaque glass windows muted the winter morning light. I fell asleep at once. An hour later, which seemed like one minute later, Rory woke me.

"You can go back to sleep this afternoon, but work starts Monday so I need you to observe a few of my classes." He retreated downstairs. The ice-cold floor jolted me awake — the only heater in the huge house was a kerosene-fueled metal box down in the kitchen. Rory's wife kept a kettle on the heater to warm the first floor. When she saw my tired face, she offered me a cup of tea.

Rory taught Saturdays from home. The rest of the week he acted as head teacher at the school. Skilled at keeping the class flow smooth and getting students to join every activity he gave them, he had been right that watching would prove valuable. After two classes, he gave me a bicycle and the rest of the day off. Shingu looked smaller and more isolated than Santa Cruz, but was more beautiful with a larger river nearby, steeper mountains, and a temple that had graced the area for hundreds of years.

Showering in the old house involved sitting on a little plastic overturned bucket set on a slatted wooden platform. The handheld shower head was attached to a flexible hose. I felt really glad to move into the house I'd be sharing with Joanna from Scotland. We had a jacuzzi-like tub, wall-mounted shower and three space heaters. Our house looked like a wooden puzzle box with sliding doors that, depending on their position, changed the size of the rooms.

Jo was an old sea captain in a young pretty woman's body. She showed minimal emotion and spoke with authority in her northern Scottish accent. Like the teacher I replaced, Jo spoke fluent Japanese. I felt embarrassed to know so little. Jo would have none of that: she said it was impressive that I had moved to another country and jumped right in.

Jeremy sent me an affectionate email, saying that he wanted to celebrate my beauty. He also called me his favorite girl, and said that he was ready to love me for a very long time. Though flattered, I got insecure about the "favorite girl" part. Were there others? Regardless, I felt excited about our possibilities and very much wanted to see him when I got back.

The year in Japan ushered in several firsts. Had I stayed in California, I wouldn't have been driving that year anyway, but since none of the teachers had cars, we all bicycled. Teaching meant speaking with confidence, which eventually I could do. I had to use English in the classroom, but living in rural Japan meant using Japanese every day outside school. I caught on to common phrases within a few weeks, but learning the more involved — yet still conversational — level of Japanese would take the better part of a year.

Making friends with women happened naturally because the social structure in the Japanese countryside remained traditional. Women and men hung out in separate groups. Students Rie and Yuka, kindhearted 20-somethings, invited Joanna and me to everything they did, and prepared special excursions for us.

Teaching became easier in time, but my first day on the job made me question my decision to take it. We had a main school as well as satellite classrooms. My first class took place in the spare room of a house in a nearby town. Rain fell all morning. I had a head cold and deeply achy menstrual cramps, and when I arrived at the classroom (by bus), I discovered I didn't have the right key. No one answered my knock. Our office manager had to drive through the downpour to bring a spare key, while young Japanese moms dropping off their daughters stared at me.

The six girls in my class, all five-year-olds, were accustomed to my predecessor and her impeccable Japanese. We were supposed to use only English to teach, yet she had depended on Japanese to get ideas across to small children. With sore muscles and a stuffy nose, I

☑ Other

tried to get the lesson going with a simple song. The girls ignored me. Two were having a yelling match, one crawled behind the furniture, and another glared at me. She shouted,

"WHY. YOU. DON'T. KNOW . . . JAPANESE!"

Jesus Christ. OK Cindy. You can do this.

"Everyone stop," I called out. The girls looked frightened. "Sit," I said, beckoning, kneeling on one of the cushions arranged around a low wide table in the center of the small room. "Paper," I said, placing a blank sheet for each girl at a place on the table and patting the cushions. They gathered around, throwing me skeptical looks before sitting down. "Pens," I said, pointing to a box of markers. "Draw," I instructed, pantomiming, and to my relief they all grabbed pens and began working.

During a round of *What is this? This is a . . .* for each drawing, the girls calmed down enough to open their study books. The morning classes, which had the youngest students, were the hardest to teach. The more proficient high schoolers attended in the afternoon. By evening, the classes were full of adults who could understand a lot more English.

Within a month I loved Japan. I felt as if I were on an extended vacation where I got paid to do a fairly easy job. Following Rory's example, I planned lessons so that each activity flowed smoothly into the next. Teachers of all kinds were very respected in Japan, and as visitors we were treated like royalty, taken on trips to see World Heritage sites and invited by neighbors to elaborate meals.

At long last, I earned more than survival money. I kept the refrigerator stocked, bought belts, purses, hats and jewelry. Having these general means amounted to sheer luxury. Ready to start chipping away at my fines, I called the Santa Cruz court to set up payments. The clerk told me to mail them because the court didn't allow criminals to pay by credit or debit card.

I sent a payment, only to get an overdue notice in return. For the second payment, I arranged for receipt confirmation, but again got a past-due notice. I made another phone call. The same gruff clerk said that they weren't receiving my mail. She suggested postponing

☑ Other

payments until I got back, and sent me a three-page form to fill out. The court, suddenly organized, received my return mail. The postponement suited me just fine. I wouldn't have to deal with crazy American bureaucracy for a year.

The teaching job in Japan provided health insurance, another first. Still in pain, I looked for treatment. Choices were limited in rural Shingu, so I went with a recommendation for sentai, which meant "bone therapy."

The waiting area of the Shintani back clinic was crammed with patients in their 60s and 70s who eyed me curiously. The air smelled of roasted herbs. A slender receptionist/nurse led me to a massage table and motioned for me to lie face down.

"Hi," she said. "I'm five minutes then practitioner."

"All right."

"So right now, electric, OK?"

"Mmmmmm, maybe OK."

"This is bidi-bidi," she explained, positioning four wired pads onto my bare back and turning up the juice. At each point of contact, a tangled ball of warm static grew, leveling out when she stopped upping the electricity. Pulses made my muscles flex and relax. Over the next several months I would come to like my weekly visits to Shintani.

The doctor was more serious and more skilled. He used a rapid massage technique that released a lot of tension. I tried my Japanese with him after a few months because he barely spoke English, but the best I could manage was that my shoulder muscles were "like steak." The next session, he tried giving me directions in English.

"Left, on, up," he would say, meaning I should lie on my right side. "Centahhhh, on, up," meant to lie on my back. Once he said, "Cindy condition bad. Bad."

After six months of treatment, my body felt better than it had in a few years. I realized that most people, who are able to turn their heads comfortably all the way to the left, or look skyward without pain welling up at the base of their skulls, were unaware of these superhero abilities.

☑ Other

The school offered a decent raise system, which enabled Jo and me to enjoy sushi often and to take frequent trips with Rie and Yuka to mountain hot springs. The relaxing mineral pools were gender segregated. I got used to soaking naked around women of all ages.

Jeremy and I exchanged emails every few days. He told me how much he missed me. We talked again about moving to San Francisco. He mentioned that every time he heard my voice, saw my picture or read my words, something in him said I was "the one."

"Well, come here and visit me then," I said. I wanted to find out where the relationship would go, not foster expectations.

He agreed to come, and just before his flight he sent an email that said, *Sending my love. I want to hold you forever.*

At the airport, I drank cold green tea and watched passengers trickle in through a white door. I spotted Jeremy, and we greeted each other with a long hug. When I looked into his eyes, I remembered how much I liked him.

"Hey," I said warmly.

"Hi," he returned. "Are you hungry?"

"Let's go eat."

Halfway through our meal, he paused and said,

"So . . ." like he was struggling to phrase something. "I didn't feel anything from you when I hugged you at the airport." I dropped one of my chopsticks.

"Me?" I said.

"Yeah," he replied, setting down a teacup. "I didn't feel anything from you."

"Look, Jeremy. I'm really glad you're here. I haven't seen any men and women hugging in eight months, or holding hands or kissing, because in the Japanese countryside physical affection is private. Maybe that affected me."

"Maybe I'm jet lagged," he said, blinking affectionately.

We stepped out of the restaurant into a warm summer rain. Clouded with dread, I couldn't remember which train to take to

☑ Other

Kyoto, where I'd booked a guest house for us. We caught it just in time.

Jeremy claimed one of the two futons in our room and fell asleep at once. I sought the company of the guests in the lounge area and joined their card games till late in the night.

At six in the morning, Jeremy said,

"Cindy, are you awake?" I sat up, woozy.

"Morning," I said. "How are you doing?" He didn't look at me.

"I still don't feel anything," he said. "I don't know. I just need a friend right now." That woke me up fast.

"I don't understand," I said. "After everything you've said."

"I don't either. I just know I need you to be a friend."

"*You* talked about 'the one' and loving for a long time. This is ridiculously abrupt."

"Sorry," he said. "If I could leave right now, I would."

"You'd *what?*" I wanted to slap him. I'd paid his airfare. The return ticket was for three weeks away.

"Let's just get breakfast. Sorry I'm . . . I don't know what's going on with me."

Suddenly he looked like Johnny Depp's idiot cousin, with a higher forehead and thinner upper lip.

"Well, this is gonna be fun," I sighed.

Kyoto, preserved from ancient times in lush green splendor, would have been amazing had I not felt crestfallen. I didn't get how someone could speak so often of love, and yet take it all back in one instant. Making matters worse, at times during his visit Jeremy would walk over, put his arms around me and give me a kiss. And I let him.

During his stay, I brought him to a wide cool river to swim, to a little island that had a hot spring in a cave (with full amenities), and to my favorite restaurants. In every photo of me during the three weeks Jeremy spent in Japan, I look resentful.

Jeremy slept on the floor in my room while I tossed and turned on a nearby futon. On the night before he left, I rose in the dark and went downstairs. Normally I prided myself on respecting people's privacy. But while Jeremy slept, I opened his bag and took out his journal.

Two days before coming to see me, he had written about staying up all night with another girl, wrapping a blanket around them both and feeling love in the dim morning light. Instead of reasoning that "love" was his modus operandi, I just slumped on the floor like a sack of used-up shoes.

No, no, and no. You didn't just keep silent about another woman while accepting a ticket to Japan. How could I have picked yet another man who had no qualms about suddenly abandoning a relationship? I didn't need any more trauma. My heart felt frozen. I wiped my eyes and took a hot shower. When Jeremy came downstairs I glared at him. Before leaving to catch the train, he mentioned that he wouldn't be moving to San Francisco after all.

"Well, I still am."

Once he'd left, I shoved away thoughts that I was unlovable, and that I would always be deserted. *That's not logical. Everyone deserves love.* I struggled to think, move, eat and teach through a searing grief. As my first support net of reliable girlfriends, Jo, Rie and Yuka gave me the hugs and smiles of encouragement that prevented a fatal fall.

I climbed a five-hundred-year-old stone staircase on a nearby mountain to the local shrine and prayed to its presiding goddess for the pain to stop. My heart was snagged on an old wound. I drew tarot cards, threw the I Ching, and analyzed my dreams, believing I could simply turn things around. I went to a salon and had more than a foot of hair cut off. I bought juggling balls and a guitar, forcing myself to practice for hours at a time. I began repeating a silent mantra. *I am now in a sound, healthy love relationship* — a chant against the humiliation of how casually Jeremy had switched gears.

I longed to know how to choose well, to be in a relationship where the ground stayed level, where I wouldn't be raised to impossible heights, only to be dropped. Looking at photos that

☑ Other

Jeremy posted online a month after he returned to California, I found that in almost every one, he posed with a different beautiful woman. Some of the ladies looked love-dopey just to be near him. I decided that, in the future, I would try dating Japanese men. Most that I'd met had an aura of politeness that hinted at more respectful behavior in general.

Time didn't heal all injuries, but it did seal off a cave of pain. After a few months, I woke to find that my heart no longer ached. I enjoyed a Saturday breakfast with Jo at a cafe. On Monday, I came up with innovative lesson plans to make up for any scholastic lag.

On Christmas Eve, our school had a Halloween party for the students, their families and friends. Neither holiday meant much in Japan. Half the attendees wore costumes, some arrived in Santa suits, and the rest dressed down. I came as a tarot reader, carrying my prettiest deck. Chiho, a middle-aged student known for her eccentricity, waved me over. She had a voice like a whistle.

"Ooh, fortune cards," Chiho trilled.

"Want a reading?" I asked. She nodded, her heavy necklaces clanking. She wasn't in costume. We sat at a corner table in the huge crowded community room. Chiho drew the Hierophant, the Three of Wands and the King of Swords.

"You have one major arcana, which is the bigger lesson," I began. Chiho looked at me expectantly, and I remembered she was an intermediate student of English. "This card," I said, pointing to the Hierophant, "is about a guide. A spiritual guide, like when you go to the shrine." She nodded. "Now is an important time to take the right path." Chiho almost jumped out of her chair.

"Yes it is!" She squealed and drew a sharp breath, looking intently at me. "Kumano Kodo," she said.

"Before you tell me about that, let's continue the reading. The Three of Wands, or Virtue, means you can lead, maybe a small group, and the King of Swords means correct thinking. Do not hesitate. Be clear." Chiho looked astounded. I almost laughed. "Have you done tarot before?" I asked.

☑ **Other**

"Once," she said. "But let me tell you about Kumano Kodo. It is a road."

"OK."

"Ancient road." She whipped out a pocket dictionary and consulted it. "Pilgrimage road. Here, Kumano area, is where the oldest gods of Japan are. The pilgrimage road became World Heritage this year."

"And your reading?" I asked, hoping she'd get to the point. "It is connected?" Chiho's face lit up.

"Yes, I am taking a group on Kumano Kodo." She smiled. "Spiritual path. People stopped. But now we begin. Sacred guide."

"That's great," I said. "You're on the right track."

"Because," she continued. "We are in the three-point-five dimensions." Here, I thought, was the charming Chiho eccentricity.

"Three point five," I echoed.

"Yes, because time is one-way." I didn't want to contradict her, though I believed time might be two-way. She straightened up. "Do tea ceremony tonight," she said. "Thank you for this reading."

"Of course."

Later, I wandered over and sat in another corner of the hall, where a woman in a kimono conducted a rite of tea drinking. She handed out dishes of Japanese sweets, then knelt, using a series of tools to make frothy tea. I reached out to receive my steaming bowl.

"Turn the bowl in a circle two times before drinking," she said. I looked up to see Rory passing by.

"Remember to take three-and-a-half sips," he said. I stared at him.

"Why that number?" I asked.

"I don't know," he laughed, walking on. I viewed coincidence, no matter how minor, as an arrow pointing the way. Maybe I would go on my own pilgrimage.

I had arrived in Japan during winter, and winter had arrived again. Our office manager Yusui asked me to sign on for another year. Apparently, a lot of students wanted me to continue.

☑ Other

"You are a popular teacher," he said. "Will you stay?"

"Thank you very much," I said. "I love it here, I just don't want to get stuck, if you know what I mean." If I stayed another year, I might stay yet another, and another. I wanted to prove I could be as successful in America as in Japan. Yusui understood.

"Will you meet next Friday at Zeh Coo?" he asked, referring to the Italian restaurant/sake bar next door.

"Absolutely," I answered and bowed. Though it was probably a matter of convenience, I felt honored that my goodbye party would be held there instead of the usual Japanese pub.

An email from my mom gave me an idea. She suggested that I "stop by New Jersey on the way back to California," even though Japan sat directly across the Pacific from California. If I kept going west, though, I could stop by New Jersey on my way to California, as well as fulfill my dream of going all the way around the world. I didn't know why I hadn't thought of it before. I told her my plan. Soon after, she sent me a package. To my surprise, I found inside a beautiful leather-covered journal, engraved on one side with a wavy sun over a tree-filled land, and on the other with a wandering shepherd who peered over the edge of the world at the cosmos. I couldn't remember the last time she had sent me a personal gift.

Yusui's father, who owned the school, made an unusual appearance at my farewell dinner. After some of the teachers gave me cards and gifts, he stood at the head of the long table and held up a book.

"I want you to have this," he said, passing a new copy of the English language version of *Autobiography of a Yogi* down the table to me. "I had a chance to meet the Dalai Lama once. He recommended it to me. I believe you should read it."

"Arigato gozaimasu," I replied in thanks, wondering how Yusui's father knew anything about me at all. At 5:30 the next morning, Jo accompanied me to the train station — a common gesture in Japan, but to me an incredible kindness. She pulled a ring off her finger and handed it to me.

☑ Other

"My parents gave me this when I went off to university," she said. The ring had two silver hands that clasped each other. She slid them apart to reveal a heart. "See," she said. "The hands hold the heart. It's for your journey." I hugged her in thanks. "We'll miss you," she said.

I fell asleep on the train until it reached the city of Kobe, where I boarded a Chinese-run passenger boat that would sail across the sea to Shanghai over the next two-and-a-half days. From the decks and windows of the small ship, I saw nothing but slate blue water and sky from horizon to horizon. The reading lounge at the top of the boat became the gathering place for passengers. I met a girl named Pepper, from England, who suggested we look for a hostel together, to make arriving in Shanghai easier for both of us. Once there, we parted ways.

Everywhere I went in China, people stared at me. After a year in Japan, the Chinese seemed really rude. Apparently, every third person needed to spit for some reason. Most conversations were shouted.

☑ Other

    Through a longstanding program called SERVAS, I stayed with people who volunteered to host travelers for free. Not only did that reduce costs, but made me feel welcome. The first hosts, a family in Guangzhou, were two optometrists. Their twelve-year-old daughter joined us at the dinner table on my first evening there. Upon discovering I had no plans to visit Beijing, she said,
    "A pity," in a beautiful British accent. At the end of the meal, her father insisted I pull out a contact lens so that he could show his family the difference from when it was right-side-out or inside-out.
    Every day I ventured around the city on foot and by taxi. Guangzhou roads bore no lane markings, creating dangerous rivers of traffic that people of all ages plodded through.
    One afternoon, I set out toward an art museum. I hailed a cab among the Dr. Seuss-like highways and city noise. My driver gunned the engine, then torpedoed into a sea of unorganized traffic. As he gained on the stopped cars ahead, the terrified face of a very young girl loomed in front of us. She towed an even smaller girl by the hand. Waiting until the last second, the driver yanked our course aside. The girl in front, now calm, continued to pull the other, dazed one behind her.
    After two hours at the museum I sat outside near a koi pond. A round, ponytailed man approached and sat too, speaking at length in Mandarin. I shrugged. He opened a large sketchbook.
    "Draw?" he asked. Thinking he might try to sell me a caricature of myself, I was about to protest when a teenager sat next to me. In halting English, he told me that the artist was his teacher, and that the others beginning to crowd around were his students, too. They invited me to their school. My host couple beamed when I told them I had plans with a group of Chinese people.
    The next day, I went to the concrete building where the students sat on tiny square plastic stools with their watercolor notebooks on their knees. Since the building had no heat, everyone drank hot tea, from plastic cups that were so thin, they were almost liquid themselves. Skilled drawings covered the walls. By the end of the next few days, I had spent so much time there that the students felt

☑ Other

like relatives. While we walked along the sidewalk after a group meal on my last day in Guangzhou, one linked arms with me as the girls do in China.

"You are my sister now," she said. My reply of *Awwww* needed no translation.

On a train, my "hard sleeper" bunk (slightly cheaper than a "soft sleeper"), was the topmost in a stack of three. I wondered if I should I put the pillow next to the door of the cabin, or next to the speaker over the cabin window, which spat out old-style Chinese music that would have been shrill had the system worked well. But the hair-trigger volume knob either turned the music off or to full capacity. The train crew had set it to "on," which meant the singers were shrieking. I had to wait until my cabin mates (which included a flashy, drinking couple and a bored young businessman) were all asleep before switching it off. Until then, whenever I reached over and turned the knob, one of them would get up and crank it back on.

The dining car boasted a full menu of delicious Chinese food and a great view of the grassy countryside. The twenty-seven-hour ride would bring me close to Vietnam. I read in my bunk to kill time. I warmed up to *Autobiography of a Yogi* from page one. Written in the 1930s, it had a timelessness that related easily to 2005. Reading the author's descriptions of extrasensory abilities, as commonly accepted in India as sports abilities were everywhere else, I began to believe that anything was possible. When I fell asleep in the bunk, my dreams took on a lucidity I'd never known. I could materialize anything, fly at will, and transport anywhere. A blaring announcement jerked me awake at 3:00 a.m. I scrambled to get my belongings as passengers streamed off the car.

In line at a station for a border-crossing train, I realized I'd left *Autobiography of a Yogi* under the pillow in the bunk. During the moment of sharp disappointment that followed, I heard,

"Hello," behind me in perfect English. I turned to see a smiling, easygoing Vietnamese man. "Pleased to meet you," he said. A grad

☑ Other

student on his way to visit his grandmother, he had grown up in Germany. He offered to cross over with me.

We took a four-hour train ride to a signless outpost, where a dirt path led to a tiny, unmarked building. No station stood there, only the continued road, so we had to walk again until we saw some cyclos (covered carts hitched to motorcycles). We bumped along with no shock absorbers through fog and dark green foliage until we reached a small station. My companion suggested we hire a car, which would be cheap and comfortable. After the driver treated us to soup (and beer with ice cubes) at a tiny restaurant, we parted in Hanoi. Neither that night, nor any night since, have I experienced the same level of lucidity in dreams as I had the night before on the train.

The Vietnamese acted much more relaxed than the Chinese. On corner after corner, people sat leisurely in tiny cafes. After what had passed for coffee in Japan and China, the old French-style brew in Vietnam tasted ambrosial. I chose a cafe full of pleasant chatter, and I grabbed a table that faced the street. The people passing by moved and gestured in the languid way I associated with the tropics. The heat unwound me, too. I sat back in my chair, unexpectedly realizing that I couldn't remember when I had stopped feeling afraid all the time.

I had imagined the cities of the world as having places that were neither for tourists nor local businesses, nor simply a park, a church, or a school. I thought there would be buildings where people just gathered to talk, paint, eat, or study, and all of it with no commercial plan involved. I had pictured old stone structures with interesting histories, or huge wooden houses with fireplaces, window seats, and music playing.

Finding nothing of the kind, I visited temples, shrines, pagodas, cathedrals, and churches from the gigantic to the tiniest, patched-together chapel. All were filled with a profoundly tranquil atmosphere.

☑ **Other**

In Saigon I stayed with Allyson from Australia. Her hosting method amounted to "hands off" and she spent no time with me. At the weekend, she told me where her friend's band would be playing. When I arrived, a table full of travelers and a few Vietnamese people waved me over. The band turned out to be novice and too loud for conversation, so we went to a cavernous bar that had a soccer game playing on several screens.

A skinny, rough-edged guy from Southern California with tattoos and a shaved head told me that he had "come back" after dying from a stab wound, and now just wanted to help people. He had started a basketball program for poor children. A young blond woman from Denmark introduced herself and said she was helping create a system to rescue young girls abducted into the sex trade.

"That's impressive, both of you," I told them. "I'm just following a dream to circle the globe."

"Most people don't even do that," said the Californian. At another bar, we sat at small tables near windows open wide to the warm night. Children approached, selling lighters, postcards and books to the tourists. The kids would stand in front of the tables and say, "Buy this, yeah?" If anyone refused, they would ask, "Why?" in the most jaded voices I'd ever heard from children. I bought a copy of *The Killing Fields* from a kid of five or six.

At the end of the week, I prepared to travel through Cambodia to Thailand. Allyson wasn't home to say goodbye to, so I left bunches of lychee fruit and a note of thanks.

I boarded a huge bus. The driver got on a highway and blasted the horn every few minutes, for hours. As soon as we crossed from Vietnam into Cambodia, verdant foliage and moist air became dusty, brown and dry. As the bus stopped to wait its turn to board a ferry, women and children rushed aboard. Some were selling small, roasted birds and grilled frogs that they carried in huge piles on trays on their heads. Some hawked cans of warm soda. Those outside the bus pressed against the windows and held up dirty, naked babies while begging. They were far poorer than the beggars and vendors in Vietnam.

☑ Other

I boarded another, sleeker bus toward Thailand. Leaning back in the seat, I noticed an English-language Cambodian newspaper someone had left. The headline of a one-paragraph story read: *Men Hack Friend to Death With Cleavers*, the operative word in my estimation being "friend."

The bus rolled into lush, tropical Thailand. In Bangkok, I stayed at Big John's Pies Guesthouse. An Australian, Big John prided himself on his savory meat pies. I far preferred the street food in Thailand, which was easily twice as delicious than the best Thai food I'd ever eaten. Big John hosted happy hour nightly, prompting guests to gather on his front patio. I met two Chinese-Canadian sisters on vacation. The older sister told me she worked in Manhattan at a sandwich shop.

"I'll be stopping on the East Coast on my way back to California," I told her. "Let's exchange email addresses."

"Send me photos of the rest of your trip," she said.

We forgot to exchange the addresses when I left Bangkok a week later.

On Koh Samui island, days and evenings blended — sky and water, beach and flowering trees. Guests at Morning Glory Bungalows spent most of the day swimming and lazing. One guest mentioned that the shore across the bay hosted a rave scene, with psychotropic enhancements and driving beats, which I found unnecessary to visit in light of soft white sand, blazing crimson sunsets and tropical bliss. Thursdays at Morning Glory were barbeque nights, featuring live musical accompaniment. As we guests dined on curried sausages and grilled chicken, a group of skinny Filipino teen boys put their all into performing ACDC covers. The singer, wearing a terrycloth wristband and platform boots, pumped his fist and yelled,

"*Tee* enn *tee*!" with no trace of parody. Another band, which had two women singers, played reggae and finished with a song I knew called *The Rivers of Babylon*. Sitting close to the tiny stage, I sang along. When they finished, one of the singers looked at me.

"You want to sing with us? Next week is fine."

☑ Other

"I might, thanks," I said. A week to practice and enjoy my bungalow on the waterfront, for three dollars a night, posed no problem. On the following Thursday, I found out, the local band would be playing at a lounge on the other side of the island. I made my way there.

The drummer, a short skinny man with long black hair and luminous eyes, told me I could sing one song before they started. I chose a Radiohead tune, and stood on the stage in front of the microphone. If I hadn't gone to karaoke a couple times a week in Japan, I would never have found the courage. Looking out over the audience while the band began the opening bars, I saw vacationers sipping tropical drinks and waiting expectantly. I took a deep breath and went for it. At the end of the song, a man leaned over to the woman next to him.

"Nice voice," he said, which kept me from thinking I'd bombed.

"Thank you. Enjoy your evening everyone," I said and jumped down. I stayed for a few songs, and made it back to Morning Glory in time for the last half of Thursday barbeque.

In a way, singing for an audience was no big deal. People did it all the time. But as the girl who, for years, could not easily raise her eyes to meet anyone else's, standing up straight and keeping a level head while expressing myself vocally signaled a whole new tier of living.

My image of Egypt was from pre-Islamic times — well before the seventh-century Arab invasion, hookah smoking, Turkish coffee and the diminutive yet near-worshipful respect of covered-up women. Many Egyptian women had men delicately holding onto their arms and staring almost helplessly at them. Such ladies smiled with the beauteousness of the adored. Sometimes I'd see women whose eyes were their only visible part. Intense and fiery, those eyes gave truth to the saying about "windows to the soul."

In Cairo, men wearing baggy white uniforms and black berets stood along certain stretches of the sidewalk. They had rifles slung over their shoulders. Several broke their serious stance to smile and

☑ Other

nod as I passed. That would have been strange if I hadn't been approached by so many Egyptian men already. Wherever the lone Western female ventured, an Egyptian male followed. At every turn, a man fell in step with me. *"Hey. Hey, woman. I like your eyes/hair/shoes. Welcome to Egypt."* Some tried to lead me into their shops, insisting we were friends and lamenting the inevitability that their daughters wouldn't marry unless I accepted a cup of coffee.

After I checked into The Claridge, the all-male staff reacted as if a wild animal had gotten loose in the hotel. I must have been the only female guest not part of a group. At the service desk, on the stairwell, and in the lobby, every employee trained his eyes on my every move. I glared at a few before remembering my manners. Men, I concluded, did not own exclusive rights to roaming solo without hassle. I kept handy a can of pepper spray I'd packed.

One hot afternoon, strolling along the crowded dusty beige street lined with beige buildings, I heard a lady's voice yelling. She came into view — a middle-aged woman wearing a scarf on her head, a long skirt, and nothing in between. Bare-breasted on the streets of Cairo, she kept up an angry tirade while a patient (but weary) man held a shirt up before her as if to suggest that she might want to put it on. Not one of the passing locals stared. I wished I could understand her speech as I left that mystery behind and checked out of my room.

Before flying to Greece, I visited the Great Pyramids by horseback. This was the Egypt I had longed for. Sahara winds tossed my hair about my shoulders as the horse dashed over the sand. I was thrilled to be riding again, especially toward the ancient monuments.

Athens also proved enchanting, as I sauntered along golden-lit hillsides that held mossy ruins and tiny, new spring blossoms. All the humidity of Asia and bone dryness of Egypt got replaced by the clear, unencumbered scent of a Mediterranean spring.

At a hostel, I met a trio of American girls on vacation. Joining them for jewelry shopping and dinner, as they chatted about cold swims and hot Greek men, I felt grateful that my newfound social comfort applied with American women.

I ferried to Italy. Once there, I boarded a train to Rome. In one enormous corner of St. Peter's Basilica stood a chapel with a vaulted ceiling and an arrangement of muscular statues high on the wall above a congregation. Only those willing to attend full mass were permitted to enter the pew area. I went in, not for Catholic reasons but because I had never heard mass in Italy (or anywhere since my grandmother had taken Chris and me as children).

Before the service began, I noticed two little girls, both about five years old, sitting with their mothers — one in the row before me, and one behind. The one in front looked like she and her mom might be from India. They waited for the service, sometimes leaning toward each other to speak in low tones. The girl behind me hummed, her shrill voice off-key. She repeatedly stood up and sat back down. At one point, she started shouting the Lord's prayer in an American accent. When she got to *thy will be done* she said,

"I will be done."

"Those men over there are going to come *get* you if you don't behave," her mom scolded. "So stop it."

"Well. I'm gonna stop so I can get ice cream. OK?" The choir, warming up, shut out her voice at last.

The only words that I understood of the priest's sermon were these few, in Latin: "I am the way and the truth and the life ..."

I walked hours and miles along the hilly roads of Rome that were crowded with intricate statuary, then dropped into my bed at the well-organized, elegant, and mis-named Fawlty Towers hostel. After two nights of dining with other travelers on its rooftop garden terrace, I woke to a heavily clanging bell. As I passed the front desk on the way to the shower, the clerk mentioned I would have to vacate my room due to full bookings. I contacted the local SERVAS volunteers; one promised he would find a host. He invited me to a group dinner for guests and Italians alike. As promised, at the end

☑ Other

of the evening the SERVAS volunteer dropped me at the door of a new host he assured me would be quality.

Maurizio looked like a younger version of my Grandpa, with the same heavy eyebrows and long nose. Cheerful even at 2:00 a.m., he pointed out the guest bedroom and the bathroom, and wished me a restful night. In the morning he left pastries and hot coffee for me before leaving for work. I loved his top-floor apartment with its huge terra cotta patio. I spent most of the day writing in my journal. Maurizio returned with an extra key and an invite to dinner. I agreed, if he would let me pay for it. He refused, so I offered to take him to coffee afterwards.

Maurizio took his host duties seriously. After dinner he brought me on a pleasant walk through an old neighborhood of passageways and courtyards to a cozy cafe for espresso and chocolate. He refused to let me pay. He politely backed off for the next couple of days, and I spent most of my time taking pictures of the archaic city.

Realizing I had reached farther than the halfway point of my trip, I pulled out a journal and wrote every Japanese phrase and word I knew, with English translations. On my last evening in Rome, Maurizio showed me around by motorcycle. I'd ridden on the back of a lot of motorbikes in Vietnam, but none like his.

I had just returned from a full day, bringing him a large bouquet of wildflowers in thanks for his hospitality. He handed me a blue and black Italian motorcycle jacket that looked bullet-proof. He said he had a surprise. Outside, he passed me a helmet and got on his bike. As I moved to sit down behind him he said,

"You will hold me, and I will not go too fast, but if you get scared, you knock me like this." He tapped his helmet. "Bam, bam, bam."

"Sure," I said, putting mine on. "But I won't be scared." Sitting behind him, I held the sides of his jacket, reluctant to wrap my arms around a stranger. As we gained speed, he slowly pulled my left hand around his waist. Good thing he did, because at the rate we accelerated, I would have flown off the back of the motorcycle.

☑ Other

Rome rushed by as darkness fell, and I found myself grinning nonstop, as if I were on a good roller coaster. Maurizio stopped the bike at the end of a street overlooking the city. In the distance, St. Peter's dome glowed against the cerulean blue sky.

"I will drive back the way we came," he said. "You should turn and watch the cathedral." As the motorcycle retreated, the dome (decked out in jewelry made of light) appeared to grow larger, as if it were gaining on us.

"An illusion," Maurizio said over his shoulder. "Because the road we are on narrows."

"You're the best host of my trip," I shouted over the breeze. "And Rome is amazing."

After making a brief stop to taste wine and stroll along the Mediterranean in the tiny seaside village of Cinque Terra, I boarded a train for France. It had been a few years since I'd seen Paris, but the city looked just as lustrous. Savannah's sister Melissa surprised me with an email announcing her coinciding arrival. We met at a little den of a bar called *Folie En Tete* (Crazy in the Head). In the midst of a boisterous conversation about globetrotting, I spilled my beer all over my purse, and onto the lap of a guy at the table next to ours.

He was tall, with languid brown eyes and sexy stubble. Without a trace of annoyance, he gazed down at me. I was puzzled that he wasn't looking at Melissa. In America, most men of his height favored tall women.

"'Allo," he said.

"Hi," I replied, extending my hand. "I'm Cindy."

"Karim," he smiled, offering a warm handshake. His friend, Yousef, kindly translated pleasantries for us. By that time, Melissa and I were ready to leave. I got Karim's number, but hesitated later that week to call because he spoke almost no English.

At Melissa's are-you-nuts urging, I called him. I had to use the remnants of my high school French. We managed to set up a meeting place and time. Karim arrived with Yousef, and the three of us went dancing.

☑ Other

A few days later, Melissa went on to England. I met up with the guys a few more times before boarding a bus for my beloved Amsterdam. I promised Karim, who had stolen kisses when Yousef was out of sight, that I would return sometime.

In Amsterdam, Tim didn't live in a squat anymore. He shared an apartment with an artist, and he worked nights at a hotel. He enthusiastically attended two dance classes per week. With his long hair cut off, he looked radiant. His only complaint was that he felt unsure that he would ever find the right woman.
"I'm sure you will," I said. "Just look at you." He laughed, saying he'd see.
Over the next few days, I visited my favorite "coffee shops" and museums, savoring every moment in Amsterdam.
Two flights would bring me around the world. First stop: New Jersey, to visit my mom as she had requested. Impressed that I had taken myself all the way around the globe, she arranged a welcome back breakfast at a nice Jersey diner. She invited ten relatives. I finally received firsthand the side of my mother's personality most people already knew — cordial, smiling, and thoughtful. The breakfast turned out lively, with cousins passing around digital photos of their kids while aunts and uncles asked about the trip. I cherished my extended family, even if I seldom saw them.

A fellow blogger I had traded comments with (but had never met) lived in New York City. He invited me to dinner, which wasn't a date — he preferred men. I said yes.
I headed to the city early. Sitting outside at a cafe, I remembered the two sisters I'd met in Bangkok. I only knew that one worked at a sandwich shop in Manhattan. Laughing, I left money on the table and then crossed town to the Korean restaurant I'd been invited to by the sweet but jaded intellectual from the Philippines. We compared notes on the exhibits at the Museum of Modern Art. As my water got refilled, I looked up and felt shocked to realize that the

person pouring it was the older of the two sisters I'd met in Thailand.

"I know you," I said.

"Oh my God, no way."

I jumped up and hugged her around the water pitcher.

"I still work at the sandwich place," she said. "This is my second job. But it's my last day here."

"Even more incredible." My dinner companion, I noticed when I glanced over at him, actually had a tear in his eye. Again, I saw coincidence as a sign that everything was lining up right.

That night, just to make sure, I mantra'd myself to sleep on Mom's couch:

I am now confident, welcomed, accepted, successful . . . completely healed . . . thriving . . . in a sound, healthy love relationship. The list grew long and I drifted off.

On my last day in Nutley, my mother said something totally unlike anything she had ever said to me.

"It's been lovely having you here, Cindy."

"Thanks," I said, surprised and a little unsettled. Warmth from her would take getting used to.

Her boyfriend arranged for a chauffeur friend to drive me to the airport. The man was a talker.

"My friend's watcha callit, parrots?" he said as he navigated toward Newark. "Just loved singing to all kinds of music, got real happy, but hated when he put on a Yankees game. Wouldn't leave him alone then. The wife used to make sweet potato pie, cause the birds loved it, with all seeds and real gourmet like. But after eating one of 'em, one of the birds dropped right to the cage floor. Even though my buddy rushed to open a window, all the birds died. His wife had bought some new ceramic baking dishes, and the gas from the heated dish, you know, odorless and harmless to people, was deadly to those birds. What a shame." Without waiting for a response, he charged on with another story, and another, all the way to the airport.

☑ Other

Returning to California involved a new style of cheap flying: no meals, and several stopovers. Passengers were now referred to as "customers."

Though I had refused the offer of a beer from the sassy, flamboyant flight attendant, he showed up with one anyway and set it on my tray.

"Did you say *yes*?" He gestured over his shoulder to another passenger, adding, "*He* changed *his* mind." Sudden turbulence prompted,

"Shaken, not stirred," from the girl behind me, who was getting tipsy with her boyfriend. I nodded.

I kept to the plan of moving to San Francisco. Melissa offered me a temporary stay at her tiny "studio" while I looked for a job. She lived in a semi-permanently foggy area of the city, in a small dim room sectioned off with plasterboard from the main part of a house that was owned by an unfriendly woman. The bathroom was so tiny, the toilet sat *inside* the shower cubicle, but at least it was a place to stay. Melissa worked bartender hours, and I soon discovered that she would flick the overhead light on at 3:00 a.m. when she got home.

"There's no other light and I have to see," she whispered the first time it woke me. I tried putting my jacket over my eyes, but it fell off. On the third or fourth night she came home and put on a movie at regular volume, a few feet from my head. When I asked her to turn it down, she told me this was *her* time. I found Traveling Melissa much more relaxed than Home Melissa. I was getting up at 7:00 each morning to go job hunting. Lack of sleep made the employment gauntlet even testier.

My spirits drooped after several interviews at English-as-a-Second-Language schools without any job offers. Melissa asked with increasing annoyance when I'd be moving out. Scrambling for work so that I could afford a place of my own, I took an ESL teaching job in Menlo Park, a 45-minute train ride away. The position was only

☑ **Other**

available for a couple months, but it paid enough for the room I found to sublet from a young Japanese woman.

I made an appointment for a court date in Santa Cruz to reinstate a payment plan for the fines. Getting to Santa Cruz without a car involved three hours on public transportation, twice what driving would have taken. The judge informed me that my case was long neglected. She didn't care for explanations of legal postponement, and I got roped into paying a "failure to appear" penalty of $330 dollars. She threw another court date into the mix, this time to confirm the payment plan. A week later I made the long round trip all over again.

I noticed that the really poor people visiting court who tried to dress properly had pitiful results: gaudy sweatshirts tucked into too-short polyester pants exposing dirty socks, for example. Each one of their faces bore a record of pain. Again I felt thankful that I had gotten the job in Japan.

Before a judge once again, this time a different woman, I brought a letter I had written in my defense. She read it over.

"OK. You have sixty days to begin payments. Furthermore, why don't we reinstate your license? I see no reason to continue the hold."

I wanted to hug her. At the Department of Motor Vehicles though, when I went to apply for a replacement license, the clerk shook her head.

"You can't just lift this hold, no matter what a judge told you." She clacked away at her keyboard and peered at a screen. "You have to pay the $1,500 and go to a year-and-a-half of classes."

It seemed a hard-earned degree had been torn from my hand. I had been hoping to revamp my life with no oppressive ray of misfortune to dread — far easier thought than done. In America I was still a second-class citizen. The wages for ESL teachers in California were less than half of what they had been in Japan — with no health insurance, of course.

On my days off, I explored the city. In San Francisco, greeting a stranger amounted to idiotic behavior. I really missed the friendly

☑ Other

people I'd met all over the world. Feeling lonely, I hung out a couple times with Raita, a student from work, but he soon returned to Japan. Dejected, I noticed absurd details in mundane places:

CHECK DRYER FOR CHILDREN, PETS, AND FOREIGN OBJECTS BEFORE LOADING AND OPERATING.

Are Americans that dumb? There has to be something I liked about this country. I stepped outside to wait while my clothes dried. Even in the prosperous Cow Hollow neighborhood, the owner of Bubbles Laundry hadn't bothered to clean the pigeon droppings off the awning. *This is a culture of crushed spirits,* I thought. Walking through busy Chinatown later, I noticed a little white-haired man standing on a wooden box on a street corner. He kept repeating,

"Everybody happy. Everybody love. Your mother and father happy. Everybody nice." The sidewalks streamed with people, but no one looked at him. A dirty bus crawled by in heavy traffic. I ate a greasy lunch of cheap dim sum. My old demons were waiting for me at home: isolation, certainty of doom, and fear, sliming its way from my stomach through my intestines. I called Mike.

"Go back to Paris," he said. "You can stay at our spare apartment for a couple months, get your groove back, and start fresh from there." Mike had married the Parisian hottie. She brought their newborn son to San Francisco, where Mike had found a nice two-bedroom. He lived less than three miles from me, but I almost never saw him. When he wasn't working a fourteen-hour shift, he was with his family. He suggested I pay half the rent at their Paris flat for a couple months, saving them money while getting the apartment for almost nothing.

I remembered telling Karim I'd visit again. I weighed my options: paying more than half the court fines at once but staying depressed, or enjoying the company of Karim and his friend Yousef. No contest.

☑ Other

"When I get back, I'm going do this right," I said aloud in my room. (I'd moved up one floor from the sublet, into the larger room with the bamboo shades.)

Oblong orbs of light ran slowly down a thick glass pitcher: reflections of the traffic below. Church bells clanged nearby. From all the places I'd been, I hoped to forge a real life from the scraps, from reverberations of mountainside temples, from echoes and scattered drops of rain. I felt excited to fly to Paris.

I figured Mike's wife would have packed up most of her belongings when she moved to America. They planned to use the Parisian flat about once a year, twice at most. Even so, I found her kitchen cupboards laden with edibles and cookery, clothing still hanging on a drying rack, several live houseplants, and bathroom shelves crammed with towels, cosmetics and jewelry. This was not the apartment of a nuptially blissful woman, but of someone planning to return.

Whether I was roaming with a camera along the skull-lined catacombs under the city, or relaxing indoors with wine and cheese, all my depression lifted. I saw Karim and Yousef a few times a week. Karim was a hardworking plumber who liked to watch soccer, cook, go dancing and drink beer. Yousef liked intellectual conversation, cooking, dancing and drinking beer. We all had the last three in common. They proudly told me that French men, not women, were known for their chef skills, prompting a cook-off.

I loved their casual putting of arms around shoulders, pats on backs for conversational emphasis, and the French hello and goodbye kisses on the cheek. I savored nights spent at Karim's, which were alternately cozy and frisky. I relished the warmth of falling asleep next to him.

They wanted me to stay for Christmas. Seeing the merry winter streets of Paris, I longed to spend the holidays there, but had to be realistic about money. To stave off the dread of returning to America, I reasoned that if I really tried, I could maintain zero division between being on the trip and being back from the trip. As

☑ Other

much as I wanted that to be true, I knew it wasn't. In a journal I wrote *I've become really good at keeping it all together, but now I have to let that go.* And as a warning to myself: *Don't put yourself in any position you don't feel really good about getting into.*

Back in San Francisco, I left the small pub downstairs and trudged up to my room, needing a shower and a good sleep. In one day I had gone from feeling attractive, interesting and fun to boring, ugly and alone.

An acquaintance I knew from Santa Cruz reggae shows, Mignonne, called and asked if I would come down and help construct a sweat lodge. (She remembered my interest in Native American culture.) We cut down willow trees along the San Lorenzo River, afterward removing the branches and tying the trunks together to form a low room we had to crawl to enter. We cast blankets over it, creating a sauna when water got poured over red-hot rocks. The extreme heat relaxed our muscles while Mignonne and her friends sang traditional songs. The pitch black hid everything, even inches from my eyes. I let the warmth and darkness hold me, believing that the time in the lodge would help me take on my shadow side, once and for all.

☑ Other

8.

Satori

I sought courage on the rooftop of my building. *Do not run away. You can do this.* Poverty threatened, even with minimal spending in effect — no internet or cable, just survival and a cheap cell phone. Now and then, I tapped a few beats on a tall antique conga drum that Mike had given me. A vague plan percolated in the back of my mind: to write a guide for the reluctant traveler. I had met dozens who said they would venture but for one snag, whether waiting for a child to be out of school, or that they were "too old," didn't want to go alone or couldn't afford it. I would call it *Just Go*.

One evening as I left the pub, Riley, my landlady's son, was about to go into the building adjacent. His thick black hair stopped just above the collar of a leather racing jacket. I hadn't seen him since the day I had locked myself out of my room. Looking at me over his shoulder, he greeted me with a jut of his chin. I nodded once.

"What're you up to?" I asked.

"Just getting in," he said. His face brightened. "Come up for a beer." I didn't want more beer, yet I followed Riley up a dark stairwell. At the top we crossed a landing edged with closed doors, climbed another flight and went into a dimly lit room with red and purple walls. I sat on a couch while Riley perched at the edge of a wooden chair, facing opposite. I don't recall much of our conversation, only that he seemed more interested in learning about me than in talking about himself. He gestured toward the soundboard across the room when I asked what he did.

"Trying to make music. Hip hop. I'm pretty good at it." I noticed how attractive he looked, every feature of his angled face well-formed.

"Well, I'm getting really tired so I'm gonna go home," I said.

☑ Other

"Hey, come through anytime. We should hang out," he said.

"Sure." I walked toward the stairs.

"Here." He handed me a slip of paper with his number on it.

It had been a couple weeks since I'd hung out with anyone. The attention from Riley soothed me in a *down so long, looks like up* way. The next morning I awoke somewhat refreshed, and applied at a temp agency. The administrator assigned to match me with positions could not have been kinder. As soon as one assignment ended, he recommended me for another. The wages covered my low rent, court payments, and a few groceries. Meanwhile, I put together a few notes for my travel guide.

"See," said Mike on the phone. "That last trip planted the seed for a great idea."

"Do you actually think it's great or just trying to encourage me?" I asked.

"Aren't those the same?" He laughed. "Yes, Cin, I like your guide idea."

"Thanks," I said. Another call was beeping in. "Talk to you soon Mike ... Hello?"

"Hey, Cindy," said Melissa. "Do you wanna celebrate my birthday at Top of the Mark? I'm inviting a few friends."

"Sure," I said. I could afford one cocktail and a card for Melissa. I texted Riley to ask if he wanted to go. He said he'd meet me there after he ate dinner.

In the lounge on the uppermost floor of Top of the Mark, a hotel on a hill, I crossed a plush carpet and made my way to a table where Melissa sat with five girl friends near a window with an impressive view of the city. Riley soon arrived, in full suit and tie, carrying a bouquet of yellow daisies and a mylar birthday balloon.

"Thank you," Melissa said, surprised. Riley handed both to her and then sat in the chair next to me. He whispered,

"The flowers were actually for you."

"She looks so happy. No worries."

We went to another bar. While we danced to underground hip hop, Riley twirled his forearm and shouted,

☑ Other

"*Yeeeeeah daaawwwwg!* That's how we *do it* in the four-one-*five* yo." Two of Melissa's friends snickered. I wanted to defend him. I had developed a motto that, I believed, revealed my nonjudgmental acceptance of people: *You have to be* really *weird for me to think you're weird.*

"Hey," I said in Riley's ear. "Wanna come by sometime this week and watch a movie?" He nodded with enthusiasm.

A few nights later, we sat on my carpet with our backs against the bed. This time Riley wore a short-sleeved cotton shirt and jeans. It was the fifth or sixth style I'd seen on him.

"Are you from here originally?" I asked.

"Born and raised," he said, a phrase I had never liked. "Been living next door since I was a baby. My dad was military, German-American and tough. He passed away about ten years ago."

"I'm sorry," I told him. "My dad died, too." Riley crossed himself and kissed his fist.

"He met my mom in Japan and brought her back," he said. "She was a charming lady at the time. I'm their only. She had some high expectations for me, back when I was motorcycle racing. I'll show you pictures and you'll see the look on her face — you won't recognize her."

"Do you visit Japan?" I asked.

"Not since I was a kid. I don't really speak the language, just a scosh."

I spoke much more Japanese than Riley. He didn't follow any old-world "code of valor," as I'd imagined my ideal Japanese-American boyfriend would. Nor did he enjoy drinking sake, cooking, watching full-length movies, traveling, reading books, going to museums, hiking or listening to anything but hip hop and rap. Living with his mother, he had everything provided for him. He spent most of his time practicing lyrics or redecorating his room. But he had brought me a rose, poured beer for me, kept himself impeccably groomed — and happened to be the only person I had met in San Francisco.

Before long he made his moves. The rejection from Jeremy less than a year before had knocked my self confidence into the gutter. Riley's touch was exhilarating, and once we shed our clothes, my body reached an intense level of pleasure hitherto unknown. But I closed my eyes when I noticed that he wore a nervous expression that betrayed his sensuous moans. It was creepy, and I felt embarrassed to be as turned on as I was.

I drifted off to sleep almost immediately. Sometime in the night, he gently woke me and said that he needed to be in his own bed. I nodded and dozed off again.

I woke up with my head and feelings divided. My body seemed to like Riley more than I did. Strange — usually it took a few tries to warm up to someone physically even when otherwise I felt interested. This time, I could see our conversations falling flat. I thrived on lively discussion while Riley veered into describing the minutia of the previous hour. He would recount the complete dialog of a phone call or a blow-by-blow description of his thoughts leading up to his choice of lyrics. He would ask about my plans for the day, only to interrupt my answer. ("Maybe I should play reggae. Nah, better stick to freestyle.") He would gaze at the ceiling for a moment as if I were not in the room. He often labeled anything I said "real talk" without adding any response. But as far as physical touch — even hugging him ranked high on the pleasure scale — I'd known nothing like him.

His mother Miyako wanted to meet me more formally. She invited me over. When I arrived at their patio door, she jerked it open.

Behind her, Riley stood in profile with one foot on a lawn chair, elbow on his knee, fist under his chin. He didn't greet me. Again he had dressed in a suit and tie. I almost joked at the scene. *What is this, sixteenth-century Japan?*

"So," Miyako said sternly. "You like my son, and he is very happy to meet you."

"Sure," I said. "And I'm glad to meet you too. Where in Japan are you from?"

"That was long time ago. Riley doesn't know Japan, now. We haven't met anyone like you." I glanced at Riley, wondering why he hadn't come to the rescue of the conversation. He still faced sideways, cutting an absurd (but beautiful) silhouette as daylight faded. *They're really doing this?* He looked like a maiden on an auction block.

"I'm getting pretty old," Miyako continued. "Running the building is a lot of work. Riley help me very well but he could use more. You could have free rent if you want to help him take care of the building."

"Oh, you need help? I can help. Work exchange for room and board would actually help me," I said. "Thanks for offering." How much work could it be?

"Not that room," Miyako said. After a pause I replied,

"Share his rooms? Nooooooo. I'm not moving in with him." *She's crazy. And by proxy, so is he.* "I'll just keep paying rent. I'm sure Riley can figure something out." He still hadn't so much as looked over. "Ah, actually, I've gotta go," I said. "Have a good night, both of you."

I turned, barely glimpsing a look of rage forming on Miyako's face. I hurried back through the door. Looking down the hall towards the ground-floor room I had first stayed in, I realized that before her tenant sublet to me, Miyako had rented available rooms only to young, single Japanese women.

Back in my room I made tea, put on Miles Davis and breathed deeply, trying to clear my mind of Miyako and her pet son, Riley.

Redoubling focus on the travel guide, I took advantage of the free internet at a nearby cafe. Going there on mornings I didn't work, I managed to distance myself from Riley. I felt weird about the intense physical pleasure I'd experienced. After sending a text I didn't respond to, he knocked on my door one afternoon.

"My mom feels really stupid," he said sheepishly. "The way she does things is obviously old school. She wants to apologize. She's making dinner tonight for both of us, if you'd like to come over." I didn't want to, but it seemed rude to refuse.

What are you doing, Cindy? I shut the door, annoyed with myself. My actions had split off even more from my thoughts. Riley's attractiveness had diminished by half since I'd met with his mother, yet I had just agreed to see him again in her company. Going to dinner at Miyako's seemed like an obligation made to a family member. I lay in bed reading until dinner.

☑ Other

Just past five o'clock, Miyako greeted me with a huge smile and a martini. She gestured toward a pleasant-enough looking man in a recliner.

"This is my boyfriend Bob," she said. He wore glasses and had a receding hairline. Raising his drink, he smiled like a kindly uncle.

"Hey, good to meet you, Cindy," he said.

"You too," I said. A football game flickered on a large old television, and hors d'oeuvres sat in rows on trays on the coffee table. Riley gestured to a place on the couch. He put together a small plate and handed it to me.

"If you're not into the game," he said, "it's all good. I don't watch a lot of sports either." He gave me a comically knowing glance. In between offering a nod or word in response to sports commentary from Bob, Riley said,

"There's a show I'd like to take you to, Cin. A cat called Equipto. They're having guest singer Mike Marshall, longtime Bay Area dude. *Really* rocks the crowd."

"I'm definitely down for live music," I said.

"It'll be a week or two. They haven't said where yet." Miyako brought out cups of green tea and a second round of cocktails. She stood watching me.

"Hmm, interesting," I said nervously under her unwavering stare. "You serve the tea with the leaves in the cup." Riley got up and took Miyako's arm, leading her back to the kitchen. I caught the word "tea" and their hushed, argumentative voices. I turned to Bob, who shrugged.

"He just wants to make sure his mom doesn't embarrass him again," he said. The moment stretched out and Riley still hadn't come back.

"Do you live in the city?" I asked. After a year of teaching conversation, I could kill an hour if necessary with small-talk topics.

"East Bay," Bob answered. "Miyako and I own a house there. But she's mostly here. Not ready to retire and let Riley run things."

"The situation is kind of strange," I said. Bob nodded.

"Believe me, I know. I'm a therapist. The father was abusive to both of them, and Miyako babies the hell out of Riley. He hasn't really grown up, but he can be a good guy. I've known him for years."

☑ **Other**

In an era where thirty was supposedly the new twenty, few people my age were considered grown-up. I decided to give Riley the benefit of the doubt, though we were polar opposites in that he had never left home while I'd been living on my own since sixteen.

He and Miyako came back from the kitchen, carrying plates of food. During dinner, everyone became subdued, eyes on the screen. I decided to go home as soon as I had eaten. Before I left, Riley whispered,

"Come back later."

While doing yoga in my room, I had the bewildering sensation that the walls around me stood guard. It seemed I had to deal with unfinished business of some sort before life could continue on its regular route.

Miyako had gone to bed by the time I returned. I climbed the stairs to Riley's rooms. He called softly from behind a partially closed door. Pushing it open, I saw him posing in a pair of black thigh-high leggings and nothing else.

In one of those rare moments of delayed surprise, I stared. It so happened that I found opaque thigh-high leggings on a man to be sexy. Riley took my silence as acceptance, and began posturing like a stripper. I froze, unsure if I was amused or horrified or what. His skin looked toned and silky smooth, all his muscles well-defined. If he had decided to flirt with me, it might have been enticing. Instead he put on a show, apparently heading for a full "happy ending" that didn't include me. I did not know what to say.

"Nobody's vanilla anymore," he said, wiping his abdomen with a tissue. "I just wanted to show you that. San Francisco girls always want a step above."

"Well," I began. "I like the attire, but the sexiness involving only you was unexpected."

"And you're not a San Francisco girl," he said. "But I like that about you."

"Uh . . . thanks."

"Let's watch this Dave Chappelle Block Party special," he suggested, picking up a DVD. He put on sweatpants. I didn't know what most San Franciscans were like, but Riley was unlike anyone I'd met.

☑ Other

I needed some semblance of a social life, so I invited him and Melissa to dinner in my room. I made roasted chicken, Melissa brought wine, and Riley showed up with candles and garlic bread. We relaxed over pleasantly forgettable conversation. Riley went home before Melissa.

"I can see why you might like him," she said. "At first I thought he was a little off, but tonight I noticed this other side. He's sweet." With that, she sleepily said goodnight.

A lull in temp work reduced my pocket money to almost nothing.

"I can't go to the Equipto show," I said to Riley on the phone.

"Oh, I can get us in for free. Equipto plays gigs with my buddy Andre a lot, so I get the hook up."

The show took place at a basic venue called Studio Z. I liked hip-hop, but had never been a fan of thuggy, bling-centric rap. I didn't know what to expect. Equipto had a polished, melodic style with heartfelt lyrics. Not bad. I started dancing along with the devoted crowd. Riley picked me up and twirled me. When he set me down he asked,

"So you like it?"

"Yeah!"

The voice of guest singer Mike Marshall struck up, galvanizing the show into something beautiful. At the end of the last song the house lights rose, and the crowd exited the venue. Figuring that Riley might have gone to the restroom, I headed to the universally known spot for post-show reconvening: out front. Two young guys were throwing down street rap with intelligent, socially aware lyrics. I nodded in appreciation.

"See?" one said. "You don't have to go to a club for good rap. We're the real underground right here." I read an incoming text from Riley.

Where are you?

Out front, I replied.

I scanned the sidewalk, but didn't see him. The crowd thinned out, and I spotted his BMW down the block. The headlights glimmered through a thick, falling mist. I waved, but Riley just stood next to his car

☑ Other

and looked angry. As soon as I started walking toward him, he jumped behind the wheel. He revved the engine and burned rubber in a fishtailing u-turn as he drove away. Someone in the crowd laughed. Having no money on me, and no umbrella as it began to rain in earnest, I felt dumb. I started walking home.

On the way, I saw an old, thin man sitting in a cardboard box, combing his gray hair in the reflection of a shop window that displayed a new bedroom set under stage lights. A few blocks later a car pulled up alongside me. The driver, a young pretty brunette, asked if I'd like to go to Power Exchange — a BDSM club that was open after hours. She and the two guys in her car wanted to know if I'd join them because that night was half off for double couples.

"No, thanks," I said, plodding onward through the rain. Around four, more than an hour after I'd left the club, I neared Union Street. Fog horns bellowed from the bay.

Instead of shrugging off the bad night and bidding *Good riddance* to Riley, I got overwhelmed by a sense of abandonment. As I slept, anger wrapped itself around my vulnerability like a snake. By morning, I had decided that Riley needed to apologize for leaving me in the rain at 2:30 a.m. I called his number. Miyako answered.

"You can come over and see him," she said.

Both the patio and main doors were wide open. I headed upstairs, slowing down when I saw debris scattered on the carpeted steps: coins next to a five-dollar-bill, a belt alongside a comb. On the landing, an ironing board lay askew. Discarded pieces of clothing made a trail to Riley's bedroom. I instantly saw the house of my early childhood after one of my father's rages.

The door stood ajar. With the same morbid fascination I had once given scenes of true crime, I entered to find Riley naked and passed out, partway covered by a blanket. He had a black eye. On the table next to him sat a pawed-through box of See's chocolates, a half-empty beer, and a key attached to a tag that read #9 — my room. I grabbed the key and put it in my pocket, hoping neither Riley nor his mother had a spare, before running out of the room.

☑ Other

All day I escaped into movies, my phone turned off, a knot of unease in my stomach. Scrounging change, I went downstairs for a beer at happy hour. The pub was empty except for the owner, James.

"Were you here last night?" he asked. "Did you hear?" He pointed toward the ceiling, indicating Miyako and Riley's.

"I didn't hear," I said.

"Oh, my God," he said. "It was after hours. A friend of mine had just left, and suddenly there was a *boom, boom* that shook the walls. I saw a car out front. You know what the noise was? Riley coming down the stairs with a baseball bat, smashing it from one wall to the other. Three guys grabbed him and started beating the shit out of him. I know he has his problems, but I couldn't let them just work him, so I ran out and pulled them off. They left pretty quick, but that noise scared the crap outta me at first."

"How horrible."

The next day, I left my phone turned off and went to the temp office in person to check on new assignment possibilities. The administrator offered me a two-week reception job at an ad agency. As soon as I got paid, I bought a round-trip bus ticket to visit PJ and Jeanette in Sonoma County.

PJ had gotten a little rounder, and wore a slightly scruffy beard. Jeanette, now a manager at a body-care shop, looked just a tiny bit older. As we prepared dinner together, I filled them in on Japan and the world trip. I said nothing about the situation in San Francisco. Just by getting a little distance, I could see how bad it was. My life had narrowed dismally when I had expected it to blossom.

After a night on the couch, I nursed a cup of coffee on their deck in the sun, listening to PJ talk about what kinds of peppers he had in the garden. He believed that he could gauge what kind of year it would be, based on which pepper plant grew the best.

"Looks like this time it's gonna be a serrano," he noted. Gazing out at the first green of spring, I sensed the absence of my far-gone Sonoma County life. I didn't feel sorry I had left, yet that morning I would gladly have stayed a month rather than return to the city. I took my time

☑ **Other**

getting ready to catch the bus. I ignored Riley's messages. He kept saying, "We need to talk."

If I thought I didn't want to go up to my room after returning from traveling, now it felt like going to prison. I trudged into the building, hung my instincts on a hook, and clomped up the stairs. When Riley asked again to talk, I told him that we could speak outside. Freshly washed and combed, he met me on the sidewalk.

"I overreacted," he said. "I'm so sorry." We walked slowly along Union Street. "I have something to tell you." I looked expectantly at him.

"I've been struggling with meth," he sighed. "Staying off it. Back like three years ago, I didn't smoke, barely drank. I tried meth once and started up with all this shit." He looked at me, but I remained silent. "The racing career bombed," he continued. "My life went down the drain. But meeting you has made it worth it." He looked at the ground.

We reached a small neighborhood park where people let their dogs play. Riley waited for me to say something. I watched a brindle bulldog chasing a stick.

"Were you on meth at the show?" I finally asked.

"No, I've been off it. I just got insecure. I saw you talking to those guys outside. It's been like two years since I've even gone on a date. I definitely overreacted." His shiner had faded to a small purple bruise next to his perfectly curved eyebrow. "There's something else," he said. "It's hard to talk about."

"Mm-hmm," I said.

"We used to rent the other two rooms upstairs to tenants when I was a kid. This guy from Ecuador, played guitar all the time, he really made me feel kind of important. My dad always criticized me, but this guy was nice. But then he got real friendly, real fast." He ran a hand through his hair. "I was raped when I was thirteen, right there in the bedroom I have now. He did it. My dad found out somehow — I don't know — and beat the guy up, kicked him out. But then he started calling me fag all the time." Tears welled up in his eyes.

☑ Other

"I'm sorry," I said. "I can relate actually. My first sexual experience was violating too. It's hard to trust anyone." Riley's face turned sympathetic.

"Aww, I'm sorry that happened to you," he said. His eyes affirmed, *I get it. I completely get it.* He rested a hand on my shoulder. His touch not only soothed me, but sent warmth down my spine.

"I'm glad you're staying off meth," I said, now thinking to help him. I mistakenly believed I could help Riley become more of the thoughtful, gracious person I had glimpsed in him. "Well, I had a long bus ride. Heading home now."

Back in my room, I opened the mini fridge and found two hot sauce packets, one stuck to the plastic shelf, and half a bottle of sparkling water gone flat. It always surprised me how quickly chaos crept in when I fell behind on housecleaning. A few misplaced items (a hairbrush on the bed or a pair of socks on the floor, like the first dislodged pebbles of an avalanche) could spawn a layer of clutter that hinted at a descent into madness.

Minor backsliding or temporary road bumps when starting anew in a major city would have been understandable. Back-catapulting, I hadn't expected. As if I were the accursed Lady of Shalott in her tower, I paced in slow circles on the roof and looked at the buildings of San Francisco as if they were the spires and flags of Camelot.

Without doubt, Riley had serious issues. But why should I judge? *You're not judging, you're discerning. He may be struggling, but that's no excuse to treat you badly. You can do better than having this guy in your life. C'mon.* It had gotten to where I would think something reasonable and true about Riley, and not react to it.

On the way out the door one morning, this time on assignment as a food server in a hostel/residence hotel, I found a brand-new copy of Hemingway's *A Moveable Feast* just outside my door. A bouquet of jasmine was propped up next to it. Inside the front cover of the book, Riley's handwriting read:

SOMETHING NEW FOR YOU TO ENJOY.

☑ Other

I'd wanted to buy *A Moveable Feast*, but hadn't been able to afford it, or any book — or, on some days, even a cup of coffee.

Putting the flowers in water and tucking the book under my arm, I dashed out the door to catch the bus. At work, I shared the dining room floor with Comi, a 28-year-old guy from Madrid. He invited me to join him and some friends for an evening of karaoke.

"We are going to do singing." Comi smiled as we set up a salad bar. "Do you like it?" He wore billowing cotton pants, a T-shirt, and Pumas. His curly dark brown hair was in a ponytail.

"I do," I said. "In Japan we sang everywhere. At bars they'll hand you microphones. You don't even have to stand up."

"In Spain I was in a band," Comi said. "But I don't want to take it so seriously, just have fun. You'll meet my friends Stefanie and Alex. Tomorrow night."

Comi's Spanish accent recalled Tarragona and the circus troupes that caravanned from town to village. I felt pleasantly nostalgic, but what I liked best about working with Comi was feeling at ease.

"Sounds good. I'm down," I said. He frowned.

"Why are you down? What's wrong?"

"Huh? Oh, no, 'I'm down' means I want to go." We laughed.

From the bus on the way home that evening, I saw a billboard that read: *Asia is now a moveable feast.* I got off at the stop right in front of my building. Riley waved as he put a bag of trash in a bin. My stomach slightly sank as I waved back.

"Thanks for the book," I said.

"You look so pretty," he said. "You look happy and your eyes are smiling." With one piston of instinct still firing, I didn't mention Comi or the karaoke plans.

"What're you up to?" I asked.

"Just had some people come through. Trying out the new mic." As I headed for the front door he added, "Hey, Andre Nickatina's doing a daytime gig at the megastore downtown Sunday. Just a half hour. Maybe wanna go?"

"That might be all right," I said, going inside. "See ya later."

☑ Other

Karaoke in Japantown, with Comi and his friends Alex and Stefanie, proved by far to be the best time I had since returning to America. Alex, from Pennsylvania, brought tambourines and maracas to accompany the songs. A skinny, young Edward Norton-type, he built miniature buildings and ships for an architectural firm. Stefanie, from Germany, had innocent-girl beauty, big brown eyes and shoulder-length red hair, nicely complemented by a clever wit. She was a manager at a nanny service, and complimented everyone she spoke to.

I noticed one thing I had in common with these three: laughing freely and often. I relaxed. Singing felt wonderful.

When I got home, I glanced up to see Riley watching from his window. He didn't wave or smile. In the morning, I awoke looking forward to the day. After work I brought my laptop to the nearby cafe to map out the next chapter of the travel-encouragement guide.

Ready? Riley's text read. It was a Sunday afternoon, and I was dusting and straightening my room. I had all the windows open because of an early March heat wave. I had forgotten about the Andre Nickatina set downtown.

Sure, I replied, hastily brushing my hair. I put on jeans, a Bruce Lee T-shirt and Converse. I grabbed my phone, purse, and a stick of gum. Before I got down the stairs, I saw Riley through the glass front door. He wore a satiny red head wrap — gangsta style. He had on a red-and-white football jersey, white jeans with "SF" stitched in red and black on a front pocket, a red bandana neatly rolled and tied around one thigh, a white leather wristband, and un-smudged red Adidas. His pressed-perfect outfit and flawless skin made him look like an action figure. It would have been appropriate if one of us yelled,

"Dance off!" and a battle whistle blew.

"How are you?" I asked, stifling a smile. We walked to his car.

"Glad to get out of the house, fa sheez. My boy's goin' off the chain. This shit is gonna be poppin'."

Have you noticed he talks like an eighteen-year-old? Doesn't work? Lives with his crazy mother? The voice of reason consistently chimed in, but the volume was turned down.

☑ Other

    Riley let me drive his BMW whenever I wanted, though he knew I still didn't have a license. Noticing that San Francisco police didn't harass most drivers, I decided to indulge myself. Besides, the car handled like a dream.
    On a tiny stage in front of fifty dedicated fans, Andre Nickatina rendered his hauntingly emotive rap. In one verse, he mentioned some old-school comics I hadn't heard of. He said,
    "Remember those, Riley?" looking right at him. Riley drew his fist to his chest and looked like he might choke up. The fervent crowd whooped and cheered as another song began.
    A pack of busty, tall women in too much makeup rushed the stage after the final song, vying for attention. Nickatina kept a poker face and headed for the door in long strides. The small crowd filed out. Smiling, but with downcast eyes, Riley whispered,
    "'Dre Dog. Well." He straightened up. "Let's go." The temperature outside had risen to the upper seventies. For a moment strolling back to the car, things felt oddly normal.
    "Do you want to get some cold beer and play backgammon in my room?" I asked.
    "Sure," Riley answered. "It's too warm to stay outside."
    I had to teach him to play — but once we got rolling, the afternoon became enjoyable. Riley had removed his headgear and thigh bandana. He talked about a falling out he had with Andre years before, and about how he hadn't been interested in "the rap game" until recently.
    "I don't wanna show Nickatina up at all. I'm new at this. Just seeing him is enough," he said. "An inspiration."
    I studied Riley's expression, which showed no signs of accumulated anger or stress. His face lacked a single crease or furrow. If I had never met him, I would have thought, *What a beautiful man.* Sometimes I wished the stereotype that women aren't "visual" concerning sex were true. The same as for men: sights could instantly trigger libido. I ignored the recoiling of my rational mind.
    Again we slept together. Riley didn't do anything out of the ordinary, but the pleasure in my body intensified — even more than the last time.

☑ Other

"Sorry," he said, sitting up.

"For what?" I asked, confused.

"I'm sure other guys were better."

"What are you talking about? Were you here a minute ago?" Riley began dressing anxiously.

"I know you don't want me here and don't care if I fuck up and take meth," he said.

"Where did you get that impression?" I drew my knees to my chest and pulled the sheet to my chin. Riley's face contorted.

"I didn't know how you'd react to someone like me," he said. "And my mom has no idea how bad my life is. I have no one to talk to." Though I felt sorry for him, I was getting sick of every conversation with Riley becoming all about Riley.

"Sex is not a good idea for us," I said. "There's too much you're dealing with and it just complicates things. Let's not do that again."

"You're right," he said, sneering. "It was a mistake." His eyes turned suspicious, then worried. "You do what's practical and right, and you don't care. Sometimes I don't know if I want to live." I felt obliged to tell him I cared whether he lived or died, but I sharply noted how twisted he sounded.

"I care but calm down a second." His eyes flared as he stepped toward the door.

"What. I'm fine. I knew you'd react this way. You're judging me."

"You just said you *didn't* know how I'd react."

"Nah," he said, yanking open the door. "I said I *knew* how you'd react. I'll just go back to my place where it doesn't matter and you can forget the whole thing." Slam.

This ain't no joke, the old man's voice in my mind said and I thought, *What just happened?* I took a very long shower. *What a baby.* The voice of logic told me to cut off all ties with Riley. *Seriously, Cindy. Just walk away from this craziness.* Yet I remained transfixed, as if I'd encountered a gang of shadows that had sprung to life and were poised for battle. I needed to face those dark figures. But what did that really mean?

☑ Other

My new work assignment brought me to a reception desk at a financial consulting firm on the sixty-fourth floor of a downtown building. My sole responsibility, routing incoming calls, left hours of free time. Bored, I accessed the internet and looked up the keywords *sudden anger* and *odd behavior*. A slew of sites popped up about Narcissistic Personality Disorder. Some of the traits sounded like Riley: *cares overly about appearance, is self-contradictory, lacks sense of humor.* A few were hauntingly familiar (though not about Riley): *makes decisions that concern you without consulting you, commits your time without asking, expresses opinions for you and claims they are yours.* Just reading those chilled my blood, but I shook it off and continued.

Sites about Borderline Personality Disorder also came up. *Do you know someone with BPD? Do you feel uneasy? Are you the focus of irrational anger, alternating with periods where they act normal and loving? Do you feel manipulated or lied to?* The BPD traits sounded Riley-like: *has moodiness that cycles quickly, expresses anger inappropriately, alternates between idealizing someone and devaluing them, talks about suicide, acts competent and controlled in some situations but out of control in others.*

Until then I had thought terms like narcissism and borderline described personality types, not serious psychological illnesses. That there were detailed traits common among the afflicted (such as chronically interrupting a significant other's sleep), perturbed me. Without understanding my relentless need to help, I looked for some positive information — ways to counteract the behavior. I didn't know for sure that Riley had BPD, but what I had read sounded like him. According to psychologists, he needed stability and assurance. Sudden

☑ Other

detachment, which I had been considering, would most likely trigger an aggressive reaction. That was the last thing I needed.

After work, dread seized my heart as the bus pulled up to the stop by my front door. I remembered feeling the same way coming home from school as a kid, afraid my dad would be drunk. I hurried up to my room and locked the door. Sipping tea, I stared out the window. All the benefits of Japanese sentai therapy had dissipated. My entire neck and left shoulder were clenched and painful. *How am I supposed to live like this?* That night, as I fell asleep, my phone's text alert startled me.

I need you, Riley had typed.

What's up? I replied.

I feel as if though I won't make it without you. I have anger issues but I never try to be hurtful.

Remember you made it all right before you met me.

Can we meet up soon? Need to see you.

Ok, I just need sleep. Gotta work in the morning.

Please don't turn your phone off. It helps me know you are there.

Ok goodnight.

I dropped off heavily. The text alarm jolted me awake again. I squinted at the phone's lit screen: 4:12 a.m.

Thank you.

A little unfocused at work the next morning, I felt glad the day was easy. When I got home, Riley was standing near the recycling bins. He looked relieved.

"I don't know what I'd do if I couldn't reach you."

"Is anything really difficult going on?"

"Just that I haven't done any meth for twenty-four days, and I'm barely hangin' on. I wanted to jump off the roof all day."

"It'll get easier. You're doing a good job."

"Because of you," he said, hugging me. I stepped back, out of his arms.

"See you soon," I said, heading inside. The following night I awoke again to the phone's buzzing.

☑ Other

25 days! Riley's text read. I groaned, turned the phone off and went back to sleep. In the morning I found fourteen panicky messages, and that my voice of reason had shut off. I texted Riley.

I was asleep. Are you ok?

He hadn't answered by the time I finished work. I called to check on him.

"Can you come over?" he asked. "Just for a few minutes."

"Sure, I'll be there soon." He was sitting up in bed when I arrived, gauze wrapped around his hand and wrist. A few spots of blood had seeped through.

"What happened?" I asked.

"I told you I didn't know what I'd do if I couldn't reach you. I'm OK though. Just please leave your phone on."

"I can, but I *really* need sleep. I don't function well on limited sleep."

"I understand," he said, but that very night the texts started up again. I thought (drowsily) that spending a little time with him in person might lessen his tendency to bug me while I slept.

Any Nickatina shows coming up? I texted before work, yawning.

Incredible timing. There's one tonight in Berkeley!

Calculating expenses, I found that my budget would fall short for the month. The thought of going to Berkeley consoled me. I would skip buying a drink to save every dollar possible and simply enjoy live music, which had long been a diversion from rough circumstances. I remembered going dancing with Eric the massage therapist in Berkeley, and how he had somehow made *Look at all the dead people dancing in the mirror* sound pretty.

Wearing his full red-and-white regalia and a large Band-Aid on his wrist, Riley met me downstairs that evening, kissed my cheek and opened the door for me. I told him I needed to be home early because I had to work the next day. He drove toward the Bay Bridge.

"I'm doing a lot better," he said in an extra calm tone.

"Good. It'll be nice to get out of town for a minute and see some music."

I glanced at him. His gorgeous profile looked vacant, as if it were missing a personality. *Ok*, I thought, finally in agreement with the voice of logic. *I don't need to help him and definitely don't need to hang out with him anymore. This is it. His problems aren't mine.* It felt good to regain charge of my senses.

"Sometimes I can really turn things around," he said, nodding. "Just like that. I feel like a batter in the ninth, about to hit a homer. So," he continued. "You like my boy Andre?"

"Yeah. He's great," I said — and Riley went berserk.

He yanked the wheel left, almost hitting a car in the next lane, then jerked it right. Back and forth he swerved, with near misses on both sides, causing horns to blast. I couldn't hear what he was yelling because I was screaming. When he slowed the car and drove straight again, the screaming gained words.

"You *know* I've been in car accidents, you *asshole*." Tears covered my face, and I was shaking. When the next moment didn't bring anything rational, shock kicked in. At least, I expected Riley to glance over at the woman he had been thanking for his very life, or look like something out of the ordinary had just happened. He appeared utterly placid, surveying the lanes before him as if he were a spoiled prince.

In an industrial area, he pulled over and parked. The street was empty except for a few dim figures huddled on the sidewalk in the night wind. Wads of paper and aluminum cans blew past. Riley said,

"I'm going to leave you here." Adrenaline pulsed through my veins, but my mind worked slowly. *I don't have any money.* Why the hell did I not have any money on me, again? It took effort to think. Now he stood, keys in hand, just outside the driver side door.

"Go ahead," I yelled, apparently not the response he expected. He got back in. *Oops.* I tried to remember where the nearest transit station was, but I didn't have the necessary $1.50 and didn't want to beg for money. I considered asking the indistinct figures down the block for directions, but felt vulnerable. Desperation crept in. Riley started the car.

☑ Other

"I want to go home," I said. "I need to get home. Just drop me back on the city side of the bridge, or this side. I don't want go anymore. Go the show yourself. I don't want to be here."

As if I'd suddenly broken off a date for no reason, Riley looked pained. He drove on. I rubbed my aching forehead. In a more populated, dining-and-entertainment area, he pulled up near a club and parked. I thought of asking strangers if they would be going back to San Francisco anytime soon, but I felt shell-shocked. I got out of the car in a daze.

Intending to find a way home, I went into the club. Riley strode off into the crowd. He didn't look back, just waved at someone onstage who waved back. Then he jogged to the side and jumped up, joining a small crew of fans. Words died on my lips every time I approached someone to ask about a ride. One of a group of guys in their early 20s barked,

"Move," and shoved roughly past me. I sank onto a couch, watching a kaleidoscope of limbs twitch and jerk under swinging colored lights.

Hand on my shoulder — I jumped, looking up to see a muscular, dreadlocked man peering kindly down from way, way above. He said his name, DJ-something, which I recognized because Riley mentioned him fairly often, someone he had known since high school.

"Hey," I said. He looked concerned.

"You aren't happy, are you?" he asked. "I saw you come in with him." He gestured with his thumb at the stage where Riley continued to cavort. I nodded.

"I know what he's like," he said. "I don't know what's wrong with him." The man patted my shoulder before walking off. Time wasn't progressing normally. The show ended.

Earlier, when I had told Riley I had to get home early because of work, he had assured me that would be no problem. Now, standing on the sidewalk in front of the club at 2:15 a.m., I saw him bounce out, grinning ferociously, only to look scornful when he spotted me. Without looking me in the eye, he said,

☑ Other

"Time to go, son," and started walking toward his car. I looked around at the people smoking and chatting.

"Anybody driving back to San Francisco?" I asked. No one answered. A few people looked askance at me. Tears threatened. I blinked them back. I had to get up in a few hours and saw no other way home. Beaten down, I followed Riley, and with a pounding heart got back in the car. I sat with every muscle tensed. Driving toward the freeway, he pulled up to a stationary police car and lowered his window. Though the officer inside looked surprised, he asked what the matter was.

"Excuse me sir, but we're just trying to get back to San Francisco," Riley said like a lost tourist. Frowning, the policeman pointed to the freeway sign a few dozen yards ahead.

"Oh, thank you, officer," Riley gushed. I pressed myself against the passenger door the whole way back, imagining bludgeoning Riley with a heavy object. Before the car came to a complete halt a block from the hellish place I called home, I jumped out, ran to the door, fumbled with the key, pushed frantically and yanked it shut. I vaulted up the stairs three at a time.

Sleepless, I stared into the dark until it was no longer dark, the edges of windows and furniture defining themselves as dawn bled into the room. Time had twisted into an enemy, issuing the oncoming day. Through a thick fog, I felt really stupid. How could I have gotten back in that car? Furthermore, why did I find it necessary to get up and get ready for the last day of the job assignment instead of calling in sick? Something urged me to keep up a good work ethic, and yet all day I apologized for mis-routing calls and forgetting what people had just said. I turned on my phone only to text,

> Never come near me or contact me again.

Bone-tired after work, I got on the bus. When I stepped off, Miyako was waiting on the sidewalk.

"You have something of ours?" she asked.

"What would *that* be?"

"The manager copy of the key to your room. It is missing. Maybe you have it. My son cannot trust you. He says he want to trust you, but he can't."

"Your son put my life in danger last night. I don't care what he wants." She chuckled.

"Riley is just frustrated. So you *do* have the key?"

Without a word, I turned and went upstairs. I fell into a dreamless slumber. Waking in the dark, I thought, *I have to get out of here. Need money.* I checked for messages from the temp administrator. Yes. He was offering a weeklong filing job. I left a return voicemail, accepting the work. About to turn the phone off again, I dialed Comi's number instead.

"Hello?" he said in his Spanish accent.

"Hi Comi, it's Cindy, from —"

"Hey, Cindy," he said. "How are you doing?"

"Not too bad," I said. "Wondering if you and Alex and Stefanie were doing anything soon?" In my shaken condition I wasn't sure if I sounded friendly or desperate.

"Just a dinner at Stefanie's. Come over. We are having food, wine, and relaxing."

"Tonight?" I had no idea what time it was.

"Yes. You can go anytime but I'll get there in a little while," he said.

"S-P-T?" I asked.

"What? Say again."

"Spanish People Time?" I said. He laughed.

"I'm bringing sangria. I don't think they need anything else. Just call Stefanie. See you there."

Stefanie cheerfully echoed the invitation and gave me her address. As I dressed, fear saturated my entire chest cavity. If I could be reduced from an optimistic world traveler and respected teacher to a trembling victim in a few months' time, what place did I have with normal, mature people?

Accustomed to presenting an upbeat expression despite feeling gutted, I stepped off the mirrored elevator in Stefanie's elegant

☑ Other

building looking as though nothing disastrous had happened. She greeted me with a wine-stained grin and bade me to follow her down a long hallway. A scent of sautéed garlic and butter increased as we approached her dining room, where Alex sat holding a round, thin-stemmed glass half full of dark red wine. He looked over with a friendly expression that reminded me of my cousins. As I helped Stefanie make a salad in the adjacent kitchen, he said,

"Kanako's coming with us to Burning Man. We're gonna make a Japanese tent and it's gonna be crazy."

"I'm picturing the girls happily covered in dust," Stefanie said. I couldn't think of anything to add to the conversation, and got annoyed with myself. I tried to breathe deeply and slowly — always a chore for some reason. I focused on slicing cucumbers.

"Have you been to Burning Man?" Alex asked me.

"Not yet," I answered. "But I'm a fan of the art and it sounds fun. Expensive though."

"That's why I went for the discount they give you if it's your first time and you write an essay. My ticket cost ninety-five."

"Nice. I might try that." Ninety-five dollars might as well have been 90,000. *Right now, an extra ten dollars is ninety-thousand.* I felt like a child in a roomful of grown-ups. Comi arrived carrying a guitar and a small bucket of sangria.

"Cindy, Cindy," he said, kissing my cheeks. I managed to smile.

After weeks of ramen and bagels, the simple meal of steak, salad and bread amounted to a feast. Comi picked up his guitar and began playing while we dealt with food comas. I excused myself to the bathroom and did a few stretches to relax my taut neck. I wished I could breathe right. Taking a full breath caused the deepest muscles at the top of my shoulders to stiffen. I quickly wiped away a few unexpected tears. I dabbed cold water on my face. Walking back to the dining room, I glanced out a window at the commanding, sixteenth-floor view.

"When I move out of my one-room place, I'll invite you over," I told Stefanie. *When I rejoin the living.* She smiled.

"You're always welcome here."

☑ Other

Later, walking home, anxiety oozed through my bones. Shutting the front door of the building, I imagined what a temporary relief it would be to slam it so hard the glass shattered. I also imagined smashing Riley's head into a wall. *That can't be good.*

In a band of morning sunlight I sat up.

"Oh, no," I said aloud. "I'm doing temp work." Signing on with an agency had always been a last resort, to be used for only a couple weeks. Here it had been a few months. I couldn't remember when I'd gotten anything done on the travel guide. Committed to the week of filing, and still short on bills, I got dressed and headed to work. The company produced catalogs or product magazines. I had to file bulky manila envelopes. Ten minutes in, I started yawning. A lady in a hip-length sweater, tube-like skirt and square heels tottered over.

"You can sort photos in the conference room if this task gets monotonous. When you get through with those and a cart of envelopes, you can go, as long as you've done four hours."

I considered it a minor miracle to escape the eight-hour shift, which tended to devour the rest of the day. Killing four hours would have been easy if it weren't for a barrage of intruding thoughts and memories: an imminent, crushing slam; the cold eyes of desertion; the need to act as if everything was fine.

The employee break room, greenish in the fluorescent lighting, appeared laden with malice. I stopped mid-preparation of a cup of coffee when two fat tears spilled down my cheeks. After blotting my face with a paper towel, I returned to filing. I tried to look as alert as possible.

That evening, as I focused on outlining a chart of hang-dry times for the traveler without access to a dryer, a pounding on my door startled me. I slid the chain latch in place. Through the fisheye-lens peephole, Riley's tiny face twisted in anger. A stream of muttering erupted. Then he shouted.

"Bitch! Pig! I hate your guts." While he continued snarling I yelled,

☑ Other

"Go away!" He retreated down the hall. My heart banged against my ribs as I paced the room. It would take a few weeks at least, if I found a better paying job immediately, to raise the funds to move out. My head felt heavy, with sharp pressure at the temples. I would need adequate rest to work, job hunt, and find a new place to live. After uneasily dropping off to sleep later, more door pounding roused me sometime in the night.

"Leave me alone!" I yelled, and heard Riley running away. Every time I fell back to sleep he would shout, bang on the door, or climb onto the fire escape and knock on my window.

I had never called the police on anyone. Though I considered it, I thought that since Riley knew the building inside and out, he could hide or lock himself in his rooms.

I went to work on about forty minutes of sleep. I barely made it through three hours before clocking out, grateful that everyone in the office acted just as polite as they had on my first day. The left side of my neck hurt so much, I could have screamed. I got off the bus and dragged myself upstairs to find Riley standing outside my door. He held a kitchen butcher knife.

"You fucked me up," he said, sliding the tip of the knife down his face and pausing near his jugular. *Really?* I thought in a surreal haze. *This cliché act?* Nerves on alert, adrenaline coursing through me — and yet still exhausted — I somehow wrangled the knife from him, and ran the length of the hallway to throw it out a window onto Miyako's patio. It clattered down and I looked tensely back toward my room. Riley was balled up on the floor, shrieking.

"You fucked me up. You fucked me up."

I wished I had enough money to stay at a hostel even a few nights. *I just need a few hours of sleep.* I stepped over him and went into the room, locking the door and sliding the chain latch over. I didn't take my jacket off or bother getting under the blanket, just rolled onto the bed.

Dream-like thoughts flooded my mind during the one minute before I conked out. *I'm a sheep in a pen. Unfit for public*

☑ **Other**

consumption. I wasn't out long when the shouting and knocking started up again. Riley's voice taunted.

"You gonna call the cops yet? Go ahead." Instead I dialed Melissa. I'd been hesitant to ask if I could stay with her again. I needed calm and comfort, and she had been impatient with me as a houseguest before. But maybe she could loan me enough to move. My fingers clumsily dialed her number.

Hi, this is Melissa, her outgoing greeting said. *I'm overseas at the moment but leave me a message.*

Mike had an infant at home, so I didn't want to bother him. Nor did I want to ask for help from any of the new people I'd met, in case they might think I was crazy. I passed the night dozing, being woken, and yelling at Riley to get away. I dreamt that I rode a tiny black horse that ran in slow motion. I tried to flee, only to find myself trapped in a doorless room.

Too weary to stay more than an hour and a half at work the next morning, I filed a cartful of manila envelopes and left. At the small park off Union Street, I sat on a bench and rested my arm across the back, cradling my head against my shoulder so I could take a nap sitting up. Pain shot across the base of my skull. I gave up and went to the cafe, wrapping my hands around a hot cup of tea until it grew cold. When the cafe closed I went to the pub, yawning over a pint of ale.

The hallway was quiet when I went up to my room. Standing inside, at the sink just behind the double-locked door, I glanced in the mirror and saw purple blotches under my eyes. Riley's voice approached from down the hall. *God, no. This can't happen.*

"Fuck all you motherfuckers," he was saying, then something unintelligible. Then, "That's right. I'll kill you. I'll break your fucking jaw, bitch."

I picked up my phone and dialed 911. As I gave the dispatcher the address, Riley climbed onto the fire escape and threw a hard object at my window. Through the drawn blinds, I saw something on fire. As the sirens rolled up, I heard him climbing back in and running away. I had never hated anyone so much in my life.

☑ Other

"You'll have to come down and let the officers in," the dispatcher said. "They're at the front door." I was surprised, having thought they'd use a universal key or find another way in.

"What if he's in the hallway?" I asked dubiously. "He was talking about killing me."

"You need to let them in," she repeated, this time in a stern tone. Some of my hate transferred to her. I opened the door a crack, crept into the hall and ran to the stairwell, rushing to the bottom. I let in the four officers who stood outside.

"He ran away," I said. "It's the guy who lives next door. He was threatening and harassing me, and he set something on fire right outside my window." Two of the men went next door.

"I've run into this guy before," one said. "Used to ride a motorcycle?" I half shrugged, half nodded. "Fifty-one-fifty," he said to the other policeman, and then looked at me. He spoke slowly. "Why would someone like you be involved with someone like him?" After a weary moment, I replied.

"Everyone makes mistakes." The other two officers returned.

"He might be inside," one said. "But his mother won't let us in. There's nothing we can do right now."

"Let's go up and have a look in your room," the eldest policeman said. They followed me and gave the place a once-over, finding a partially burned hat on the fire escape.

"I see you have this nice little bungalow here," the same officer said. "But I would strongly recommend moving out. This guy is nothing but trouble."

"I agree. Working on it. Thank you for coming."

Burrowing into the bedcovers, I put a pillow over my head and passed out, waking after fourteen hours. *Shit. Late.* The phone rang. It was the temp agency.

"Cindy, I have some bad news," the agent said. "Our team is being replaced under new management. So you'll be reporting to another person, but I just wanted to thank you for signing on with us."

☑ Other

"Oh . . . you're welcome. And sorry to hear that," I said. "Hope you find another good position soon."

"Me, too," he chuckled. "So listen. I called your current assignment and the manager couldn't say enough good things about you. If you want to be on their top-pick list, just let the new supervisors here know."

"Wow, thanks." I had no idea who the manager of my current assignment was, but to get a glowing review when I had left the premises without finishing the shift, twice, gave me hope. I might have been in hell — but therein existed invisible helpers, nameless people who showed up, assisted and disappeared. Without them, I would have fallen into a wide-open abyss of despair. I finished out the week of filing, glad the staff didn't care what time I came in to do the work.

Taking one last assignment while searching for a better job seemed best. I went to the temp office to meet the new management. They were nothing like the previous staff. A middle-aged woman in thick, boxy business wear frowned over my file.

"I don't think we have anything for you," she said, shaking her head. "Hmm, they did put a smiley face next to your name." She looked bewildered.

"I was recommended by one company as a top-pick and always got offered good assignments," I said. Defiance had crept into my voice.

"Yes," she replied, distracted. "We'll call you." She closed the file and smiled over my shoulder to the next waiting person. My face blazed. I felt I had been subject to a low-level yet devastating injustice, like getting denied access to a voting booth.

I had lost count of how many times I'd ever gone job hunting, but the loathsome task could not be ignored. Restaurant serving would allow me to move out the fastest. I hadn't waited tables in a few years, but I had basic knowledge of Japanese cuisine and language. I applied only at Japanese restaurants, and got hired at Hime (Hee-may), an upscale sushi place in a nearby neighborhood.

☑ Other

On my first night, a second new employee — a tall, pretty redhead with a South Carolina drawl — also showed up to start, even though the hiring manager had told me they only needed one server. An arrow of doubt plunged into my stomach. We glanced at each other, our guards up.

The manager, Jimi, sported a faux-hawk, a business suit and heavy silver skull jewelry. He told us to run food, fill water, clear and reset tables. We would inform the servers of any table's status. Meanwhile, we had to identify small pieces of raw fish presented by too-cool-for-school Jimi. The restaurant was packed by 7:30.

The Carolina beauty and I weaved around the tables and each other like tomcats, each striving to perfect her job performance. To gain an edge over her, I called the slivers of fish by their Japanese names. To her advantage, she looked at Jimi, blinked slowly and said,

"I'm actually a sushi artist." Withholding feedback until the end of the shift, he finally beckoned us over.

"You two are very capable," he said. He looked back and forth between us. "We've decided to hire you both." She and I smiled at each other for the first time.

Ample funds were my golden ticket out, and working at the restaurant would provide them. Early evenings, setting tables in the lacquered dining room lit by candles, I could feel part of something other than the craziness of Riley and Miyako.

Riley had not made an appearance since the night I called the police, yet I remained wary. Everywhere in and around the building was enemy territory. I tried to focus on my new job and keep fear from taking over, though every few nights I had nightmares. I was stalked, chased, and threatened — my dreams tried to hunt me to extinction.

The owner, a short Japanese man named Isamu, directed his staff in B-male-trying-to-be-alpha style, mainly by yelling and shifting all blame to staff members when mistakes were made, regardless of facts. Already on hyper-alert for sudden aggression, and extra sensitive to being yelled at, I was determined to stay under his radar.

☑ Other

I used all the Japanese protocol I could muster, helping customers make sake choices and navigating the more obscure points of the cuisine.

Poking my head out of the poverty hole, able to buy toothpaste, contact lens solution, dish soap, and batteries all at once felt glorious. So did the first chiropractic adjustment in months. My neck no longer had an invisible ice pick wedged in it.

"Hey Cindy," Comi said one afternoon on the phone. "There's a teaching job at the English school I go to. I want you to meet our director Frances. You'll love him." *Two jobs? More income. No problem.*

"Absolutely," I replied. As it turned out, the hours of teaching perfectly complemented the hours of serving. Frances — sweet, gentle and fair — hired me to teach advanced English. As a cultural as well as language teacher, I could bring the class anywhere in San Francisco for outings. I got paid to go bowling, visit museums, and walk across the Golden Gate Bridge.

Apartment searching proved more challenging than I'd expected. Affordable, quality studios were grabbed up. Even for the less desirable abodes, competition was fierce. Renting a room in a house involved roommate interviews that spread out over a few weeks with the scant time I had available to attend them.

One afternoon I came home to the feeling that something wasn't quite right. After a moment I figured it out: my conga drum was missing. The five or six tenants on my floor were hermits. The first floor still housed several polite young Japanese women. I doubted any of them had stolen the drum. Refusing to contact Riley, I called Miyako.

"This is Cindy. I'm calling because something has been stolen from my room."

"Ah," she said. "Riley want to do a nice favor to you." My jaw clenched and I growled,

"No. I don't want — what favor? My drum is gone."

"He is fixing it," she said.

"Just give it back or I'll report the theft."

☑ Other

"He is at music store today. Why are you complaining?"
"If I don't get my drum back by tonight, I'm reporting it." I had to be at Hime at 5:00. Miyako waited till 4:00 to call back.
"It's here. You can come get it."
"No," I said angrily. "He needs to give it back."
"On the patio. He is inside. You take it. I don't want you to call the police. You are making trouble for us. When are you moving out?" I tossed my phone on the bed in exasperation.

The door to their patio stood ajar. When I pushed it open, I didn't see the drum. Riley slid open their back door.
"What're you doing here?" he demanded.
"Give my drum back," I said, turning to go back up. I didn't want to be anywhere near him. Suddenly a long, thick piece of glass, which Riley used as a tabletop, came soaring through the air toward me. Surprised he had been able to throw it so forcefully, I protected my head with my arms. It struck my thigh and thudded onto on my foot. I limped upstairs.

A huge purple bruise formed on my leg, and a darker, smaller one on my foot. I dressed for work. Trying to get out of a shift last minute equated to not showing up, in Isamu's eyes. Not showing up meant getting fired. I had reached a point beyond crying, beyond anger — strictly in survival mode. I felt numb. On autopilot at work, I took orders, brought food, and cleared tables. I stopped feeling pain in my leg and foot until I got home, when it returned twofold.

I found the conga drum on its stand in front of my door. The old hardened skin had been replaced. I hauled its bulky weight inside and double-locked the door. I booked a few nights at a hostel at Fort Mason. Grabbing toiletries and clothes, I limped out of the room with relief.

Waking in an unfamiliar bed felt disorienting until I realized the surroundings were peaceful. I inhaled the aroma of coffee. The dining room at the hostel overlooked the sparkling green bay, but I couldn't zone out on it long because I had to prepare lessons for the first class of the morning.

☑ Other

With the stress factor off the chart, cracks formed. I got no complaints about my job performance, but the pressure of planning, teaching, and waiting tables took its toll. I was finding that by the end of a shift, I had done everything well except one important detail — losing a student's homework or forgetting to order drinks for a table.

The hostel had a two-week-stay policy. I went back to the room on Union Street while I saved for deposit and first month's rent. Riley quit interrupting my sleep, but he haunted my dreams. He would appear behind me with a gun. Or I'd be trying to escape his and Miyako's house, turning one locked doorknob after the next.

By the end of the week, I decided I had better move despite not having quite enough. Riley was the craziest person I'd ever known, and it deeply shamed me to have gotten involved with him. Checking on housing listings several times a day and submitting a slew of applications to landlords, I started packing. On a Saturday night, I heard bar-goers passing on the street below. They shouted and laughed as they made their way through an evening out about town, in a forgotten reality, worlds away.

The next morning, I made breakfast and continued boxing my belongings. I noticed a complete lack of traffic sounds. The hated voice and hated footsteps approached. My chest tightened, my appetite cold. Riley's slurring voice shouted outside my door.

"If I sszee my mom crying one more time, I'll shoot her in the temple." My blood turned icy. Something crashed against the door. "I *like* to be bad to you," Riley yelled. *Need to get out of here right now.* I reached for my phone, and as I dialed the police for the second time that month, the door blew off the wall. The entire frame shattered, wooden shards bulleting past me as I gaped. The 9-1-1 dispatcher asked for my address.

"*He's right there,*" I said, panicked. "There's nothing between me and him. I can't get out. There's nothing." She had to interrupt.

"Your address. We can't help you if you don't give it to me." I rattled off the address and then went back to babbling, nearly in hysterics.

"I have no protection, he's right there. The door is *gone*."

"You need to calm down," the dispatcher said. I wanted to slap her. "You'll have to let the officers in." Riley picked up a bottle of brandy he'd set on the floor. Only a quarter of it remained. As he took a long swig, I realized it was Easter Sunday.

"I'm not walking *toward* him," I told the dispatcher. "No way."

"We can't help you if you don't let them in," she said.

I let the phone fall to the floor. Recognition flared in Riley's bloodshot eyes as voices floated up the stairway. *Thank you.* He turned and ran, but too late. I witnessed officers cuffing his wrists as he faced the wall.

I went to the cafe, got online and found a single-room-occupancy building with availability in another neighborhood. The property manager told me he had to do a credit check the following day, and then I could move in.

☑ Other

9.

The Return

Before even opening my eyes the first morning in my new room, I felt utterly safe. No ocean breeze or mountain air could rival that first breath of freedom. I stood up, a little weak in the knees, as if I'd survived a near-fatal crash. As I gathered soap, towel, toothbrush and shampoo, I found myself thinking, *I'm a person. I'm a person.* I stepped into the wonderfully hot water of the shower. My new building did not feel like a sanatorium displaced in time. It had no mysterious pull, nor any tone of dread.

I knew Riley wouldn't look for me, and that we wouldn't run into each other. When he wasn't home, he only went to friends' houses or to clubs. Never to cafes, parks, restaurants, bars. And never to North Beach, where I'd moved.

At nearby Caffe Trieste, where some of my favorite authors — Richard Brautigan, Alan Watts, and William S. Burroughs — had once met to write and talk about life, I relished sitting down to coffee. I glanced at my hands to make sure they still looked like mine. Everything appeared draped in splendor: the vintage photos of merry customers from the '50s; the saxophone-and-piano combo tuning up in the back of the cafe; the warm, earthy Italian roast.

North Beach vastly outshone the previous neighborhood. While Cow Hollow crawled with skinny housewives in overpriced yoga wear who walked tiny dogs festooned in ribbons, North Beach featured creative bohemians strolling European-narrow streets among cathedrals, oak trees and wine bars. Washington Square offered a block of grassy serenity. From the Italian restaurant next door to my new building, I ordered pasta to go. While I waited outside, an Italian man at one of the sidewalk tables called out.

"Sit down!" He gestured to an empty chair.

☑ Other

I envisioned the stepping back, out of Riley and Miyako's world, as if I were retreating up the tube of a giant microscope. The sickeningly up-close visit to that twisted reality panned back, revealing the larger surroundings. The world teemed with the movement and sound of leaves rippling in the breeze; foot traffic along the sidewalk; the clank and clatter of silverware on plates. I took a seat and happened to glance at an ashtray on the table. The man, who had bristly gray hair, spoke with the gravitas of the aged.

"Smoking is dirty in San Francisco," he said. "But homosexuals are clean."

"Modern times," I replied. Another old man approached and spoke in Italian.

"He is talking about the whores," the seated man said.

"The what?" I asked. The man mimed by holding two fists in front of his chest and moving them back and forth. About to get up, I realized he had said "horse," but with lazy pronunciation.

"He plays the horses," I said. The old man nodded. A woman in a black vest and white shirt walked toward us. She carried a crisp brown paper bag folded over at the top. "My food is ready," I said.

"You will get everything you want," the man said. "In time."

I brought my ravioli with walnut sauce upstairs, balancing the bag on my knee while unlocking the door. Taking a few days off had a calming effect, but it also made me realize how time-consuming it was to hold down two jobs. It had made sense when I wanted to escape Riley, but eight shifts a week now seemed crazy. My appetite went cold. *This much work will run me into the ground. I don't know what I'm doing and I'm in my 30s.*

A few mornings later on the bus to the school, I brushed aside the wisps of anxiety that curled around my heart. *You're fine. Everything's OK. Don't worry.* At one crowded stop, a deep voice rose above the noise of passing traffic. A scruffy man with graffiti on his jeans boarded, alternately muttering and drinking from a smudged bottle of Francis Ford Coppola merlot. His pitch and tone were now familiar, even if he wasn't. He clomped toward the empty seat next to me. But before he could sit, I jumped up and dashed to the door. He gave out a harsh laugh.

"Oh yeah?" he said, and I pushed out of the bus before it drove on. *No more.* I walked to work, stopping on the way to buy a bag of pastries for my class. As I planned the day's lessons, my mind revolved around the disordered. They could be found on buses and sidewalks, in stores, in offices and homes. Before, I had just thought, *Crazy.* Now I understood that every crazy person had a specific mental condition or a combination of them. The world was very strangely populated.

The image of Riley's face shoved its way into my thoughts. His eyes, so alluring at first, had often taken on a birdlike gleam. His expression could become as vacant as a boarded-up window. While his bodily systems functioned normally — his heart beat, his glands excreted, his lungs filled and emptied — it seemed that no one operated the control room of his mind.

That I had been drawn to such scariness led me to believe I was way more broken than I'd thought. I worried that I might not actually have a will of my own, and that possibly I hated myself.

I remembered that I used to judge people who got into bad situations, without considering their horrendous circumstances. Before meeting Riley I had thought, *How can that person be so dense? Get away.* Though I now understood the dance with the disordered better, I felt ashamed because that was just it — I had seen Riley was trouble, and weird, but got involved anyway. My conscience had told me to avoid him, but my wounded self obeyed a rule of salvages: *Take on what is right in front of you, whole.* By the end of the day, I needed a nap. I was glad I wasn't scheduled at Hime that evening.

"Cin," Mike sighed over the phone. "They cut my wages almost in half." Across the country, layoffs were increasing.

"At least you still have the job," I said.

"Do you know how much it costs to support a family?" he asked.

"No. Sorry you're having a rough time."

"I think my wife is going to take our son back to Paris."

"Mike, don't let her. That's your son, too."

"I know."

☑ Other

"You know you'll still be paying to support them."
"She isn't happy here."
"What about your happiness?"
"I don't remember what that is, except when I'm around my son."

I had always found Mike passive concerning his significant others, but who was I to judge? That any relationship or marriage could be healthy and balanced now seemed improbable. That both my sets of grandparents stayed together for more than fifty years was boggling.

The next night at Hime, our head chef announced that we would be closing early and driving to San Mateo. Isamu owned another restaurant there, and the staff had prepared a surprise birthday party for him. Our crew packed into a few cars. We arrived to find a dozen platters of sushi, a giant pot of miso soup, and several cases of beer. The head chef took out a bottle of cheap vodka and told a teenaged server to pour it.

"Big boss birthday," he said. "We drink." The girl poured the rotgut vodka for Isamu, Jimi the manager, the head chef and his sous chef. They pounded glass after glass while the rest of the staff ate. The head chef was a composed drunk, but the other three had trouble controlling themselves. Japanese society had revived the fad of streaking — but instead of running naked through a crowd, a party-goer would disrobe for a few minutes of naked sipping and chatting. The sous chef left the room and reappeared wearing nothing. Minutes later, he heaved all over the floor.

Our lead server Natsumi, a graceful and calm young woman, cleaned the mess with a mop. Isamu meanwhile charged across the restaurant and tackled the head chef. They wrestled until forcibly separated. Jimi, unable to sit up without wobbling, face-planted onto a beer bottle and then cupped his blackened eye, wincing. He, too, vomited, which Natsumi cleaned. Jimi staggered to his feet as Isamu rolled onto his back on the floor and passed out, mouth open.

I helped clear dishes at the worst staff party I'd ever attended, then stepped outside to smoke. Glancing down the sidewalk, I saw Jimi. His arm rested heavily on the shoulders of the teen server. Natsumi walked

☑ Other

along his other side and held his elbow. Jimi suddenly grabbed Natsumi's long hair and yanked her to the ground. My mouth opened in shock as he drew his booted foot back and kicked her as hard as he could in the stomach. I ran to where she lay clutching herself and howling. Jimi shuffled to the other side of the street, again leaning on the girl.

"Natsumi," I said, crouching near her. "Let's get you to a hospital."

"No," she said. "I'll be all right." She sat up with effort, crying. The sous chef, somewhat sobered and redressed, came over to help her up.

Go away, she said. "I want the girls around me." Another woman employee had run over, concerned.

"I was bringing Jimi ice for his eye," Natsumi said. "I just wanted to help."

"And he assaulted you," I said. "Do you want to call the police?"

"I want to do something, but I don't want them to think it's an emergency," she said.

"You can call the non-emergency number," I suggested. She agreed, and within a few minutes a squad car pulled up. Jimi was sitting across the street on the curb. Remaining workers huddled in small groups. Isamu still lay passed out inside. The sous chef shooed us away from the door and locked it.

"Why?" he asked, looking confused. "Why Natsumi call the cops?"

"Why shouldn't I?" she shot back. The officer approached. Natsumi began explaining, but when the officer asked if she wanted to press charges, she declined. The officer looked around.

"I see this as a mass arrest opportunity," he said. "All of you, clear out."

Back home, I couldn't rid my mind of Jimi dragging Natsumi by the hair to the ground, his foot swinging back and kicking her with the full force of his weight. Violence now seemed to leap out of nowhere, and I hoped it would stop.

In the morning, plump, middle-aged Chinese ladies shoved each other in their rush to board the bus first, then stood blocking the aisle. I squeezed through and sat on a hard plastic seat. We inched through Chinatown. A frail boy sitting just ahead of me tugged his mother's

☑ Other

sleeve and whined in German or Austrian. She ignored him, and his features became a mask of pouting indignation. Storefronts and street signs outside the window looked filthy and pitiful.

Focusing on planning exercises for my students took a Herculean effort. Basic grammatical structures turned mysterious. Verb complements joined noun clauses in a guarded procession. The longer I stared at words, the less decipherable they became. I questioned what business I had teaching the advanced class. Relying on the textbook, I made it through the first hour and moved on to conversation practice.

Isamu called me in to work that night. I didn't expect Jimi to show up, but there he stood at the reception podium with his black eye, heavy jewelry, suit and tie. The tall redhead from South Carolina hadn't gone to the staff party.

"What happened last night?" she asked quietly as we set up for dinner service.

"Jimi whacked his face on a beer bottle and attacked Natsumi when she offered him ice," I said.

"*What?*" Her eyes widened. "I guess that explains why four people quit."

Focusing didn't come any easier at the restaurant than it had at the school. I kept deleting and re-entering orders, and twice brought food to the wrong table. Jimi approached me as I stood at the bar waiting for an order.

"You're causing problems," he said.

"I'll stop making mistakes," I said.

"No. You're telling people what happened and it isn't a good idea," he said, one eyebrow raised. "You should stop or I'll have to let you go." He glided away. I gave notice at the end of the shift. Jimi just shrugged.

☑ Other

    Before becoming an adult, everyone has an image of what adult life will be like. In the scenario I had spent years building, I saw myself in a sunny, two-level apartment near the sea. Inside, toward the back of a central area with a 15-foot ceiling, a spiral staircase rose to a loft where a wide bed fit perfectly. A skylight framed an array of stars to gaze at while I fell asleep next to my sweet-tempered, passionate, creative husband. Downstairs we would have an open kitchen with a combination of antique and modern features. Also on the ground floor: a studio for art, with easels, canvasses, musical instruments, and a writing desk. Our living room would have a fireplace and plush rugs over polished wooden floors. Occasionally we would host dinner parties where our closest friends would gather for hours of tight-knit revelry. After we had bid them goodnight, my sexy man and I would make transcendent love by the last curling orange flames. Somehow we would find time in our busy lives to be revolutionaries. We would topple the American regime, restoring full, free health care, civil rights and education to all citizens.

    Instead, I watched cultural documentaries alone in my 7-by-10 room and had nightmares where Riley rushed at me like a silverback gorilla. I dreamt of having to wait on sections of twenty or thirty tables at a time. I carried trays that writhed with small live mammals. Leopards followed me on dirty, foreign streets and bit me. A hippo in a muddy pond swallowed people whole, leaving a spreading pool of blood.

    "What's with the animals?" I said groggily one early Monday. Worse than the dreams, fear flashed like lightning through my nervous system throughout the day. *Calm down,* I kept telling myself. Occasionally I went to dinner or wine tasting with Comi, Alex and Stefanie. They seemed to find me fun, but I felt hollow and inferior. It took great amounts of energy to carry on meaningful discussions or playful banter. Students telling me they liked my classes or thanking me for helping them surprised me. I worked hard at making challenging and entertaining lessons, yet I declared myself unworthy.

One student in her late 20s, named Aki, always looked like she'd just dragged herself from bed to class. One afternoon, she asked me over.

"You live in North Beach, right?" she said. I nodded. "Me, too. We are on Green Street."

Aki lived with her boyfriend and two roommates in a converted warehouse with a kitchen that looked like the set for a food show. Granite countertops complemented a huge steel oven and refrigerator. The rest of the place had particle-board floors and thin walls. Paintings from the giant-sized to the miniscule hung in every room. An upright piano stood along one wall. Aki offered me a seat on a tall stool at the kitchen counter.

"This is Jesse," she said, introducing her boyfriend. He had round brown eyes framed in long thick lashes, and a tall build with a slight paunch.

"Hi," he said in a Texan drawl. "Wanna beer?"

"Sure," I said. Aki and Jesse were staring at me. I glanced from one to the other.

"We are looking for a roommate," Aki said. "One is moving. It's a really big room and not too much."

"What's the rent?"

"Eight-hundred." The same as I was paying for the tiny space.

"Can I see it?" I asked. Aki showed me to a huge room.

"This comes with it," she said, gesturing to a queen-sized bed with a massive wooden frame. "Do you like it?"

"It's really nice. What're the other two roommates like?"

"One is a bartender," Aki said. "At first I didn't like her. Kelley." Jesse walked into the room.

"I've known Kelley for years," he said. "She's solid."

"And Matt. He's from Boston. He works at the same restaurant with Jesse."

"He's hilarious and cool," Jesse said.

☑ Other

"All right," I said. "I'll move in." Aki and Jesse beamed, tipping their bottles toward mine. As readily as I had resisted moving in with Riley when his mom suggested it, I agreed to this move. At least some aspect of my subconscious knew a good idea from a bad one.

Mike came over to help. My 5 foot 3 seemed even shorter when I hugged his 6 foot 4 frame hello.

"Damn, Cin," he said as he stepped back. He looked sleep deprived.

"What?"

"Good to see you."

"You too."

After the quick move, we went to lunch.

"How're things?" I asked.

"As I thought. She's going back to Paris. My son is going to be in France while I'm staying here. I'll move over there when I can. But right now I have too much debt."

"So, you're getting divorced?"

"No. I know. It's strange." I hoped Mike would someday leave his unappreciative wife and find a good woman. Toward the end of the brief meal he said, "I've got to get back home. We're getting up early."

"Get some rest," I said.

All my new roommates worked in the food-and-beverage industry. Kelley, who had Betty Page hair and got a new tattoo every few months, earned the most. She tended bar just across the street from our place, at a dive that was improved by its fine selection of draft beer. I joined Jesse and Matt there once or twice a week and became part of their crew of regulars, whose occupations ranged from sound engineer to health board official to computer technician. Soon enough, they greeted me by name. I still had nightmares and jolts of fear regularly, but my self-esteem meter rose from the very bottom up one notch.

Jesse and Matt earned a comfortable three grand a month waiting tables a block from home. My teaching job paid about a third as much. I looked for a replacement position among the dozens of North Beach restaurants. Interviewing with the owner of L'Osteria del Forno, a busy Italian eatery, I asked if the management was supportive to the staff. I needed that. The French-born Italian co-owner, Richard, looked puzzled.

"Supportive?" he asked. "Well, no one is complaining." After a brief pause, I decided it wouldn't hurt to give the job a try.

On the night Richard asked me to "stage" a shift, which restaurant-industry people pronounced *staahhj* (and which meant working for zero pay), he told me he loved my performance. Hired for five nights a week, I quit teaching.

I couldn't shake a certainty, though, that I would mess up. Waiting tables required constant multi-tasking. I'd always been able to do the job. Now I felt sure that, at any moment, something horrible would happen. Karen, Richard's skinny blond wife, was also the host of the restaurant. Naturally, she noticed.

"Why can't you focus?" she sniped.

"I can," I assured her. "I'm still learning how everything works here." That night, a couple ordered a bottle of wine by pointing to one of the thirty reds on the menu. Only after I presented, opened and poured the wine did the woman say,

"That's not the bottle we ordered." I brought the menu to her and pointed to the same bottle they had indicated, but she shook her head. Karen beckoned me over and asked what had happened. When I told her, she insisted I pay the $19 difference.

"This must be your last mistake," she said. Frustration surged in my chest.

"No one's perfect," I said. Even the long-term servers made mistakes. Richard himself had brought wine to the wrong table more than once that week.

"Yes, you must be perfect," she said, with no trace of a smile. Terror invaded my blood. I feared becoming the target of anger. When Karen left for the evening, the other server approached me.

"She was in the wrong," she said. "That was bullshit. You're doing a great job." I tried to take it to heart, but from then on I walked on eggshells whenever Richard or Karen were present. Richard took every opportunity to hassle me about it.

☑ Other

"You carry the plates too awkwardly," he would say. Or, "You look lost. What the hell is wrong with you?" Or, "This job isn't hard. Why can't you do it?"

He knew it was no easy task to wait on several full tables at once, to keep them all happy and to offer in-depth knowledge of regional dishes and wines whenever asked. I would take a deep breath and tell him I *could* do it and that nothing was wrong, but I'd leave worried, with aggravated neck and shoulder muscles.

I still hoped my injuries could be healed. With plenty in the bank, I searched for a body therapist who could treat long-term damage. I found a woman who had been doing just that for twenty-five years. She told me over the phone that the force from the car's impact long ago had gotten lodged in my body, and that myofascial release was designed to free that energy. She reminded me that sometimes emotions, too, got unstuck during massage.

"Five minutes of crying on the table is worth at least an hour of regular crying," she said when I arrived at her office. "What you'll have to do is let your body move however it wants to. Myofascial brings you back to the original accident, then releases it. You'll also need to tell me what feelings and words come up for you."

This was not how I anticipated healing: paying to cry in front of a stranger and convulse on a table. Even though the massage therapist looked like a high school gym teacher with her short hair and jogging pants, I wondered if she was planning to do an exorcism.

"Lie face up with your head off the end of the table," she instructed. She sat behind me and wound her hand in my hair, holding my head up indirectly and rolling it in random directions. At one point my hand twitched.

"Yes," she said. "Move." My arm flopped sideways. I felt timid.

"I feel like ... " I remembered that I was supposed to tell her what came up. "I feel like a chicken embryo."

"Hmmm," she said. "Birth stuff."

"I was born with a dislocated hip." Heat rushed down my limbs. I felt angry. "A voice is saying, 'leave me alone.'"

"Say it," she commanded.

☑ Other

"Leave me alone," I mustered like a scared kid on a playground.

"Louder," she urged. "Say it louder." I tried. She told me to push at her with my hands. This was a woman who stored rolled towels in her treatment room to stick in patients' mouths if they needed to scream. I figured she'd seen plenty of embarrassing behavior. I pushed and kicked while she encouraged me. "OK," she said as the treatment wound down. "Come sit in this chair."

I was able to turn my head all the way to the left without pain. The whole area had loosened up. I made another appointment. By the time I returned, two weeks later, my muscles were tight again. The massage therapist scowled. She said that myofascial wasn't the right treatment after all. She looked at me.

"You aren't breathing right," she said.

True. For years, I'd struggled to take a full breath comfortably. "It's like you have a disability no one can see," she added, vocalizing what I'd felt my entire adult life. She switched to a technique called Bowen: a method of simple touches and movements. The procedure supposedly "reset the nervous system." By the end of the treatment, I was breathing more easily and my muscles had unclenched.

I went every two weeks and noticed steady improvement. What had seemed impossible had happened. I became pain free. Previous attempts to fix the injuries faded away like the memory of a bad song, maybe "Raindrops are Fallin' on My Head" or the cringeworthy "Dream Weaver" — songs that, as a child, I thought were made crappy on purpose to be played in dentist offices, where B-list tunes go to die.

The summer I got Bowen therapy marked the first time since I was a child that my body didn't constantly hurt. Unfortunately, that didn't last. Each treatment cost $150 dollars, and my position at L'Osteria Del Forno was growing more and more uncertain. Richard stepped up his barrage of insults until I practically tripped over myself doing any task at all.

"No one fucks up like you do," he hissed in my ear on a busy Friday night. Never mind that I had only left an empty tray on a chair. Instead of saying, *People make mistakes every day, Richard, including you,* I absorbed his bullying and really believed that I couldn't do the job. On the way to a table, I knocked over a bottle of wine, spilling it onto a customer. Burgundy gushed upward onto my shirt and downward all over the floor.

"That's it," Richard roared. "You're done." I ran the two blocks home and tore off my soaked shirt, sobbing as I fished through drawers. I shut my bedroom door when I heard Kelley and Matt come into the apartment. *Unfit to work* floated through my anguished mind.

"No, you aren't," I told myself. The whole Riley mess had caused even more damage than I'd suspected. I needed down time. *I can apply for unemployment.* Feeling a little better, I went to wash my face. I passed behind Kelley and Matt playing video games in the living room.

"Hey Cin," called Matt. "Play bowling with us."

"Sounds good," I said when I got back, picking up a game controller.

"How do you ladies feel about some homemade mac and cheese with bacon and mushrooms?" Matt asked.

"Yeah, baby," Kelley crowed as her imaginary bowling ball struck all ten virtual pins.

"How about I make a salad to go with that?" I offered.

"Well, look at you," he said with a good-natured nod. "Cin, the chef. Let's go to the store after this game."

My new housemates liked to eat together, watch movies together, and go out in the neighborhood together. I would have enjoyed it much more if I hadn't expected Matt, Kelley, Jesse and Aki to find me stupid or laughable. I felt sure I would be betrayed, attacked or suddenly alone with no cause — a level of inferiority I hadn't had to cope with in a long time. I took soothing baths and listened to recordings of Tibetan bowls struck with mallets. I tried to meditate the anxiety away.

Over-the-top stress makes people do strange things. I would set a bag of laundry by the front door, and then walk by it as I headed out to the laundromat. Or I'd be searching for my keys, but not notice them sitting on my desk the whole time. It scared me because these glitches often happened right after one of my attempts to *reduce* stress. Little slip-ups didn't matter so much in a home with pot smokers. But how would I hold a job if sometimes I couldn't see what was right in front of

☑ Other

me? The thought that I might not be competent enough to earn a living terrified me.

Riley lurked in my subconscious. In one dream, he pushed me out the window of a tall building. The faraway street rushed up, and I jolted awake. A stubborn intruder, he resisted banishment despite my "positive thinking" during waking hours.

Regardless, my social life blossomed. I remembered that Bryan, someone I'd met in New York City at Hunter College, lived in San Francisco. When I contacted him, he was thrilled. He wanted to introduce me to his friends, who were mostly artists. As empty as the first year in San Francisco had been, my days were now filled with painting exhibits, outdoor parties, long dinners and city hikes. Balancing the inner chaos and the outer enjoyment was like juggling a chainsaw and a feather.

I dated here and there — an Italian friend of Julio's, then a nerdy video store clerk who played guitar in a tango band. They were dead-end relationships that served the purpose of putting distance between Riley and me. Months slipped by. I believed all my focused relaxing was helping me recuperate. In truth, I had gotten used to feeling doomed. I just noticed it less.

Every morning I climbed atop the armoire in my room, where I had placed a thick cushion. I played the recordings of singing bowls and meditative bells. The effects of Bowen therapy were wearing off, but I convinced myself that I would maintain the lack of pain I'd reached. I thought it might be fairly easy to let go of fear, too, and to stop jumping at any sudden loud sound. However briefly I sat on the armoire, I would climb back down thinking I'd accomplished something.

I spoke with Peter, the manager of the restaurant where Matt and Jesse worked. He looked like he recently had spent time in a buried coffin. His new brown suit highlighted, rather than camouflaged, his pasty skin. Peter was the kind of manager who took naps on the couch in the office during service. He hired me on the spot.

I needed to shake a feeling that I was disposable. I memorized the menus relentlessly, down to the detailed characteristics of each wine, and every ingredient in every dish. When Peter gave us a written test, I got the highest score. I ironed my shirts carefully, came to work early, and did my best.

Despite all that, I seemed to have a cowering, bleating scapegoat tattooed on my forehead. *Blame me-e-e-e, pl-e-e-ease.* Peter would throw away a cappuccino I had just made and remake it (even though I could've sworn that it looked the same as what the other servers prepared). He would interrupt me at a table to tell me the chef needed to talk to me. But when I went to the kitchen, they would say nothing was wrong and that Peter was just in a bad mood. He glared at me with his black-ringed eyes.

"You're clearing too many dishes off the tables before you drop the check. We don't do that. Just leave it."

I was making the table too clean? Other servers cleared theirs. Why tell me not to? By the end of the month, my name wasn't on the schedule. No termination — just a quiet removal. To keep perspective, I had written down every handshaking thank-you and sincere praise from customers, to prove to myself that Peter was wrong.

I had to reinstate unemployment. I felt like an utter failure. *Life isn't supposed to get reduced to this: hanging onto a crumbling cliff, scrambling to regain solid ground.* I reminded myself that my roommates and friends wanted to spend time with me, that I had traveled the world and attained a degree. *Everything can be fixed. You're going to be OK.*

The U.S. economy was tumbling into a huge recession, which made the task of getting a job much harder. At restaurant interviews, hordes of applicants vied for scarce positions. After a few weeks with no callbacks, I was shocked to find out that my roommates and I had a month to move. Our landlord hadn't renewed his lease. He was known to withhold deposit money indefinitely.

Alongside fewer jobs, rents had gone way up. *Breathe, Cindy.* In response to my self-soothing voice I snapped, *Breathing doesn't get me a job and an apartment.* Wearily, I spent half of every day looking at online classifieds and submitting my resume. Bryan swooped in with an idea. His housemate would be subletting her room cheaply for a few months. As the head tenant, he could choose who would take the room. And voila. He assured me an affordable place to live, at least for a short time.

"Look who's here!" Kelley shouted as I walked into the bar on Green Street. Jesse and a few others made room for me in "our" corner. I basked in the refreshing wave of welcome from the little group. I was also glad, because recently the city had passed Healthy San Francisco, a measure that provided inexpensive medical care — and free counseling — to those who didn't have insurance. I was matched with a therapist who specialized in trauma recovery. No surprise there. She usually charged $140 per session, but with Healthy S.F., I could see her for free. With a little mojo back, I sang along with Matt to a jukebox song.

"Be right back," I said and got up from the barstool. In the restroom, after concluding necessary actions, I pushed aside the heavy red drape that curtained off the toilet. I stepped up to the sink. My eyes met their reflection in the mirror and I recognized that something in my life had shifted. However far the oasis of home territory still lay, right at that moment I felt certain I had touched shore at last.

A week later, I got a call from someone named Phil, who said that he had my resume in front of him — and that he knew me.

"Really?" I asked, certain he must have confused me with someone else.

"You dropped a resume at Kiji Sushi, right? And your name is Cindy?"

"Yeah."

"I worked with you at Hime. I got hired right before you quit."

"Oooh, OK. I worked with you for like two shifts."

"Yes! I'm assistant manager at Kiji now. I would be more than happy to put a word in with Eddie Hong, the owner. Just come in tomorrow at five."

"You don't know how great this timing is," I said. "Thanks."

When I arrived, Eddie seemed taken aback that he had an interview to conduct. Phil, who would have looked appropriate in a marching

☑ Other

band, whispered something to Eddie, then beckoned me over. We sat at a low black table across from each other.

"So. What kind of sake would you serve with an oilier fish?" Eddie asked.

"Either a junmai or a full-flavored ginjo," I answered, drawing on general Japanese cuisine standards.

"I'd do just the opposite," he said.

"Well, the delicate flavor of a daiginjo wouldn't stand up to the fish," I said. I could feel my confidence sagging.

"It just works," he barked. "What is yellowtail called?"

"Hamachi."

"Salmon roe?"

"Ikura." His rapid-fire questions went on for half an hour.

"Thank you," he said and got up. I slowly rose and waved goodbye to Phil, who gave me a call an hour later.

"Eddie was impressed with you."

"Good. I couldn't tell."

"He'll call you Friday."

Friday came and went with no call. Desperate, I phoned Kiji on Saturday. Phil answered.

"Eddie meant to call you, but he had an emergency. You're on the schedule. Come in on Monday and wear black."

I thanked whatever gods had undeniably helped me.

On my first shift, I worked with a petite Japanese man: another casualty of the failing economy.

"I used to be manager at the best Asian gay club in the Castro," he told me. "But we went bankrupt this year, so now I'm a server here. Let's set the tables." Eddie arrived just before dinner service. He looked grim.

"Hey!" Eddie shouted. The server flinched. "You needed to take the red wine out of the cooler half hour ago."

"Sorry, sorry," he said, rushing to the cooler. When Eddie disappeared into the kitchen, I approached the poor guy and put a hand on his shoulder.

"You all right?"

☑ Other

"I'll be fine. In fact I'm going to step outside for a cigarette." He drew himself to his full height (of about 5 foot 6). "We open in ten minutes."

Who the hell kept red wine at 41 degrees? Eddie came back from the kitchen. His dead-tuna eyes flicked in my direction.

"No training," he said. "You start taking tables right now."

We opened, and the restaurant filled up. I had to enter orders on a computer set up by the unbalanced Eddie Hong — a process resembling the rabbit hole of quantum physics. I had to request the customers' patience, but I made it through the evening with no mishaps. On my second shift, the next night, a customer on the phone asked for the price of a sashimi combination plate.

"Hold on." I turned to Eddie for the answer.

"Mind blowing," he said. "You don't know? Come over here."

"Yes?" The caller was still on hold.

"You should know all the prices," he said, deadpan. He shoved a menu toward me. After quickly locating the sashimi combo plate, I went back to the phone to inform the caller. To Eddie, I said,

"It usually takes a week to memorize a menu of this size."

"No," he replied. "You should have learned the whole thing in one day."

I didn't know why every San Francisco restaurant owner that I'd worked for acted abusive, but the sampling hinted at an epidemic. I didn't want to stay at Crazy Eddie's, but I needed to shore up money. Bracing myself, I took six shifts a week and moved into a studio.

Eddie didn't pick on everyone. He treated heterosexual men and Korean women with respect. I was one of the harassed, which added even more stress to my life. But since Eddie didn't fire me — instead he asked me to cover shifts after firing other servers on a whim — I worked as much as possible.

Through a fog of exhaustion, a beacon blinked. Therapy, therapy, therapy.

Julie had a welcoming expression and thirty-five years of practice. She was a slight, alert woman in her sixties. In the first five minutes, she pointed out something I'd always known about myself: I didn't like to let people get very close.

"I can see that you prefer to be self sufficient," she said.

"How can you tell that?" I asked.

"Mainly by how you carry yourself," she said. I didn't want to sound dumb by adding *But I'm sitting down,* so I tried to nod thoughtfully. Julie had a gentle, you-can-relax-here smile. By the end of the session, she mentioned post-traumatic stress.

"I don't find that prescribing medication is very helpful for the condition," she said.

"Good. I've never wanted to go the pharmaceutical route."

"Our time's up for today," she said.

At home I looked up PTSD. I had always associated the syndrome with war, but found that many types of trauma could trigger it. Just one endangering incident could result in prolonged symptoms, and I had endured several: *physical injury, accident, rape, verbal and emotional abuse, being threatened with severe physical harm.* I knew the results: constant fear, a certainty of doom and an uncertainty that I would ever feel the love of anyone who loved me.

Julie had extensive training in one of the most effective therapies for trauma. It involved delving into the mind (and into memory) in order to rob the past events of their power. She told me that, usually, this type of therapy was used over a period of several sessions to deal with one traumatic incident. I had quite a list. Overcoming it would take serious effort and time. I didn't care. I absolutely could not go through life feeling inferior and afraid.

"One thing that really bothers me," I said a few sessions in. "Why would I decide to stay around Riley all those months?"

"You know how it works with unresolved family issues. You still felt a need to help your dad for some reason, and also needed someone to *be* a dad, but the only one you'd known was abusive. Riley and his mom were the fill-ins for your parents."

"How disturbing. I thought I knew better than to get involved with unbalanced people." My stomach went cold. *Who am I?*

☑ Other

"You bypassed what you'd learned about judging character. You let your child self run things, and you tried to deal with unfinished business. You ended up with no money, or very little, and felt powerless — like a child."

"But the issues weren't dealt with — I was re-traumatized," I said. "That whole do-it-over function didn't work at all."

"You went with what you knew early on." Judy looked at me tenderly with her luminously blue eyes. I wanted to squirm. "You recognized the crazy realm and therefore could freely be yourself. You just opened right up to it."

"And to more damage."

"We're going to work on that," she said in a soothing tone.

Bryan invited me to Burning Man, the art festival in the Nevada desert. He went every year, and said I could camp with his group.

"Definitely," I answered. "I can hold out at Kiji while I save up, and hopefully the job market will get better." At work when I steered clear of Eddie, he targeted me outright.

"You can't be serious," he said as I wiped down the sushi cooler. I ignored him. "I can't believe it." He followed me as I moved along the bar-length case. "You're doing that all wrong."

"It's spotless," I said when I had finished. "Look."

"You don't tell *me*" — he started. Then, "I'm hiring Vincent back. He wants Fridays and Saturdays."

"I already have Fridays and Saturdays," I said. Phil stepped over.

"Cindy is doing a really good job," he said. "Maybe Vincent can have one of the money nights and she can keep one. Or they can both work weekends."

I went home annoyed. Who was this Vincent, stealer of prime weekend shifts? No matter. As soon as I could find a better place to work, he could have them — and lunatic Eddie.

While reading in bed, I massaged my stiff, sore neck. The upcoming trip to Black Rock Desert for a week of art and music would be the prize for enduring all this. And I'd get two Julie sessions in before then.

☑ **Other**

Kiji's front door clanged open early one evening. A short guy hurried in. He had a shock of hair the color of crow's wings. Unwinding a dark gray scarf from his neck, he flashed a friendly smile.

"This is Vincent," the other server on duty called across the room. "Vincent, Cindy." We exchanged "heys," and then they talked about scheduling while I folded napkins.

I'd reached a point of indifference toward romance and dating. I didn't take notice of Vincent's flirting on his first shift. Keeping up friendly conversation as we stood at the service station, he asked where I was from.

"New Jersey originally," I answered. "You?" I looked over and noticed for the first time how handsome he was. His face reminded me of the hand-carved figures in the South American chess set that my parents bought Chris when he was nine years old, during a family trip to Tijuana. Each of those chessmen was an indigenous work of art. My fondness for Native Americans spanned both North and South America, and I looked appreciatively at Vincent. He said,

"I was born in Peru. But I grew up in Maryland and Virginia, near D.C." He carefully carried a teapot to a table. I had the earlier shift, so I did my side work and got ready to leave.

"I'm hungry," I said, thinking aloud.

"There's a really good place a few blocks away," Vincent commented. "Beretta. If you're looking for a partner in crime, I can join you when I'm done."

"I'll go there," I said, putting my coat on. "Come by if you want."

I was halfway through a cocktail and a few small dishes when the hostess brought Vincent to my table at Beretta.

"This place is delicious," I said. "Thanks for the suggestion."

"I know what's good," he said playfully, launching a conversation that covered the topics of travel, religion, and the upcoming Burning Man festival. Fifteen minutes into it, I was startled to realize that I had left my wallet at home.

"I promise I'll get you back after work next Friday," I assured Vincent when the check arrived. I noticed he looked happy about that.

☑ Other

Before going to bed that night, I closed my eyes and envisioned myself in a hammock between two low-slung palm trees. I imagined the quiet surf of a jade-green bay on a warm, clear afternoon. I brought in breezes to caress my arms and face. *Everything is OK. You are healing.* I fell asleep believing it.

The following Friday, I managed to leave home with all necessary personal items. I owed Vincent an after-work meal, and he suggested a late-night Japanese eatery. Unwinding from work felt fantastic. Over sashimi and miso soup, he showed me the photos he had stored in his phone.

"They're really good," I said. "The symmetry, the water, the reflections."

"Thank you," he purred.

"I love taking pictures too," I said. "But writing better. And I read a ton."

"I read, but not a lot of books," Vincent said. "I *have* a lot of books, though."

We ordered more dishes. I asked him for the story of leaving Peru. He told me that he was the youngest child of a widowed mother living in the tiny district of Manazo. On mountainous land in a village with unpaved roads, they shared a long history as natives who now suffered economically. His mom drank a lot. Missionary nuns found Vincent, who was three years old, asleep on the ground as it rained one morning. Wanting to give him the best chance they could, they petitioned to have him adopted by an American couple. He grew up in a conservative, Catholic household, but he later became liberal and agnostic.

My inner reasoning voice chimed in, volume back on: *It takes time to know someone's value system.* There I was, post-Riley, guarded and even less able to trust. It helped to remember that I wasn't just a collection of negative experiences. It helped, too, that in reducing the importance of *must find a good relationship*, I'd become less of a people pleaser. What sweetness it was to understand that I didn't have to bend to everyone's whim in the belief that it would make me likeable.

"Strange," I said to Vincent during dinner. "Usually I would've had a cigarette on the way here, but I quit."

☑ Other

"I'm glad," he said.

"Long shift at Crazy Eddie's tonight," I commented. He held up his drink and said,

"To somewhere else." I clinked in agreement.

Few buses were passing by the time we left. We stood at a curb to flag down taxis.

"What're you doing Wednesday?" Vincent asked. "Want to meet up?"

"If we hang out, you should know I'm not in a big hurry to date."

"Understood. How about a day trip to the East Bay? We can take photos."

"Sure," I said as I slipped into a cab. "Goodnight."

Society in the first decade of the new millennium played out like a script written by a demented individual. More and more people frantically texted all day, and stayed glued to their social networks. They boasted hundreds of "friends" they had never met, yet fumbled whenever they interacted with actual people.

Robots were being developed to look and sound human when it would have been just as easy to make them another shape so they wouldn't get rival ideas about what it meant to be human.

We thought we were the smartest animal, and yet we knowingly released thousands of tons of carbon dioxide every year into an already taxed atmosphere by chopping down what was left of the forests.

☑ Other

I couldn't fully enjoy a hot November day in places where it was "supposed to be" cold at that time of year. Even if the breeze was refreshing, even if people were in good moods because of the sun, I thought of the past when we could trust that November was late autumn. I have found the unsustainable lifestyle of the modern world suicidal. Those who insist that technology will save us have faith only as legitimate as a religious person's faith.

I saw a few improvements, though, during that first decade. Less damaging energy sources were getting researched. Rapists were prosecuted more often. Cannabis started shifting from a drug to a medicine. Advances took time. As with global challenges, I couldn't expect to resolve my own overnight, no matter how hard I tried.

Julie did everything she could to help me recover, and I did my best to assist. Have you ever tried to change core damage or early conditioning in yourself? I found staunch resistance. Imprints remained rooted, so every day I shifted just a few grains from the doom pile to the optimistic. Advancement would prove glacial — symptoms would spring on me twofold after a period of hard-won improvement.

In Julie's office, I rooted deep into the strata of erroneous beliefs that I had formed as a kid (such as *I don't deserve continued good*). I would resurface with new conviction: *I have a right to live happily, a right to dignity,* only to wake up the next morning throttled with near terror. Something in me acted like a trained brute ready to slice my throat open, just because I had dared to try to heal.

I hadn't expected this. Imagine waking to an enraged Rottweiler's snapping jaws just inches from your face, the frothing dog barely held back by a weak leash that might snap at any moment. Imagine eating breakfast while the beast growled and howled, with pure hatred in its eyes. Imagine going to work as the dog somehow followed and kept lunging at you. *Focus. Keep focusing.*

On those mornings, instead of getting dressed I'd shuffle around my studio reminding myself that I deserved to enjoy life — but it would be a thought, rather than the feeling it had been at Julie's. I'd review the "light arrows" lesson from the spiral-bound book that Tom

Toohey had given me years before. For perhaps the thousandth time, I'd try to think lightness into being: *I am aware of myself. I appreciate myself. I accept myself.*

With the rabidly mad dog in tow, I'd muster the courage to go to work, pasting on a smile. The ramped-up fear needed an outlet, so I'd shoot daggers from my eyes into Eddie's back throughout the night. The Rottweiler would back off very slowly, and I'd go home exhausted, yet thankful to feel a tiny bit sturdier.

Meanwhile I found myself having a lot more fun with Vincent than I had expected. On the surface, we differed. He had an edgy, spiky, black-attire style (much like mine had been in high school), while I had an artist-like persona with occasional steam punk thrown in. He favored computer games and horror movies; I enjoyed historical dramas and flash mobs. Still, our two worlds met comfortably. We both loved going dancing, climbing over boulders near the ocean, trying unusual wines, and crossing the city by foot in heavy rain. We preferred about the same amount of social time and alone time.

Attracted to Vincent's indigenous good looks, I pondered the pros and cons of "friends with benefits" until he went courtly on me with flowers and a nicely planned picnic lunch on the beach. So much for my casual approach. My reasoning voice was on and functioning: *Enjoy this, but don't hurry. Keep getting to know him.*

We kept busy getting ready for Burning Man with separate groups of friends. As soon as I had enough savings for the event and a few months' living costs, I quit Kiji. Now I could relax and look forward to the vacation. The annual "temporary city" in Black Rock Desert had humble beginnings. A few people lit a wooden effigy afire on a beach. Eventually, "the burn" became a huge gathering for creativity, community and self-reliance. Everyone brought their own supplies to survive a week in a dry dusty lakebed in Nevada. Music, costuming and art played big roles, but a lot of attendees came to Burning Man for no other reason than to get high and have sex with strangers. I wondered (politely, I thought), if Vincent might be one of those.

☑ Other

"Not at all," he said. "Just 'shrooms. And I'm not there to hook up. I like the freedom to be whatever you want, without the limitations of regular society. It's a world I never got to experience."

"I agree it's not easy to have that much freedom in the mainstream," I said. "I love off-the-beaten-path gatherings too."

Arriving at Black Rock Desert after a six-hour ride with Bryan and a few of his friends, I wanted nothing more than to unpack, set up my tent and eat. As soon as we got out of his car, though, fat raindrops fell, drenching our clothes and spattering dust all over our shoes. The unusual summer shower passed after a cold ten minutes, and the clouds opened to reveal a gigantic double rainbow. People half-clad in fake fur rose from their tents and frolicked under the emerging sun.

Bryan had gotten a text that morning detailing the new location of our campsite. Instead of "E and 6:30," we were at "D and 4:00." With no cellular signal, I left a handwritten sign at the original site so that Vincent, due to arrive the next day, could find us.

"Glad you made it out," Bryan said, pausing mid-tent setup to squeeze my shoulder. He wore his usual plaid shirt, and looked skinny in shorts instead of the loose dark pants he often wore. I returned his grin and nodded. I loved that we had all week to do whatever we liked.

Bryan had his well-known favorite places to go while I set out to explore Black Rock City for the first time. In heavy bicycle traffic I pedaled along a network of dirt pathways lined with towering figurines, tricked-out art cars, people dancing, sudden plumes of fire, and dust. I feasted my eyes on the wide beige sea that met the sky at the far horizon in every direction.

Bryan and his friends had been coming to Burning Man for more than a decade. The group, whose occupations ranged from bank teller to dance instructor to flight attendant to property manager, enjoyed a fair amount of partying, but they were great at taking care of every detail at our camp. I could tell I would feel right at home in this casual compound. Having made it past my cripplingly shy years, I could enter into conversation without hyper-awareness of how I was performing every second.

☑ Other

In no time, the camp group whipped up a wooden shower stall, outlaid with tarps so that the soapy runoff would evaporate instead of soaking into the ground. We positioned our tents around a central shaded lounge area where, the second morning, I smiled to see Vincent walking toward us. He looked nice in a white cotton shirt (torn off around the ribcage, sleeves rolled up) and knee-length shorts.

"You found us," I said. "Did you see the sign I left?"

"No," he answered, taking a seat next to me. "I just looked until I saw you." All around us, activity revved up despite the intensifying sun.

Vincent and I took turns going to each other's camps all week. I felt just as comfortable biking through little swirling dust devils and climbing huge metal structures with him as I had going for a beer or movie in San Francisco. We slipped away for hand-in-hand strolls across the nighttime carnival playground. Neon-lit bicycles cruised past in random directions.

For the better part of a day, I waited out a blinding dust storm in a campmate's portable garage. I valued breathing comfortably and seeing clearly. Vincent and his friends, faces wrapped in bandanas and goggles, preferred to charge around dust-sieged Black Rock City, posing often for photos. I have one of Vincent and me on the last day. Nestled side by side against a red wall, we share the exact same tranquil gaze, all cares swept away.

The first few days back from the desert, I delighted in little things with momentary amazement, like turning a knob and having temperature-controlled water pour right out of a faucet. I eagerly inhaled dust-free air. The initial ugly hint of returning to a daily grind: rent. Before I could get frustrated about the languishing job market, Vincent offered to spruce up my resume. I halfheartedly submitted the improved version to Twenty-Five Lusk, an upscale restaurant that was scheduled to open soon. They granted me an interview.

☑ Other

"Let's practice before you go in," Vincent suggested, and met me at a cafe to motivate me with suggested questions.

"You're good at this," I commented, giving him a long hug and a kiss on the cheek before going inside. His encouragement buoyed me up in no small measure.

Since Vincent loved plants and unusual flowers as much as I did, when I got the job I bought him a big bouquet of pincushion sunbursts and fiddlehead ferns.

I enjoyed his company more and more, even though we hit a few road bumps. We both admitted that we weren't quite sure what we were doing relationship-wise. I had only just launched trauma recovery, while he had some early abandonment issues. Sometimes we both dropped the ball. The first time we went dancing, I had told Vincent that I would be leaving early because I had to catch a train the next morning to visit my brother. A few of Vincent's friends had also come to the club. I cheerfully waved goodbye to everyone around eleven. A few days later when I called to chat, he asked coldly,

"What happened the other night?"

"What do you mean?"

"You just left."

"Remember, I said I'd be taking off early so I could visit Chris in the morning."

"Oh," he said after a long pause. "Yeah. I couldn't sleep that night. I thought you just blew me off."

"Never," I said.

The evenings we spent dancing were some of the most fun, and most of them ended well — though not all.

"I'm going to the bathroom," Vincent shouted over DJ music one evening. I walked with him off the dance floor and sat at a table to cool down. I waited until, glancing toward the bathroom, I saw it unoccupied. He hadn't gone back to the dance area, so I went to the larger one downstairs. After a once-around, I walked back up a different staircase and spotted him talking to a very stoned-looking guy with long hair. I stepped up, nodding hello.

☑ Other

"You didn't just go to the bathroom," I said when they paused in conversation.

"I went to the one downstairs," Vincent answered as his acquaintance turned away. "I thought you were still dancing."

"Even though I walked with you off the dance floor?"

"I didn't know you were waiting for me," he said. *Hmm. Tonight started out feeling like a date...*

"What if you came back and I wasn't there?" I asked. He shrugged.

"We'd run into each other."

"You think so?"

"Yeah."

"All right," I said and walked away. Neither of us had our phones on us. Joining the dancing downstairs, I stayed a long time. When I returned upstairs I found Vincent looking grumpy, sitting near our coats.

"I couldn't find you," he said.

"See?" I asked, feeling a bit immature.

"But I knew you had to come back here," he sighed, taking my hand in his. "Sorry, Cindy. I was playing it cool," he admitted.

"That threw me off," I said. Unexpected distance raised an orange flag for me. I had to remind myself that most of the time Vincent was kind, upfront, thoughtful, and *there*.

The next morning we had a long talk about intentions and feelings. We both had challenges. I wasn't sure I could "do" relationships right, or even tell someone the dangerous "I'm really starting to care about you." For Vincent's part, he hadn't dated anyone in a couple years and had resigned himself to flying solo, though not entirely happily. I didn't want to stop seeing him, but felt uncertain that I could make a right choice in men. I would carefully see how things went.

I hoped and prayed that the management at the swanky Twenty-Five Lusk would be nice, and that I could blend in with my new coworkers without getting picked on. The new restaurant wouldn't open for a few weeks, but I had enough savings to get by.

☑ Other

Our staff met daily to prepare. The managers discussed "Chef's" techniques, what language we could use when talking to guests, and what minimum-cost large parties would be contracted to pay. They didn't talk about the steps of fine dining service, which all the other servers seemed to understand already. When we opened, I didn't know my *mise en place* from my *mignardise*. Feeling like the ghetto kid who had slipped in under the radar, I kept my mouth shut and my eyes open.

The first week of business ran like elimination rounds on a reality TV show. A server got fired immediately for texting in sick rather than calling. Another was let go for having too many non-work-related conversations on the clock. One more dropped off by the end of the week after getting two customer complaints in one shift.

Most of the waitstaff and managers ignored my greetings, which pressed "you don't belong" buttons. Some were willing to answer questions. I lasted through a few rounds of firing, and then a few more.

Service was tricky. We stuck to a strict coursing style, but the new kitchen staff wasn't organized. Starters came out in a few minutes, yet entrees would take half an hour, or more. Complaints rolled in, and it was up to the servers to soothe the guests. Timing was a constant issue. If wine didn't hit the table before food, the sommelier — a beefy, bald, heavy-jowled man — went apeshit. If we waited to enter food orders, the kitchen angrily demanded what the holdup was.

The wine menu listed 250 bottles. I attended weekly wine meetings (without pay) and learned more than I wanted about oak barrels, beneficial mold, and secondary fermentation. The sommelier lost his composure over any infraction of wine service. Though I could open a bottle fairly gracefully, I felt more comfortable pulling off the entire piece of foil at the top instead of cutting a portion neatly away.

That is unacceptable!" he bellowed.

I struggled for weeks to make a 360-degree cut in the foil quickly, cleanly and evenly with the tiny serrated knife on my wine key.

☑ Other

Finally I could do it and he stopped yelling at me — until I brought Bordeaux glasses to a group that had ordered nebbiolo.

I think of his disapproving voice whenever I pour wine made from nebbiolo, a thin-skinned grape best enjoyed in Burgundy glasses. I remember him loudly scolding servers for even the slightest lack of wine knowledge. He was the sole impediment in the surprisingly easier-to-navigate world that fine dining service turned out to be. Bussers filled water and cleared every unused plate. Food runners brought all the dishes out. The sommelier lent his own version of support by talking to guests who needed to know what direction the wind blew on the slopes of northern Rhone in April.

He treated customers with respect, but belittled any server who wasn't equipped to handle bullying. Every time he roared at me, it took a full hour to recover from feeling shaky inside (while I put on a capable demeanor for my customers).

I did consider that working at a high-end restaurant in an internationally known city might be too much for a person suffering from a trauma-related stress syndrome. I also acknowledged that I was getting therapy, and that I was determined to overcome my issues.

On the upside, I made way more money than ever. Not only had I lasted through several rounds of firing, I joined the top sellers on the staff. While I was waiting on one of the owners, who dined there often, a manager pulled me aside.

"He just gave you some *really* great compliments."

"What did he say?" I asked.

"Just trust me," he answered. I did. So you can imagine my shock when, after eight months of dedicated service, I got fired for making a mistake.

When the restaurant launched its brunch program and asked for volunteers, I let management know that I wanted to work just dinners. Serving at brunch meant moving as quickly as possible to wait on grumpy, hungover patrons and fussy, hard-to-please matrons. After the first brunch shift I was asked to cover, I reminded the scheduling manager that I wanted to stay on dinners only. He obliged.

☑ Other

One Saturday evening about a month later, a coworker breezed past me and said,

"Thanks for tomorrow." She left for the night. I wasn't on the schedule for the next day. When I asked what was up, the floor manager said they had put me on brunch to cover my coworker. Apparently she had asked for her birthday off at the last minute.

"We forgot to tell you," he said.

"I don't work brunch," I replied.

"Just this once," he said. "We're in a bind."

I should have refused. When I showed up, we were down by two servers. My section, which was enormous, quickly filled. I struggled to serve two parties of eight, eight tables of two, and another of four — impossible conditions for fine dining. I flagged down the head server for help. Juggling five immediate actions (and planning five more), I forgot to order a first course of gourmet donuts for a table where an amateur food writer happened to be sitting. The general manager lost his temper. He was also the scheduling manager: the one who had assured me that he wouldn't put me on brunches. When the restaurant cleared out, he cornered me.

"I have to let you go."

"Really?" I complained. "That section was impossible to run."

"Well." He waved his upturned palm in a slow circle as his eyes slid to the right. "I've been getting a lot of feedback that you aren't attentive at your tables."

"I often get thanked for my attentiveness," I said, anger rising. He gave his lapels a little tug and stood up straighter.

"Your lack of attentiveness only scratches the surface of what's wrong with your service," he said smugly.

"Then there's no way I would have lasted here this long or get above 20-percent tips as often as I do."

He walked away without another word. I trudged upstairs to clean out my locker. I folded the apron they had leased me and set it, a little too forcefully, onto the GM's desk. I wanted to punch a wall.

I calmed myself with deep breaths as I biked home. I was dismayed to realize that I had gotten trauma-triggered. Fear and doom re-cemented themselves. No matter what I accomplished or how competent I became, I would be thrown away. I struggled to gain control over my emotions. For some reason I felt that I was fighting to stay alive.

"I don't know what to do," I said in tears to Julie. I'd never wanted her to see my cry, but now I didn't care. She reminded me that flashes of terror and a slew of bad dreams were normal, in my circumstances. She granted me an extra long session. As we talked, I realized that in a move of self-sabotage, I had set myself up to lose the lucrative job that, deep down, I didn't believe I deserved. I had forgotten the donuts for a guest who was considered a VIP. I hadn't messed up on some minor table.

The mind had so many layers, like a forest where phantoms lurked and sprung at the exact wrong time. Therapy allowed entrance to those dark woods, but I had to forge the will to continue.

Reluctantly I told Vincent about getting fired. Though we had grown a lot closer, I had convinced myself that he would find me less than lovable. He responded with warm hugs and a "get back on the horse" optimism. We had managed to keep dating for the better part of a year and had decided to find an apartment together. My savings was well fortified, thanks to Twenty-Five Lusk. To ensure that we had enough space for breathing room and creativity, I suggested a two-bedroom.

"We could have a living room/bedroom and a studio each," I said as we discussed plans over breakfast.

"That could work," Vincent said. He took a hearty swig of coffee.

"I'm so glad you're into the idea," I said. I'd never understood how couples could live in a one-bedroom or a studio without getting on each other's nerves in the limited space. With that extra room we could each create whatever atmosphere best suited us, listen to different kinds of music without resorting to earphones, and get the time alone we both seemed to require. We found a barely affordable place on a hill on Hayes Street, with a cityscape view and a park nearby.

☑ Other

Even with Julie's help, it took a few months for the trauma symptoms to subside. I lost my keys often, got startled at any loud sound, and dreaded the next inevitably horrible situation. I kept expecting Vincent to pull the familiar "see ya" move. When he didn't, foreboding increased even as I welcomed him in my life.

Sometimes, of course, we went out separately. During the first year that we lived together, if I was home when he left for an evening out, I'd cheerfully kiss him goodbye. But as soon as the door shut I'd think with absolute certainty, *Well, that's it. I'll never see him again.* As irrational as that sounded, it felt true. In the months before my old wounds were healed enough, panic cut through my body like a knife. I didn't share my frightened thoughts, but Vincent had an inkling.

"I'm not going anywhere," he would say, putting his arms gently around me. "I'll take care of you."

I tried to take his words to heart.

"We'll take care of each other," I answered.

I hoped we would. We did have our share of arguments, but always followed up with a long talk to set things right. Having someone keep loving me up close felt like falling out of control toward deep water, but I managed to go forward (while worrying that I might have false hope).

Mike called on a warm, windy afternoon with big news.

"I'm finally doing it, Cin," he said.

"You got a job offer in France," I replied, excited.

"Yup. In Marseilles."

"That's perfect! You love the south of France. You are going to fit in so well."

"We'll see," he said. "This may or may not be the break I've been waiting for."

"It is. I'm so happy for you." Mike had been suffering month after month away from his family. He talked with his son by webcam every week, and yet he worried that his absence would damage the boy. After more than a year of fruitless job searching, he had almost given up on moving to France. Finally, he could do it.

☑ Other

I also wanted a better job. I felt trapped in the restaurant industry, but I soldiered on. Just as I hadn't wanted America to defeat me, I didn't want unfair management to win. That, however, would take a few more tries.

While I thought about resurrecting my guide-book project, I landed a job at yet another eatery, this time a pan-Asian one. To my pleasant surprise, the manager treated me nicely, which made his tendency to reduce some of the servers to tears seem all the more outrageous. He owned the restaurant, so there were no higher-ups to complain to.

Meanwhile, I worked on the travel book, writing and rewriting until it turned into what you are now reading. I still wanted to encourage people, but for more than just trips overseas. Every story of how a person blooms — earlier or later — is the tale of a voyage. Some flowers come up with confidence and ease. Some need flames to find their way into this world. Either way, anyone who is here, belongs here. Suffering that breeds compassion can be grist for the mill. Even though I still had daily neck pain and a load of healing work ahead of me, I had moments of gratefulness. I could make some sense of my turbulent life by appreciating the ground beneath my feet.

For what felt like an eternity, I had wobbled and *whoah-whooah-whoooaed* on a high wire. On one side lay the old way, where I fell into victim mode and where terrible things happened. On the other side waited a good life where I would thrive. At times I agonized over the possibility of never escaping the dark. My self-saboteur did not want to give up.

I had avoided managerial abuse at long last, but my mind marauder found a work-around. A customer who said online that she adored "being pampered" wrote a caustic review of our restaurant and of me, apparently. The manager emailed her, asking what time she had come in and where she had sat. Was her server male or female? The woman, who had dined in my section on the night in question, hadn't wanted a server — she needed a personal servant.

She wrote about how she had pointed to the appetizer on the table next to hers. She conceded that I had obliged to describe the dish, but

☑ Other

she complained that I didn't ask her if she wanted one, too (like you would with a three-year-old). Admittedly, if customers jabbed their fingers at a meal that others were trying to enjoy, I did not indulge them. The woman posted complaints about everything from our "horrible" parking situation and "unbelievable" lack of purse hooks under the bar, to how I was unwilling to spend extra time with her. And just like that, the manager took away all my dinner shifts.

I declared self-sabotage. I knew we had our share of narcissistic clientele, yet I had refused to fawn over them — until one lashed out.

This'll never stop happening, I thought. I was back to square one with my finances. I saw a vision of myself, a couple decades in the future, with pruney skin and stooped shoulders, limping up to tables in some greasy spoon. Resolved to wait tables without getting fired, but escape the industry before that horrific vision came true, I forged on.

A well-respected restaurant needed a private-dining server, a much less stressful position than regular waiting. I would only have to set up chairs and tables, serve a pre-set menu, and put everything away afterward. Though the pay would be less, I took the job while looking for a better one.

When Vincent and I reached the two-year mark, I started to think that maybe, possibly, we made a good couple. We did share some key qualities: loyalty, flexibility, and playfulness. We had earnest talks whenever necessary. Neither of us wanted children, our housework was divided evenly, and our levels of affection and passion remained strong. When Vincent's parents, two soft-spoken souls in their seventies, visited from Virginia, I got along with them easily.

Needing to stay in my emotional comfort zone, I searched astrology for reasons why we might *or might not* work. With a mid-July birthday, Vincent had grown up a Cancer. I liked the devotion to home and family known of "the crab," but had qualms about a watery nature clashing with my Leo fire. Vincent, though, did not have those wavering Cancerian moods. Generally calm and steady, he sometimes became pessimistic, but mostly acted hopeful and determined. He

☑ Other

could be stubborn — meeting any new idea with resistance at first. It wasn't until I looked up Southern Hemisphere astrology that I realized the Peruvian sky showed Capricorn in July. At any rate, pondering complicated star charts was just an excuse to avoid navigating unknown relationship waters. Despite doubts, I didn't jump ship.

To celebrate our two years we went to Hawaii, sailing through long airport waits and car rental paperwork. We relaxed in the tropical warmth by horseback riding, swimming and zip-lining. In the hotel room, sometime during the trip, we passed by each other and said at the same time,

"I don't want to leave." Laughing, we leaned in for a long kiss. Moments like those made me forget the PTSD-induced belief that my boyfriend was merely pretending to love me.

I had started to have faith that I could be lovable despite my faults, but my nervous system had adapted to the expectation of getting discarded. Sometimes a friend or coworker of Vincent's would mention that he adored me, yet the wounded part of me insisted on thinking the worst.

I had to find out where my self hatred cowered before it targeted the relationship. With Julie, I confronted the inner villain. Leaning back on her couch and diving into myself, I discovered that the saboteur was actually an overlooked, sad girl with no hope in anything.

I felt a strong distaste for her before empathy, at first seeing her as a monster in a cage. She couldn't speak, and had sharp long teeth dipped in blood. She appeared half dead. I could tell she viewed people as dangerous, and that she poured every ounce of energy into hammering herself down in the hope that others wouldn't. She had been the one who summoned destruction every time my life started getting better, because better was an uncomfortable garment.

She needed help. And love. The crucial practice of telling her that *I* loved her would take some shifting of perspective. She represented an unhealed part of me that, at times, I bitterly hated. It took several tries to say sincerely, *You matter. I want to give you whatever you*

☑ Other

need. Every day I had to assure myself at the core that it was OK for me to be here, and that I deserved good things. If I skipped even one day, the newfound sense of safety slipped, and little flurries of terror snuck back in. I walked myself back, sometimes a few dozen times a day.

Sometimes — say, after a week of extra pain flare-up and a return attack of the Rottweiler — I'd sink into a hopeless anguish, huddling in bed for hours. As when I was a child, I read books to escape reality. When too many of those weeks occurred within a few months, I'd doubt full recovery was even possible. But occasionally, out of the blue, some kind of providence intervened and restored my ability to hope.

One night after work, bone tired from eight hours of setting up for a wedding (and serving during the reception), I got off the bus and dragged myself up the three flights to the apartment. Once there, I realized that my wallet was gone. I groaned, thinking about the process of getting a new ID, ATM card, and whatever else needed to be replaced.

The next night after my shift, as I walked to the bus stop, my phone rang. I usually ignored calls from unknown numbers, but this time I picked up. I was passing by the Japanese restaurant where Vincent and I had enjoyed our second dinner together. Recently I'd picked up a few shifts as a bartender there, but had since given up the idea of working two jobs again.

"Hello?"

"Cindy?" said the owner of the restaurant. "Where are you?"

"I'm right outside your restaurant," I said. "Where are you?"

"Here. We have your wallet."

"Oh? I'll be right in." I walked inside to see a MUNI bus driver holding my wallet.

"Here, miss. You dropped this last night on the bus," he said. As I strode toward him, a huge grin formed on my surprised face.

"You are the best bus driver in the world," I said.

"I saw you had a paycheck with the name of this place on it," he said.

☑ Other

In my experience, a MUNI driver tracking someone down and showing up in person to return a wallet was unheard of. That, and the fact that I'd been passing by the restaurant at the exact moment he was there, bolstered a belief in something divine.

Despite this urban miracle, after years in a metropolis I needed calm. San Francisco's constant wind, blaring sirens and high prices started grating on my nerves. Vincent was open to a more relaxed setting, and we decided to move across the bay to Berkeley. We found another two-bedroom — smaller, but cute, and much more affordable. Everything in the East Bay cost less, the sun shone way more, and people were nicer on the whole.

At long last, I got a server job where no one bullied or scapegoated anyone. At the tapas-and-wine place where I started waiting tables, all the employees were treated with dignity. The managers opened good wine for us on long, busy nights. Everyone who worked there, from the servers to the bartenders to the chefs to the owner, gave me a genuine welcome. I could have cried with relief.

Berkeley was a good move. People sauntered rather than scurried. The air smelled fresh. At night, I could once again see stars. I liked that the campus had long drawn civil-rights activists, and that the city held out against huge corporations taking up space within its limits.

Vincent, still waiting tables also, got the green light to hang some of his photos in a cafe. He also wanted to escape the restaurant industry after a decade of serving.

He had first set out for the West Coast from the East by going to Seattle before coming to San Francisco. A few months before we met, he had tried to move back to Seattle, but couldn't find work there. If I hadn't decided that a belief in pre-destined love was foolish, I would have counted that as fate.

I would have given more weight to how, for the first year and a half, we had naturally celebrated the start of our relationship on the thirteenth of every month. I might have attached too much meaning to how our decorating styles matched so well, and how we sometimes finished each other's sentences. Instead I focused on *healthy*. First and

☑ Other

foremost: a healthy state of mind. With that, I thought, I could get a clearer picture of the love that was blossoming between us.

Taking leave of the familiar streets of hell, I didn't exactly charge off like a horse out of the gate. I slowly mapped out a renovated life. Placing a plush area rug and a few cushions in the center of my room, I made a comfortable place to start each day. Several slow, deep breaths, a check-in with my state of being, and a few minutes' acknowledgement of the positive in my life helped minimize emotional downturns throughout the rest of the day. Taking note of reactionary anger *(That person didn't say hi back to me!)* put warped thinking in perspective.

New attitudes formed: *There's nothing wrong with turning down an invitation for a night on the town to take a long bath and watch a feel-good movie. You don't have to prove your worth. Keep doing this important work.*

Sure, all that mending and repairing took up a portion of every day that I could have been doing more enjoyable activities, and results were far from immediate. But like a low-impact workout you think is accomplishing nothing, after awhile you start to feel like a new person.

One of the first noticeable payoffs of my daily commitment to healing was that the saboteur finally put away her tripwires and wrecking balls. Whether I was out with friends, at work or at home, nothing nightmarish happened.

At long last, when I looked in a mirror, I didn't focus on my flaws. I could actually like the person there. One of my oldest enemies, fear, took a few steps back. There had been countless times I thought it never would.

Now that I wasn't walking around scared all the time, I could think about the reasons I had chosen to be born. Perhaps one was to understand, someday, why so much atrocity and cruelty existed. Surely there were channels I could follow to help people recovering from trauma, or to advocate against the abuse of wildlife. Part of me longed to move onto a boat and sail with Vincent to marvelous lands

— to seek peace of mind in places where people still shared beaches with turtles and starfish.

While the world can sometimes be a frightening place, nothing is quite as scary as feeling unsafe in one's own mind. I've come to believe that if I can chase away my demons, including the abusive and the raping, others can too. Even after decades of hounding. There is yet time. Youth-glorifying culture might hint that life ends at maturity ... but it doesn't. Time brings a deep understanding not gained any other way. Despite what every bombarding ad image and shiny blockbuster movie tells us, the 20s aren't the pinnacle of adult life. They're only the beginning.

I have seen many more sunsets than sunrises, which for me makes dawn the more wondrous. Once in a while, I muse over waking before first light, the scent of jasmine floating in on a warm breeze. I want to stand on a rooftop as the eastern sky turns from black to murky indigo. Just before sunup on a clear day, a few remaining stars always hang along the western horizon. Whenever I happen to see the first streaks of green, blue, red, and orange blazing up from the east, I feel as though I am witnessing the primordial morning. Light spilling into every cleft and crevice of the landscape, daybreak makes the world appear as if from nothing.

I like to think of all the moments that have ever happened as if they are held together somehow, trillions and trillions of them, in an awareness big enough to grasp them all. I feel lucky to be alive,

☑ **Other**

because in the end we will vanish. All of civilization, a momentary spark in geological time, will become a fading silhouette against the brilliant, ebbing day.

www.ingramcontent.com/pod-product-compliance
Lightning Source LLC
Chambersburg PA
CBHW032030290426
44110CB00012B/738